The Mathematical Structure of
Raster Graphics

The Mathematical Structure of Raster Graphics

Eugene L. Fiume
Department of Computer Science
University of Toronto
Toronto, Ontario
Canada

ACADEMIC PRESS, INC.
Harcourt Brace Jovanovich, Publishers
Boston San Diego New York
Berkeley London Sydney
Tokyo Toronto

ACADEMIC PRESS, INC.
1250 Sixth Avenue, San Diego, CA 92101

United Kingdom Edition published by
ACADEMIC PRESS INC. (LONDON) LTD.
24–28 Oval Road, London NW1 7DX

Library of Congress Cataloging-in-Publication Data
Fiume, Eugene, L.
    The mathematical structure of raster graphics.
    Based on the author's thesis (Ph.D.)—University of
Toronto, 1986.
    Bibliogrpahy: p.
    Includes index.
    1. Computer graphics.   I. Title.
T385.F58 1989   006.6   89-344
ISBN 0-12-257960-7

Printed in the United States of America
90 91 92   9 8 7 6 5 4 3 2

To Susan and Laura

Contents

Acknowledgements

This book is based on my 1986 Ph.D. dissertation at the University of Toronto. As such, I owe a debt to all those who were involved in my Ph.D. studies. My thanks to my former co-supervisors, Alain Fournier and Rick Hehner, and to the members of various committees, including Derek Corneil, Joachim von zur Gathen, Leo Guibas, Charlie Rackoff, Martin Snelgrove, and Safwat Zaky. The individual contributions of each of these people are too numerous and varied to enumerate, but the salient fact is that were it not for their efforts, this work would most certainly be of much lower quality.

My thanks to Alice Peters and Amy Strong of Academic Press for their advice on the format and preparation of this book, and to Mary Wilson of University of Toronto Computing Services for babysitting the phototypesetter.

I am grateful to the Natural Sciences and Engineering Research Council of Canada for seeing fit to award me with a University Research Fellowship, and for providing me with an operating grant. Thanks are also due to the Information Technology Research Centre, sponsored by the Province of Ontario, for its financial support.

The First Word

It will take time until empirical recognition, experimentation, and concept formation in computer science (in all of which computation itself is essential) reach the point at which theorems, proofs, and the other apparatus of mathematics are effective in the more complex fields of computer science. It's perhaps unfair and the wrong case of comparison to make, especially in these pages, but the biological sciences are also complex in this sense; they have yielded only very little to useful mathematical representation (although mathematics abounds). We all have to get smarter, try harder in these areas of intellectual activity, and continue to believe that many things (but not all) go better with some mathematical understanding.

—H. Cohen[1]

Throughout history, mathematics, that "old queen" of the sciences, has acquitted itself admirably in clarifying imprecision and ambiguity. While it is certainly true that its efficacy depends on its user, it cannot be denied that numerous sciences have benefitted from mathematical characterisation and analysis. Often, otherwise unseen lines of thought have been inspired by efforts to use mathematics to explain existing ideas. Even the introduction, and subsequent rejection, of inappropriate notations has the virtue of forcing one to think about precisely what the essential aspects of a concept are.

---

[1] H. Cohen, "Mathematics Today—Sprucing up the Old Queen", *Comm. ACM 26*, 12 (Dec. 1983), 1037-1038.

A mathematical characterisation of an interesting concept is never perfect. Something always appears to be left out, or is expressed clumsily, or, worst of all, cannot be expressed. The mathematical characterisation of a field is in this sense evolutionary. To accommodate perceived insufficiencies, changes may occur in the notations, in the minds of researchers, or in the very objects being characterised. When Dana Scott strove to characterise data types by the use of lattice theory and the λ-calculus,[3] the novelty and rigour of the approach was not easy to digest. Today, Scott's techniques are in the toolchests of most programming methodologists, as are the techniques of Hoare and Dijkstra. In fact, a curious transformation has occurred. So great is the confidence in these notations that if the semantics of a new programming construct is difficult to express, the doubt is now cast on the construct itself, rather than the underlying notations.

This book presents a mathematical characterisation of the structure of raster graphics, a popular and diverse form of computer graphics. It would be arrogant and somewhat optimistic to suggest that the notations introduced in this book will have a comparable effect to computer graphics that Scott's work has had to programming methodology, but it is hoped that the notations will help to clarify some of the concepts generally considered to be fundamental to computer graphics. Raster graphics is rich in *ad hoc* mathematical techniques, but within it there is little sense of unity. This is understandable. Raster graphics is being continually blessed with exciting new technological goodies. Researchers and practitioners (the author included), in their haste to make prettier images, have left behind a convoluted jumble of concepts and techniques. As in the other disciplines of computer science and mathematics, a balance must be found in computer graphics between practice and theory. At the moment, there is precious little of the latter, although there are some encouraging signs. In a recent conference entitled *Mathematical Foundations of Computer Graphics and CAD*,[4] it would appear that the notion of "theoretical computer graphics" coincides with "computational geometry". The two are of course related but not identical. Computer graphics has an inherent natural *structure*, some aspects of which can be captured by computational geometry. This book will show that the entire structure of computer graphics can (and should) be mathematically considered. It is hoped that the reader will be persuaded that it is important to do so. Given the proliferation of graphics standards, it is clear that a deeper mathematical understanding is not just important: it is critical to their success.

There is no need for practice and theory to be at odds. We shall see, for example, that practical algorithms and suggestions readily arise from the framework

---

[2] D. Scott, "Data types as lattices", *SIAM Journal of Computing 5* (1976), 522-587.

[3] *Mathematical Foundations of Computer Graphics and CAD*, NATO ASI Series F, Volume 40, Springer-Verlag, Heidelberg (1988).

presented in this book. This is due to the fact that our mathematical structure of raster graphics consists of two mutually supportive components: a *semantics*, in which we precisely define the essential characteristics of raster graphics, and a *theory*, in which we explore the implications of our semantics. Neither of these issues can possibly be pursued to exhaustion in a single book, particularly by a first book on the topic. However, this book does lay some of the foundation.

Our focus will be on 3-dimensional raster graphics, as it offers a wide variety of important problems to consider formally. Of course, the term "3-D graphics" is itself ambiguous, for it is not clear whether "3-D" refers only to geometric primitives, or to display primitives as well. We shall assume, in fact, that it refers only to geometry, and that the display is two-dimensional. This being the case, the major issues we shall consider are: scene representation, visibility, rendering, bit-mapped graphics, and illumination models. The contributions of this book to the semantics of raster graphics are: the development of a unified semantic framework for raster graphics, the semantic separation of scenes and images, a precise characterisation of bit-maps and operations over them, and the use of measure theory to capture rendering techniques and their approximations. The contributions to the theory of raster graphics are: proofs of the computational complexity of visible surface determination and of a global illumination model implemented by "ray tracing", proofs of the accuracy and convergence of rendering approximations, the specification and analysis of interesting renderings and "rasterisations", the properties of line-drawing schemes, and a development of a theory of transformations which operate uniformly over both images and scenes. Some interesting open problems are also suggested.

Lastly, a few words regarding the intended audience are in order. This book is intended to be accessible to anyone with some basic computer graphics background who is willing to put up with a few definitions and symbols. A little exposure to second-year mathematical analysis and algebra, and to a third-year theoretical computer science course would be helpful. A more mathematically-minded reader may find that this book provides a useful introduction to the concepts of raster graphics and some interesting problems in the field, although it is not intended to be an introductory textbook. This book is also suitable for a graduate-level "topics" course in image synthesis. It is certainly of interest to researchers involved in the formal specification of graphics systems, in that it provides a mathematical basis for the formal specification of graphic primitives and operations on them.

Notation

$\mathbf{R}, \mathbf{R}^n$ the real numbers, n-tuples of the real numbers.

$\mathbf{N}$ the natural numbers $\{ 0, 1, 2, \cdots \}$.

$\mathbf{Z}$ the integers $\{ \cdots, -2, -1, 0, 1, 2, \cdots \}$.

$\mathbf{C}$ the complex numbers.

$[a,b]$ the real closed interval $a \leq x \leq b$.

$[a,b)$ the real semi-closed interval $a \leq x < b$.

$|x|$ the (positive) absolute value of $x \in \mathbf{R}$.

$|X|$ the cardinality of (finite) set X.

$\langle x \rangle$ component-wise rounding of $x \in \mathbf{R}^n$ up to nearest integer n-tuple;

$\langle f_n \rangle$ a sequence of functions $f_1, f_2, \cdots$.

$\varnothing$ the empty set

$\cup, \cap$ set union and intersection

$\wedge, \vee$ logical *and*, logical *or*.

$\in, \notin$ *is a member of, is not a member of.*

$\forall, \exists, \exists!$ *for all, there exists, there exists a unique.*

$\subseteq, \subset$ *is a subset of, is a proper subset of.*

χ_S characteristic function of $S \subseteq \mathbf{R}^n$.

Π partition of a set $A = \{ A_1, A_2, \cdots \}$ such that $A = \cup_i A_i$.

$\chi(A;\Pi)$ coverage mask of $A \subseteq \mathbf{R}^2$ with respect to partition Π.

$=_{df}$ *is defined to be.*

$\sim$ *is approximated by.*

$\Sigma, \int$ summation, integration.

$\ni$ *such that.*

$O(f(n))$ "at most $f(n)$": $\{\, g(n): \exists c, n_0 > 0 \ni |g(n)| \le cf(n), \forall n > n_0 \,\}$.

$\Omega(f(n))$ "at least $f(n)$": $\{\, g(n): \exists c, n_0 > 0 \ni g(n) \ge cf(n), \forall n > n_0 \,\}$.

$\Theta(f(n))$ both $O(f(n))$ and $\Omega(f(n))$.

Z_O spatial extent of object O, $Z_O \subseteq \mathbf{R}^3$.

I_O colour intensity of object O over Z_O.

S_O screen extent of object O, $S_O \subseteq \mathbf{R}^2$.

$\mathbf{P}$ a pixel prototype or prototile, $\mathbf{P} \subseteq \mathbf{R}^2$.

$\mathbf{T}_u$ tiling of $\mathbf{R}^2$ using unit square tiles.

$\mathbf{T_P}$ tiling of $\mathbf{R}^2$ using prototile $\mathbf{P}$.

P_{ij} pixel (i,j) in an image. Normally, P_{ij} has an extent $S_{ij} \subseteq \mathbf{R}^2$ on the screen, and colour intensity I_{ij} from some colour space.

$\mathbf{B}(\Omega)$ class of Borel sets over domain $\Omega \subseteq \mathbf{R}^n$.

$\mu(A)$ Lebesgue measure of $A \in \mathbf{B}(\Omega)$.

$\mu_s(A)$ Lebesgue-Stieltjes measure of $A \in \mathbf{B}(\Omega)$ with respect to function s; also, a *sampling process.*

μ_{ij}^I intensity measure about pixel (i,j) with respect to scene illumination function I.

$\delta(x)$ Dirac delta function/functional.

$R[X]$ rasterisation of $X \subseteq \mathbf{R}^2$.

$\otimes$ intensity blending function; also, a general boolean operator.

0 Motivation and Overview

Mathematicians expedite their special business by deviating from ordinary language. Each such departure is prompted by specific considerations of utility for the mathematical venture afoot. Such reforms may be expected to reflect light on the ordinary language from which they depart, and the light reflected is all the brighter for the narrowly utilitarian character of the reforms. For in each case some special function which has hitherto been only incidentally and inconspicuously performed by a construction in ordinary language now stands boldly forth as the sole and express function of an artificial notation. As if by caricature, inconspicuous functions of common idioms are thus isolated and made conspicuous.

–W.V. Quine[1]

Synopsis. In order to reason meaningfully and precisely about raster graphics systems, it is argued that a unifying rigorous framework for these systems is required. Since the perceived quality of images produced by a graphics system involves largely subjective criteria, it is important that any semantics of raster graphics be sensitive to such pragmatic issues. With this awareness in mind, a basic overview of the framework is described. Subsequently, the scope, contributions, and form of this book are presented.

---

[1] W.V. Quine, "Logic as a Source of Syntactical Insights", *Ways of Paradox* (Harvard University Press, Cambridge, MA), 1966.

1

0.1. Raster Graphics

Suppose we have a picture in mind that we wish to see displayed. A *scene* is a mathematical representation of it, and an *image* is a representation of the scene on a display screen. A *graphics system* provides a user with the facilities to:

- model pictures as scenes, providing a set of graphic primitives and mechanisms for combining and manipulating primitives into more complex structures.

- apply transformations on scenes such as various geometric, viewing, orientation, or perspective transformations.

- display some approximation of the scene on a display screen subject to parameters such as how the scene is to be illuminated.

The basic problem in graphic output is *rendering:* given a scene, construct an image that, within the constraints of a display device, is visually satisfactory. A number of other important problems also arise in most graphics systems. These include determining visible portions of objects, scene illumination, and texture mapping, to name a few.

As any textbook on computer graphics will indicate, there are two common forms of graphics display systems, often diverging conceptually due to the differing atomic *display primitives* employed by each technology [NeSp79; FoDa82]. *Line graphics* is the body of concepts and techniques applied to graphics systems which draw line segments as their primitive display operation. With only a few specialised exceptions, line graphics has been subsumed by the focus of this book, *raster graphics*. A *raster display* is made up of a densely-packed (typically rectangular) array of intensity spots called *picture elements* or *pixels*. Each pixel in the display is a display primitive. Usually, a pixel can be individually addressed, and it can be set to any colour intensity from a prescribed *colour space*. The most common example of a raster display device is the television set.

When confined to raster graphics, the problem of rendering amounts to determining a suitable intensity value for each pixel, given a scene specification. In many raster graphics systems, such renderings can be highly realistic. Because of its richness in intuitive concepts and techniques, the unification of raster graphics into a formal framework is a challenging task. This book embodies the first attempt at a mathematical characterisation of the major concepts of raster graphics. This chapter discusses the scope, goals and applications of the framework, as well as an overview of the strategy taken in this book.

0.1.1. Semantics and Pragmatics in Raster Graphics

In the essay of which the above quotation was the opening paragraph, Quine provides a series of examples illustrating that the precise, "artificial" notation of mathematical logic is useful in clarifying common constructions in ordinary language. This book has an analogous goal: to use a more precise notation to analyse constructions of the "ordinary language" of raster graphics. Before proceeding to this task, if only to demonstrate the author's biases and motivations, it is of some importance to discuss what we shall mean by terms such as "semantics" and "pragmatics". We shall be brief, and shall by no means do justice even to the basic tenets of the philosophy of language, on which the following thoughts are based.

In informal terms, a *language* is a set of expressions over a set of signs (e.g., over words, pictures, speech, or gestures). More precisely (and somewhat restrictively), a language L is a subset of the free monoid Σ^* generated by a set of signs Σ. Elements of L are called *expressions*. The *syntax* of L consists of a set of rules for constructing acceptable expressions from signs. A *semantics* supplies an interpretation for L by associating a context-independent truth condition with each expression of L. The *pragmatics* of L is the intensional meaning of expressions as they are uttered (spoken, used, etc.) in a specific context.[2] If two expressions have the same semantics, then they are *synonymous*. [Gazd79] informally defines pragmatics by the following equation:

PRAGMATICS = meaning − truth conditional semantics.

Not all philosophers of language agree on this terminology.[3] There is also a persuasive movement away from this Frege-inspired semantic/pragmatic dichotomy.[4] However, this simplification will help us to compare the issues underlying a semantics of raster graphics to those encountered in the semantics of programming languages and other computing systems.

In ordinary language, it is easy to construct expressions which have the same semantics (extension), but by virtue of context or idiom have different pragmatics. Consider the expressions:

"A glass of ice-cold beer."
"A glass of freezing beer."

A semantics might well prescribe the same truth conditions to these sentences, but their pragmatics are not the same (at least not to the author after a long game of soccer). One might argue from this example that pragmatic distinctions arise only

---

[2] See Carnap's "Meaning and Synonymy in Natural Languages" [Carn58: p233ff].

[3] For example, Quine instead distinguishes between naming and meaning rather than between semantics and pragmatics (cf. "Notes on the Theory of Reference" [Quin80: 130-138]). His terminology makes more apparent the contrasts between extension and intension, or equivalently, between denotation and connotation.

[4] Cf. Barwise and Perry [BaPe83], who present a theory of meaning called "Situation Semantics" to account for the highly-complex situational uses of everyday language.

from the idiomatic use of language (or because of thirst-crazed soccer players). This is not correct, for compare the predicates:

"X is an equilateral triangle."
"X is an equiangular triangle."

Clearly, both predicates denote the same set of objects, but their apparent intent is different. Similarly, two programs may be synonymous with respect to a programming language semantics, but their pragmatics may be different. For example, one program might be more efficient, use a more natural set of input/output devices, more gracefully degrade, or give more consistent response time. To their users, the *perceived* meaning of programs is influenced by such situational factors. Even to programmers, it is possible that two synonymous programs may have dissimilar perceived meanings, due to issues such as programming style and organisation. This is not to say that a programming language semantics should account for these factors. Indeed, programming methodologists have been careful to make the semantic/pragmatic distinction as clear as possible, so as to ensure that a specified process can be performed on a wide class of computing mechanisms. There is no magic in this: certain notations have come to be accepted as adequate for expressing the context-independent meaning of programs. The situation in computer graphics is not as well understood.

Like the programming methodologists, we desire a view of raster graphics that separates pragmatics from semantics, that separates specific situational issues from those that must be universally true. One is not likely to ever be able to define a predicate prescribing all the "good", and only the "good" scene renderings, for this type of judgement requires highly-specific evaluative criteria regarding the appearance of an image on a particular display device. The perceived quality of a rendering can depend on whether the viewing monitor is correctly adjusted, on the viewing-room illumination, on the colour of the viewers' clothing, on the mood of the viewers, etc. It is similarly difficult in programming methodology to define a predicate which captures all the "good" and only the "good" implementations of some process, for this is subject to equally personal interpretations. What can be done, and what this book accomplishes, is to develop a framework that allows a vast set of rendering techniques to be specified. The word "rendering", in its everyday use, is an intuitive concept much like the notion of a "computable function". One must therefore be hesitant about saying that *all* rendering techniques can be captured. However, it is certainly true that all *known* techniques can be easily specified, which provides some evidence that the framework is a good one.

Variety and flexibility are crucial to the success of a graphics system. Just as there exist many plausible rendering techniques, there are many ways to define scenes, several kinds of texture-mapping, graphic transformations, and illumination models. Our framework strives to give a unified account of all possible instances of a concept without unduly limiting its variety. Our semantic formalism is often referred to as a *framework*, because it is a mathematical analogue of the structure of typical graphics systems. The framework is *unified* because the concepts presented in this book are defined relative to the same set of graphic abstractions, namely relative to graphic objects and scenes in $\mathbf{R}^n$.

0.1.2. Theory and Structure in Raster Graphics

In logic, a *theory* is a set of formulae which is derivable from a set of axioms and rules of inference. A *model* maps well-formed (i.e., syntactically correct) formulae to a set of truth-values. Under a suitable model, a theory might say something sensible about the real world. In this book, the word "theory" shall connote a somewhat looser but similar concept. A *theory of raster graphics* refers to properties of raster graphics systems which may be mathematically stated and proved. Considered below are several reasons why a formalisation of raster graphics is desirable. Of greatest importance to the author is the fact that a formal characterisation of the main concepts of raster graphics allows their theoretical properties to be investigated. One criterion on which a formal framework can be judged is its efficacy as a basis for proving interesting properties of some relevance to real-world issues. The fact that many such properties are proved below attests to the utility of this framework.

Taken together, the theoretical results gleaned from the application of mathematical tools to the semantics of raster graphics will provide a greater understanding of the essential mathematical *structure* of raster graphics: the properties that must be true of all graphics systems regardless of their technological composition.

0.2. The Need for Formalism in Raster Graphics

The general accomplishment of this book is that it demonstrates that computer graphics can be made rigorous, and can be thought of as a discipline with a firm mathematical foundation. Why is this important? To the author, any formalisation that brings increased understanding is intrinsically valuable. However, this book is not intended to preach only to the already converted. We therefore enumerate several applications of a semantics and an accompanying theory of raster graphics.

0.2.1. The Need for a Semantics of Raster Graphics

Graphics Standards. Several graphics package standards have been proposed: ACM-SIGGRAPH's Core System Proposal, produced by the Graphics Standards Planning Committee [GSPC79]; the Graphical Kernel System (GKS), originally devised by the ISO Technical Committee for Computer Graphics, and now modified by ANS Technical Committee X3H3 [GKS84]; and PHIGS and PHIGS+

[vanD88]. While they differ in content and applicability, their basic aim is identical: to provide "a set of basic functions for computer graphics programming usable by many graphics producing applications" [GKS84:i]. A graphics standard is intended to enhance portability and therefore should be free of biases due to programming environments, computational mechanisms, and graphic devices. Unfortunately, these standards retain device-specific biases.[5] Since these proposals are subroutine-oriented, the "semantics" of a standard is essentially a description of the calling sequence of each routine, with some supplementary usage information in English. Nowhere in any standards document is there a precise characterisation of an image, nor the effect of rendering a scene in a particular way.[6] Thus the true semantics of a graphics system, the image produced in response to an input scene, is left entirely up to each implementation. One wonders what value a standard has without a precise semantics. Fortunately, some work has begun on formal specification techniques for the GKS standard. It must be pointed out, however, that since GKS only supports 2-D scenes, the deeper, more interesting problems of 3-D graphics such as visibility determination, texture mapping, rendering techniques, and illumination models are not considered. Indeed, when GKS is extended to 3-D graphics, rigorous definitions of these concepts will be required. Unfortunately, if we look at the example of PHIGS and PHIGS+, which are inherently 3-D standards, the definitions of these concepts is not particularly rigorous.

Graphics Programming Languages. Recently, there has been some research into embedding graphic data types and operations into programming languages [Mall82a; MaTh81]. One can reasonably expect this trend to continue. In this case, the need for a semantics of raster graphics fuses with the need for a programming language semantics. Surely, for example, the process of proving the correctness of a program should require demonstrating that the computed image conforms to its specification.

---

[5] For example, the *segment*, or simple list of graphic display primitives (defined formally in Chapter 1), is the only graphic data structure employed by GKS and CORE. PHIGS contains more sophisticated structuring facilities. The origin of the segment goes back to the days when line-oriented displays dominated the industry. Extra hardware was often installed in these devices to permit fast segment rendering. Today, with the advent of VLSI and special-purpose microprocessors, much more general and useful structures can be, and are being, handled. To remain within a standard, however, graphics programmers are forced to use an obsolete mechanism as their basic graphic data-structuring facility. As a standard gains acceptance, this may also have unfortunate consequences in the graphics hardware community: hardware manufacturers may be reluctant to produce more sophisticated devices, for fear of being "nonstandard".

[6] The documentation for PHIGS+ begins to address this matter when discussing issues such as shading, but the description lacks rigour.

Diversity of Implementations. The variety of graphics hardware is experiencing accelerated growth. Many special-purpose graphics engines, parallel processors, and pipeline systems are commercially available to compete with traditional von Neumann computers. Regardless of the computational mechanism employed, the outcome of rendering a scene should be the same. Currently, it is not at all clear that this can be guaranteed. A mathematical semantics directly expresses the required relationship between a scene and an image, and is independent of the possible computational intermediaries.

Basis for Evaluation. A mathematical semantics of raster graphics provides a basis for formally evaluating alternative rendering techniques, illumination models, and other graphic models. For example, many papers on rendering discuss the *observable* differences among various rendering techniques. However, is it clear that these differences generalise to all raster display devices? Are they instead specific to a particular device or device class? These questions are currently impossible to answer with certainty.

Basis for a Theory of Raster Graphics. Formal models which capture the semantics of a graphic concept can be subsequently used to explore theoretical aspects of raster graphics. As indicated above, this consideration is of greatest interest to the author.

0.2.2. The Need for a Theory of Raster Graphics

Mathematical Credibility. Raster graphics is a discipline which contains abundant mathematics, but has no unifying mathematical basis. A mathematical semantics will allow us to ask precise questions about raster graphics. The use of traditional mathematical techniques within the framework will facilitate finding answers.

Investigation and Classification of Pragmatic Issues. Earlier we indicated that there is no formal measure of an adequate rendering of a scene. Based on the semantics of particular rendering techniques, a study of the correlation among renderings judged to be adequate by viewers could lead to their classification and to improved graphics techniques.

Determination of Complexity and Computability. Once a formal statement of a problem is given, work can then begin on a study of its computability or complexity. At present, the complexity of a new graphics algorithm is rarely given, and when it is, it is often based on vague or suspect assumptions.[7] This contrasts with

---

[7] A recent paper by a respected researcher in a well-known (refereed) computer graphics conference proceedings recently asserted that sorting is an $\Omega(n^2)$ process (translating the writer's words into the standard notation). A likely explanation for this apparent error is that the writer was implicitly assuming the use of a particular sorting technique, namely bubble sorting, which is commonly used in computer graphics. On the other hand, many intuitions held by computer graphicists often turn out to be provably correct. For example, Sutherland, Sproull, and Schumacker long ago mentioned that the

the area of computational geometry, for example, where problems are usually well-posed, and solutions are given a rigorous analysis.[8] Moreover, it is both practically and theoretically important to determine the minimal set of computational "features" required to solve efficiently a problem in raster graphics.

Approximations and their Accuracy. Many problems in raster graphics are computationally expensive. Therefore, approximations are often employed. A mathematical framework will provide a basis for determining their adequacy, accuracy, and reliability.

This book is particularly concerned with the first, third and fourth of these issues.

0.3. Related Work

A general outline of some of the goals of this book were originally presented in [FiFo84]. Many of the basic results were originally developed in the author's Ph.D. dissertation [Fium86]. Despite its potential utility and mathematical interest, semantic and theoretic issues in computer graphics are receiving minimal attention. Several avenues of research, however, have been inspirational or are relevant to this book. These will be outlined briefly in this section.

As was mentioned above, a number of graphics standards have been proposed to cope with the wide variety of graphics hardware now available. The success of the effort remains to be established. However, some interesting notations for scene specification have arisen as a result. This includes the work of Mallgren [Mall82a,b], Carson [Cars83,84], Gnatz [Gnat84], Duce *et al.* [DuFi84; DuFM88], and Marshall [Mars84]. These approaches will be considered in the next chapter. Generally speaking, our approach to scene specification is more flexible, since it uses the full power of set theory over $\mathbf{R}^n$. On the other hand, since these scene specification languages are meant to be applied to graphics standards, they have a more refined (and often more rigid) syntax. We instead shall accept as valid any notation which allows one to express objects over $\mathbf{R}^n$.

In [Spro82], Sproull re-develops a well-known algorithm to draw line segments. His contribution is not the algorithm, but rather in his use of a sequence of *program transformations* to proceed from an inefficient but correct specification, to a very efficient, correct implementation. The use of program transformations in other areas is certainly well known. However, this was the first serious suggestion

---

complexity of sorting was somehow related to that of visibility determination [SuSS74]. In Chapter 2, we shall prove such a relationship.

[8] Unfortunately, the models of computational geometry are themselves often overly vague or unrealistic.

that it may be of value to computer graphics. Sproull also proved interesting properties of his implementation, such as the fact that a line segment's endpoints are always included in the line segment drawn.

Another formative area of study that has some relevance to this book is the recent work of Fournier and Fussell in the complexity of graphic problems, and in graphic primitives [Four84; FoFu88]. Loosely speaking, *graphic primitives* are atoms out of which scenes and images are constructed. Fournier briefly presents a programme for classifying graphic primitives and giving them a semantics [Four84]. The scene specification language outlined in Chapter 1 is neutral to such classifications, but was directly motivated by the need to facilitate semantic characterisation of arbitrary graphic primitives and their manipulation. Fournier and Fussell define an abstract graphic device with the aim of determining the complexity of well-posed graphic problems with respect to the limited computational power of that device [FoFu88].

With the increasing proliferation of bit-mapped graphics (see below), an interesting area of study is the degree to which direct pixel manipulation can be integrated with standard graphics systems. The first attempt at informally defining such an integration is by Acquah *et al.* [AFSW82]. The lack of progress in this important area of study is an indication that insights may be gained by a sharper mathematical analysis of the problem. This book does not solve this problem, but the treatment of pixel (i.e., image) operations and scene operations on an equal footing is an important first step.

Notations for expressing graphics functions which operate on pixels have been in existence for some time [NeSp79]. However, the relatively recent work of Guibas and Stolfi is the first to describe a full pixel-manipulation language [GuSt82]. This proved to be an inspiration to the author for two reasons. First, the development of a semantics for such a language would be a useful exercise. Second, it is of mathematical and practical interest to determine the richness of such a language. Chapter 4 reports the results of pursuing these issues.

0.4. Overview of Book and Its Contributions

The presentation of this book is built around the basic flow of operations in a traditional *graphics pipeline* as illustrated in the figure below. Although the mathematics used to characterise these concepts may not always be familiar, the development of our framework around this conventional structure should aid intuition and ensure its relevance.[9] A chapter is devoted to each block in the

---

[9] The notion of a "graphics pipeline" does not commit us to a pipelined computer architecture, nor, indeed, to a specific instance of a graphics pipeline.

figure. The semantics of important concepts pertaining to each block will be presented, and often some interesting theoretical properties of these concepts will subsequently be explored. The topics to be discussed in this book will now be outlined.

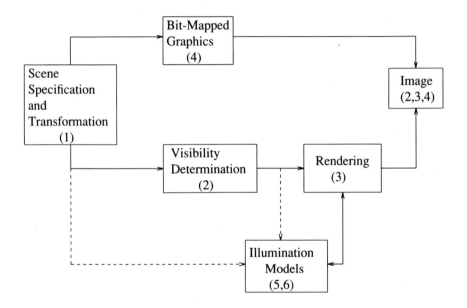

Figure 1. A graphics pipeline. Relevant chapter numbers are in parentheses.

Scene Specification. There are many ways to construct scenes. Chapter 1 presents a basic set-theoretic notation for defining them. A *scene* is a collection of *graphic objects*. Reflecting common practice, general mechanisms for constructing graphics objects from a set of *primitive graphic objects* (PGOs) are defined. The choice of primitives is entirely up to a graphics system designer. Our framework simply provides a neutral mechanism for their definition. Several examples of common (and uncommon) PGOs will be presented, to illustrate the flexibility of the notation. The semantics of several useful composition operators is then given. Various scene *transformations* are defined, including orientation transformations and perspective. The main contribution of this chapter, which is otherwise well-understood material, is a presentation of the semantics of *texture mapping*. Also considered is an interesting application of conformal mappings to texture mapping. The material in this chapter forms the foundation for the remainder of the book.

Visibility. The problem of determining the *visible* portions of each object in a scene, given a specific view point and viewing direction, is an important facet of most graphics systems. Chapter 2 defines its semantics, and subsequently establishes upper and lower complexity bounds for simple forms of the *visible surface problem* with respect to two intuitive models of graphic output. The main contributions of this chapter are that it presents:

- the first formal semantics of visibility which correctly deals with interpenetrating surfaces.

- several complexity bounds for instances of the visible surface problem over rectangles, which have immediate practical implications.

Rendering. A renderer is the heart of every raster graphics system. As indicated above, a great number of rendering techniques exist. Chapter 3 presents a measure-theoretic framework which is shown to capture all known rendering techniques such as filtering, point-sampling, area-sampling, and stochastic sampling. It turns out that any such rendering technique has a simple characteristic measure. This measure can be "snapped into" the framework, and a semantics of the specific rendering technique can then be derived. This semantics gives a precise indication of how a scene is mapped to an image. Measure theory is again used to develop good approximations to various rendering mechanisms known to be computationally expensive. The performance of these approximate techniques under various conditions is then proven. This chapter is occasionally somewhat technical, as it is based on techniques from measure theory and real analysis. Its contributions are:

- a formal model of an image, which is distinct from the model of a scene as presented in Chapter 1. It seems self-evident that one should separate semantically the notions of scene and image. However, this is a point that has been constantly overlooked by researchers.

- the ability to characterise any known rendering technique or approximation using a very concise and powerful notation.

- a formalism for specifying rendering approximations, which is sufficiently powerful to facilitate rigorous proofs of their accuracy.

Bit-Mapped Graphics. With the advent of cheaper memory and special hardware, many systems now have the capability to manipulate representations of raster images directly, rather than a higher-level scene. Such representations are known as *bit-maps*, so-called because they are often placed in store that is quickly mapped to the screen. Bit-mapped devices have become popular in several well-known personal computers and workstations. Many bit-map operations, or *rasterops* are possible. The simplest example would be to copy a portion of a bit-map elsewhere. Functions that take two bit-maps as arguments and produce a third are often built into hardware. One aspect of bit-maps and rasterops that is particularly worthy of study is the extent to which bit-map operations can replace scene operations. For example, under what conditions is a set of rasterops equivalent to rotating a scene and re-rendering? If the latter process could be replaced by the former, then many transformations could be performed much more quickly. It is therefore worthwhile to develop a semantics of rasterops and subsequently attempt to answer questions of this nature. This is pursued in Chapter 4. Other theoretical issues considered include line-drawing algorithms that satisfy certain desirable formal properties. In addition to presenting a thorough formal semantics of bit-mapped graphics, this chapter contains many interesting theoretical results regarding properties of 2-D rendering, line-drawing schemes, and image transformations.

Illumination Models. The degree of realism in an image is strongly influenced by the way in which a scene is illuminated by light sources. Chapter 5 presents a semantics of so-called *local illumination models*, which define the intensity of each point in the scene using only information local to that point. Also considered is a *global illumination model* called ray-tracing, which is based on classic ray optics. In ray-tracing, the illumination of any visible point in the scene is computed by following the paths of light rays as they are reflected or refracted throughout the scene. A very general semantics of ray-tracing is presented in Chapter 5. The semantics of Whitted's ray-tracing model, which is a coarse but useful approximation to global illumination, is presented as an example [Whit80].

Complexity of Ray-Tracing. Chapter 6 presents an interesting result: an abstract form of ray tracing is PSPACE-complete. This is proved over an abstraction and simplification of the global illumination model defined in Chapter 5. Only the abstract model is required to understand the results. Consequently, the reader interested in the complexity results but not in the more general semantics may proceed to Chapter 6 immediately after reading Chapter 1.

0.5. Conventions and Assumptions

Few prerequisites are required to understand the material in this book. Readers with some exposure to undergraduate mathematics should have little difficulty. Prior graphics experience may aid intuition but it is not mandatory. An understanding of basic undergraduate computation theory is helpful for the complexity proofs in Chapters 2 and 6.

This book should be read sequentially. However, terms from previous chapters are often introduced again (perhaps less formally), so that readers wishing to omit a chapter should find it possible to do so. The index may aid such readers in finding other references to an unknown term. As mentioned earlier, Chapter 6 is self-contained and can be read at any time.

1   Scene Specification

The less a science has advanced, the more its terminology tends to rest on an uncritical assumption of mutual understanding.

–W.V. Quine[1]

Synopsis. A general framework for specifying and manipulating scenes is proposed. Basic graphic entities, called *primitive graphic objects*, are defined using a simple notation over a euclidean space. Primitive graphic objects may be combined using various operators, forming complex entities called *graphic objects*. *Scenes* are collections of graphic objects. The semantics of graphic transformations over scenes composed of these objects is defined, as well as the notion of a *scene semantics*. This formalism is employed in the rest of the book to capture the semantics of other important operations on scenes.

1.1. Introduction

The central themes of this book are to distinguish between *scenes* and *images*, to characterise large classes of both, and to define the important mappings between scenes and images. As a first step, this chapter presents a simple framework for specifying and representing scenes. The development of a complete scene specification language, while surely an important goal, is of secondary interest in this book. This is because the set of primitives required of a scene specification language is application dependent. It is certainly fruitless to attempt to specify all

---

[1] W.V. Quine, "Truth by Convention", *ibid.*

13

possible graphic primitives. Instead, we shall develop a framework that facilitates their definition as required, without introducing undue biases regarding the kinds of primitives that may be specified. This framework could then be customised by a graphics system specifier, who would add the appropriate application-dependent syntactic sugar to the notation to form a satisfactory specification language.

Briefly, our scene specification framework defines:

- *primitive graphic objects*, which are specified using a mathematical notation over $\mathbf{R}^n$.

- the semantics of operators which combine primitive graphic objects into complex structures called *graphic objects*.

- the organisation of graphic objects into *scenes*.

- the semantics of transformations of graphic objects and scenes.

- the notion of a *scene semantics*.

Previous work in formal scene specification languages is limited but growing. The next section briefly describes this work, and its influence on this chapter. Most formal scene specification languages only allow the definition of 2-D scenes. This book is concerned with the problems of 3-D (and 4-D) raster graphics. In addition to the standard geometric transformations, it is desirable to have a framework in which the semantics of other well-known mechanisms can be captured. Some of these mechanisms include texture mapping, stochastic modelling, colour mapping, and set-theoretic object composition. It will be seen that our framework readily permits their semantics to be specified in a concise, uniform manner. The rigour of the framework will also allow us to explore an interesting application of conformal mappings to texture mapping.

1.2. Related Work

Most of the work in the formalisation of computer graphics has thus far been concerned with the development of formal scene specification languages. Since this area is still in its infancy, research has concentrated on the characterisation of 2-D scenes. It is therefore of some importance to review this work, and to indicate how it has affected this book.[2] Some general comments are worth outlining at this juncture. The work done so far is to be applauded for several reasons:

- It is now possible to attach a rigorous semantics to 2-D scenes.

- There is a growing understanding regarding what a scene specification should contain.

---

[2] The reader may wish to return to this section after reading the remainder of this chapter.

- Some formalisms have progressed sufficiently far to allow some rudimentary properties of scenes to be proved.

On the other hand, there are some general criticisms that also should be mentioned. First, most efforts so far fail to distinguish between a scene and an image. Second, it is not clear that any existing formalisms can be extended beyond their present scope of 2-D scenes. Three-dimensional computer graphics involves more than simply adding an extra axis. A myriad of problems which are not at issue in 2-D graphics become very important in realistic 3-D graphics. These problems are central to this book.

One common and somewhat effective strategy in the development of formal scene specification languages has been to borrow an existing specification technique from programming methodology. The earliest such attempt is the work of W. Mallgren [Mall82a,b], in which graphic data types are defined using a highly-modified algebraic specification technique [GuHo78]. Mallgren defines two basic graphic data types, a *point* and a *region*, both over $\mathbf{R}^2$. The graphic type *point* is characterised in the classic algebraic manner: a set of axioms is used to define the behaviour of all operations (such as geometric transformations) on instances of that type. However, the notion of a *region* is somewhat problematic to express algebraically, and Mallgren is forced to depart from the algebraic scheme, defining regions set theoretically.[3] Several useful regions such as rectangles and line segments are defined. A mechanism to form aggregates of graphic types and operations is also introduced. Using these formal tools, scenes can be defined in a rigorous manner. Unfortunately, since a scene specification is technically just a tree-like structure of graphic data types, it is not generally possible, within the formalism, to prove if two such structures denote the same scene. It is similarly impossible to determine if two programs generate the same image. To address this problem, Mallgren introduces the notion of a *continuous picture*, which is defined as a side-effect of evaluating an algebraic scene expression. The equivalence of scenes and the correctness of programs is proved with respect to such continuous pictures.

In justifying his use of this indirect scene/image representation, Mallgren asserts that "the central problem in verifying the correctness of graphic programs is to capture the 'side effect' embodied by an image on a display device" [Mall82b:699]. He then goes on to use continuous pictures as representations of *images*. This approach is limited for at least two reasons. First, while $\mathbf{R}^2$ provides a good basis for representing 2-D scenes, one must exercise care in representing the structure of images over $\mathbf{R}^2$ alone. Simply put, images are discrete, finite things. By way of analogy, imagine attempting to do numerical

---

[3] In [Mall82b:704], Mallgren remarks that a region is a data type whose algebraic specification would be overly complex. It is not at all clear that such a specification is even possible.

analysis while ignoring number systems, finite precision, and round-off errors. Therefore: infinitesimally-thin line segments would be invisible, even if they were realisable; in a raster display, line segments often appear "jagged", not perfectly straight; the nature of the "jaggies" depends on the shape of the pixel; the order in which graphic primitives are displayed often makes a difference; a transformation over a scene is not usually equivalent to transforming an image (see Chapter 4); equivalent scenes may not denote equivalent images. Second, a "side effect" is not required to represent an image. For example, one can easily imagine a Hoare-style partial correctness semantics directly characterising display operations on an image representation.

The overall appeal of Mallgren's approach lies in the fact that it provides a solid formal foundation upon which to build 2-D scenes. However, the specifications can be extremely tedious and non-modular. The addition of a new operation, for example, requires a large set of new axioms over all other relevant operations and types. Moreover, the view of an image as a continuous picture is inadequate, and the indirection required to put a continuous picture together is not necessary.

Considerable interest has been expressed in the problem of developing a suitable specification language for a proposed 2-D graphics standard, GKS (see above and [GKS84]). We shall discuss two approaches: the extended algebraic techniques of Carson and Gnatz [Cars83,84; Gnat84], and a technique based on the Vienna Development Method by Duce *et al.* [DuFi84; DuFM88].

The technique espoused by G. Carson and R. Gnatz is similar to Mallgren's, in that it contains elements of an algebraic specification technique [Cars83,84; Gnat84]. The main philosophical difference is that while Mallgren remains within the algebraic model until he is forced to draw on alternative notations, Carson and Gnatz happily employ richer mathematical techniques in their specifications whenever it is helpful. Briefly, scenes are constructed from a set of primitives defined over $\mathbf{R}^2$. Graphic primitives and subsequently scenes are described using a combination of the algebraic technique together with *ad hoc* mathematics. The notion of a *graphics pipeline* is informally introduced, which allows their specifications to be isolated to particular modules within the pipeline.[4] Specifications therefore tend to be nicely encapsulated within a given module in a pipeline. However, this does raise the potential spectre of over-specifying the operation a graphics system. On the whole, their trade-off seems to be a good one since all GKS implementations are assumed to have this structure.

---

[4] Their graphics pipeline differs from that described in Chapter 0, in that theirs is specific to GKS-related functions.

Both Carson and Gnatz make an attempt to distinguish a scene from an image by the use of so-called *combining functions*. While they are not defined formally in the above papers, it appears that combining functions are transformations that take an implementation-independent scene into an implementation-dependent image. As a paradigm, this seems more satisfactory than Mallgren's, since there is a possibility of providing a useful characterisation of an image. However, since combining functions are provided by the implementor, it is unclear "who" would, in a 3-D extension of this framework of this semantics, take responsibility for visibility, rendering, and illumination, since all of these notions could require some knowledge of the expected display device.

In this formalism, a scene is in effect a state in a graphics system which is modified as new graphic primitives are specified. Overlaps among graphic objects in $\mathbf{R}^2$ are settled by a last-come, first-served priority. While this is acceptable for 2-D scenes, a more sophisticated visibility scheme is required in 3-D to handle problems such as interpenetration and transparency.

In summary, the approach of Carson and Gnatz is more flexible than Mallgren's. Moreover, it may be possible to characterise the behaviour of a graphics system in terms of its actual outputs: images. However, as indicated, there is some doubt that the approach will successfully extend to the more interesting case of 3-D graphics.

The approach that most successfully remains within an existing specification methodology is perhaps the work of Duce *et al.* [DuFi84; DuFM84; DuFM88]. In their approach, a technique known as the *Vienna Development Method* [Jone80] is employed to define the semantics of graphic operations on a combined scene/image state. The semantics of various operations are characterised in a predicative manner by their effect on this state. As in the above efforts, some simple graphic types such as points and line segments are defined. This paradigm is rather appealing, for given an appropriate scene/image state representation, it is likely that effective specifications can be written. However, as described by Duce *et al.*, the image state is likely to lead to several difficulties. As represented, an image is simply a transformed version of the scene, and consists of a list of lines and points over a continuous space. However, there are no formal rules provided for overlapping lines, or for determining image equality. When (or if) extended to 3-D scenes, this situation is bound to be greatly complicated. For example, since an image and scene are built up concurrently with the specification of graphic operations, at what point should rendering, texture-mapping, visibility determination, or illumination be performed?

When all is said and done, the central difficulty does not lie with with developing a single notation that is convenient for defining scenes. After all, mathematicians have coped nicely with many different formulations for the same object. In computer graphics, we know that free-form surfaces have many mathematically-equivalent representations, and that no modelling system would be complete without offering several of them. Similarly, if we were dealing only with the issue of specifying scenes, then many languages would be adequate for describing them. The real difficulty lies in clearly defining the transformation of a scene as described by a specification language into an image. Most existing formulations are not sensitive to this issue.

We make the following conclusions regarding the properties our framework should exhibit:

(0)   the use of mathematics as its basic specification tool.

(1)   the ability to specify, in a uniform notation, graphic primitives that are more complex than points and lines.

(2)   a flexible syntax.

(3)   a clear distinction made between scenes and images.

1.3. Object Representation and Mathematical Preliminaries

For the work to follow, an object O must have two properties:

- a *spatial (or spatio-temporal) extent*, Z_O.
- a function I_O which assigns a colour intensity to each point in Z_O.

Definition 1. A *static object* O is a tuple (Z_O, I_O), where $Z_O \subseteq \mathbf{R}^3$, $I_O : Z_O \to \mathbf{C}$, and $\mathbf{C}$ is a colour space.

Definition 2. A *colour space* $\mathbf{C}$ is a subset of $\mathbf{R}^c$, where $c \geq 1$.

The most common full-range colour space views a colour as an (r,g,b) tuple, where r, g, and b denote the intensity of the red, green, and blue components, respectively, making up the colour. In this case, then, $c = 3$, and $\mathbf{C} \subseteq \mathbf{R}^3$. Every full-range colour space in current use has three dimensions, although there are good reasons for using colour spaces of somewhat higher dimension. A greyscale or *monochrome* colour space has, naturally enough, one dimension. In this case, the intensity value $I_O(x,y,z)$ reflects the degree of white (or other colour) to be attributed to $(x,y,z) \in Z_O$. The intensities in a colour space are usually non-negative.

To incorporate colour spaces with possibly non-orthogonal or otherwise dissimilar colour dimensions, one might wish to generalise the definition of a colour space to some subset of $\mathbf{R}^n$, subsequently defining a map from the space into a monochrome or so-called "tristimulus" colour space (e.g., a red/green/blue space over $\mathbf{R}^3$ or the unit cube). Examples of such colour spaces are the HSV or YIQ colour models [FoDa82]. Indeed, one might wish to model "colours" as continuous spectra. In this case, a continuum of colour "dimensions" is required and could be defined over an infinite-dimensional Hilbert space rather than $\mathbf{R}^n$. See also the section on colour mapping below.

Later, the possibility of defining other attributes on objects will be considered. Our focus in this book will be on static objects, but we shall give examples of dynamic objects momentarily. We shall make no further assumptions about objects, although it would be easy to specify that objects must be connected, or convex, or measurable (see Chapter 3), for example. Our notation for objects is meant to reflect well-known, intuitive notions in computer graphics.[5]

An often more useful representation for the spatial extent (and many other sets) is an implicit one in terms of its *characteristic function*, χ_{Z_o}.

Definition 3. For an arbitrary set $S \subseteq \mathbf{R}^n$, the *characteristic function* of S is the function $\chi_S : \mathbf{R}^n \rightarrow \{0,1\}$, such that

$$\chi_S(p) = \begin{cases} 1 & \text{if } p \in S. \\ 0 & \text{if } p \in \mathbf{R}^n - S. \end{cases} \tag{1}$$

According to this definition $Z_O = \{ (x,y,z) \in \mathbf{R}^3 : \chi_{Z_o}(x,y,z) = 1 \}$. For any two sets $A, B \subseteq \mathbf{R}^n$ having characteristic functions χ_A and χ_B, respectively,

$$\chi_{A \cap B} = \min(\chi_A, \chi_B) = \chi_A \chi_B$$

$$\chi_{A \cup B} = \max(\chi_A, \chi_B) \tag{2}$$

$$\chi_{\bar{A}} = 1 - \chi_A.$$

Moreover, the characteristic function of a set can be used to restrict the range of an arbitrary function f:

$$\chi_A(p)f(p) = \begin{cases} f(p) & \text{if } p \in A. \\ 0 & \text{otherwise.} \end{cases}$$

---

[5] More specifically, it will be seen later that scenes are ultimately transformed so that they can be rendered from a distinguished origin and orientation. When in this form, the projection of Z onto a plane parallel to the xy-plane is precisely the portion of the object overlapping with the screen; the spatial extent Z is used in visibility determination, and I is used in rendering. This intuition is reflected by (Z,I) tuples.

Definition 4. A *dynamic object* O is a tuple $O = (Z_O, I_O)$, where $Z_O \subseteq \mathbf{R}^4$, and $I_O : Z_O \to \mathbf{C}$, for colour space $\mathbf{C}$. For any point $(x,y,z,t) \in Z_O$, (x,y,z) is its spatial position at time t, and $I_O(x,y,z,t)$ denotes its colour.

At this juncture, the reader is justified in wondering how objects defined over $\mathbf{R}^n$ can ultimately be mapped onto a display image (or temporal sequence of images), which is at best a small, discrete fragment of $\mathbf{R}^2$. After all, Z and I are potentially many-valued for a given $(x,y) \in \mathbf{R}^2$. In fact a similar problem can arise when objects are combined. We shall begin our consideration of these issues when object composition is defined, although a full resolution of the problem is not given until the next chapter.

1.4. Primitive Graphic Objects

In order to be of use to an application requiring some type of graphic display, a graphics system typically provides the following:

- a set of basic modelling primitives from which a scene is constructed.
- a mechanism for combining, making aggregates of, or otherwise operating on, modelling primitives.
- a set of functions that can transform primitives and therefore scenes in various ways.
- mechanisms for displaying a scene or mapping it into display-oriented primitives.

Our goal over the next few sections is to consider several ways in which the first three issues may be formalised. We shall not attempt to specify all possible primitives, since this set is certainly infinite, but rather to create a neutral framework in which any primitive desired can be specified as required. We shall only insist that primitives be expressible as sets in $\mathbf{R}^n$. For now, we shall just deal with static objects and consider the differences when dynamics is introduced.[6]

Definition 5. A set Ψ of *primitive graphic objects* (PGOs) is a distinguished set of objects of the form $O = (Z_O, I_O)$.

---

[6] At this juncture, we shall not consider "semi-graphic" objects such as text, symbols, and graphs. A system specifier is welcome to define these objects as sets in $\mathbf{R}^n$, but it is not clear that operations on these objects such as transformations, visibility determination, composition, etc., have the same mathematical definition as they do with true graphic objects. For example, scaling operations on characters are often nonlinear processes to account for perceptual effects.

Normally, a set Ψ of PGOs would be the atoms of a scene definition. Instances of PGOs would then be combined to form more interesting graphic objects. A typical graphics package would presumably require PGOs such as lines, polygons, polyhedra, curves, and surfaces.

Example 1. A line segment. Let C be a colour space, $Q_1 = (x_1, y_1, z_1)$, $Q_2 = (x_2, y_2, z_2) \in \mathbf{R}^3$, and $i \in C$. Then

$$O = \mathbf{LineSeg}(Q_1, Q_2, i) = (Z_O, I_O), \tag{3}$$

where

$$Z_O =_{df} \{ (1-t)Q_1 + tQ_2 : t \in [0,1] \},$$

$$I_O =_{df} \chi_{Z_o} i.$$

The points on the line segment are assigned a colour of i (and points off the line are assigned 0).

Example 2. A point. Let $(a,b,c) \in \mathbf{R}^3$ be the location of the desired point, and let $i \in C$ be its desired colour. Then

$$\mathbf{Point}((a,b,c,i)) = (Z_O, I_O), \tag{4}$$

where $Z_O =_{df} \{(a,b,c)\}$, and $I_O =_{df} \chi_{Z_o} i$.

Example 3. An ellipsoid. Let $(x_o, y_o, z_o) \in \mathbf{R}^3$ denote the desired origin of the ellipsoid, and let a, b, $c \in \mathbf{R}$ be the desired radial thicknesses in the x, y, and z, directions, respectively. Lastly, let $i \in C$ be its colour. Then

$$\mathbf{Ellipsoid}((x_o, y_o, z_o), i, a,b,c) =_{df} (Z_O, I_O), \tag{5}$$

where

$$Z_O =_{df} \left\{ (x, y, z) : \frac{(x - x_o)^2}{a^2} + \frac{(y - y_o)^2}{b^2} + \frac{(z - z_o)^2}{c^2} \leq 1 \right\}, \tag{6}$$

and $I_O =_{df} \chi_{Z_o} i$.

Example 4. A sphere. Let $(x_o, y_o, z_o) \in \mathbf{R}^3$ and $i \in C$ denote the desired origin and colour of the sphere, and let $r \in \mathbf{R}$ be the desired radial thickness. Then

$$\mathbf{Sphere}((x_o, y_o, z_o), i, r) =_{df} \mathbf{Ellipsoid}((x_o, y_o, z_o), i, r,r,r). \tag{7}$$

Example 5. A worm. Suppose the PGO $\textbf{Curve}(Q_0, Q_1)$ denotes some interesting curve from point Q_0 to Q_1. We can define an even more interesting object, which drags a sphere along that curve to form a tubular worm. Let $r \in \textbf{R}$ and $i \in \textbf{C}$ be the desired radial thickness and colour of the worm, and let $Q_0, Q_1 \in \textbf{R}^3$ be its endpoints. We define a worm as follows.

$$\textbf{Worm}(Q_0, Q_1, i, r) =_{df} \bigcup_{(x_o, y_o, z_o) \in \textbf{Curve}(Q_1, Q_2)} \textbf{Sphere}((x_o, y_o, z_o), i, r). \qquad (8)$$

We assume this union is performed component-wise over the (Z, I) sphere tuples. The union is well-defined over the intensity functions since all spheres are of the same colour.

Example 6. A wiggling worm. Let $Q_0 = (x_0, y_0, z_0, t_0)$ $Q_1 = (x_1, y_1, z_1, t_1) \in \textbf{R}^4$, $t_0 < t_1$, now also have temporal components, and that $\textbf{Curve}(Q_0, Q_1)$ now defines a family of curves over time (i.e., a surface) Any individual curve is obtained by holding time constant. That is, curves are drawn from (x_0, y_0, z_0, t) to (x_1, y_1, z_1, t) for $t \in [t_0, t_1]$. Then without any further changes, the worm defined above in Eq. (8) is now a 4-dimensional worm, or alternatively a 3-dimensional worm that wiggles over time $t \in [t_0, t_1]$.

Example 7. Fractals. The term *fractal* was coined by B. Mandelbrot to describe sets embedded in $\textbf{R}^n$ whose so-called Hausdorff-Besicovitch or fractal dimension differs from their topological dimension [Mand83]. These two measures of dimension agree on most sets in $\textbf{R}^n$, but in the case of a fractal set F, its topological dimension would be $m \in \textbf{N}$, where m is the smallest natural number such that $F \subseteq \textbf{R}^m$; on the other hand, its Hausdorff-Besicovitch dimension would be a fractional number $q \in \textbf{R}$, $q < m$. Fractals and other stochastic modelling techniques have been used to generate impressive simulations of terrain, mountains, clouds, plants, and fire. It is fitting, therefore, that some fractals be considered primitive graphic objects. This is by no means a novel suggestion, for Fournier, Fussell and Carpenter suggest fractal primitives such as fractal polyline, fractal polygon, and fractal surface [FoFC82]. There are many ways of defining fractals [FoFC82; Nort82; Mand83; Smit84; DeHN85]. We shall employ the mathematically simplest technique, which is to define fractals as the sets resulting from repeated applications of one or more maps[7] from $\textbf{R}^n$ to $\textbf{R}^n$. Very interesting shapes and patterns arise by considering the *attractor set* of a set of maps (the set of points to which iterated mappings converge), or the set arising from following the mapping of several distinguished points. Both [Nort82] and [DeHN85] give ways of constraining the results so that they are not too unpredictable. We give two simple

---

[7] The semantics of graphic transformations is discussed below.

examples of this approach, which should illustrate the general technique.

Example 7(a). Probabilistic iterative maps. This example is taken from [DeHN85]. Suppose we define two mappings of **R**: $f(x) = x/3$ and $g(x) = (x+2)/3$. We shall consider the set traced out by starting with an initial value, $x_0 \in \mathbf{R}$, and iterating f and g on x_0. At any stage in the iteration, one of f or g is chosen for the mapping according to a pre-specified probability of choosing one or the other. Let p_f and p_g denote the probability of choosing map f or map g, respectively, at a given stage in the iteration. For example, if we start with $x_0 = 2$, and choose the sequence of iterations f, f, g, f, then we get the sequence of points 2/3, 2/9, 20/27, 20/81. It can be shown (certainly not by the author!) that if $p_f = p_g = \frac{1}{2}$, and if $x_0 \in [0,3]$, then the resulting set converges to the so-called *Cantor set* on $[0,1]$.[8] This set has fractal dimension $\log 2/\log 3 \approx 0.6309$ [Mand83].

Example 7(b). Iterative maps over PGOs. Fractals can be defined by iterating a map over virtually any geometric primitive. Thus we could build fractals from other PGOs. Consider a simple example. The Koch Island described in [Mand83] can be generated by a simple rule: transform any line segment of length s such that middle third of the line is displaced to form an equilateral triangle of length $s/3$. Graphically, the transformation is depicted in Figure 1. The iteration begins with a single line segment and continues *ad infinitum.*

Figure 1. Koch Island transformation rule.

Let **L** stand for **LineSeg**. The required transformation, T, is

$$T\,\mathbf{L}((x_0,y_0), (x_1,y_1)) = \qquad\qquad\qquad\qquad (9)$$

$$\{\, \mathbf{L}((x_0,y_0),P_1),\, \mathbf{L}(P_1,P_2),\, \mathbf{L}(P_2,P_3),\, \mathbf{L}(P_3,(x_1,y_1)) \,\},$$

where

$$P_1 = \left[\frac{x_0+x_1}{3},\, \frac{y_0+y_1}{3} \right]$$

---

[8] This set can be thought of as all elements in $[0,1]$ whose ternary fractional representation does not contain a 1. Equivalently, this set can be constructed by removing the middle third of the interval $[0,1]$, and then the middle third from each of the two subintervals, $[0,1/3]$ and $[2/3,1]$, and so on *ad infinitum* [Mars74].

$$P_2 = \left[\frac{x_0 + x_1}{2} + d_x, \ \frac{y_0 + y_1}{2} + d_y \right]$$

$$P_3 = \left[\frac{2(x_0 + x_1)}{3}, \ \frac{2(y_0 + y_1)}{3} \right].$$

The values d_x and d_y are the appropriate displacements in x and y for the midpoint of the line. The Koch Island has fractal dimension $\log 4/\log 3 \simeq 1.2618$ [Mand83]. Observe that less regular fractals may be obtained by stochastically modulating d_x and d_y. This intuition underlies the work of Fournier, Fussell, and Carpenter in their development of efficient algorithms for generating stochastic objects [FoFC82]. The semantics of their approach is well presented in their paper and does not require a reformulation here. It is worth noting, however, that their notation can be directly incorporated into our framework.

So far, we have presented a formalism for capturing the spatiotemporal aspects of basic graphic objects. An issue not addressed in our semantics of graphic objects is their physical properties. This is clearly an important aspect of a realistic model. After all, a crystal ball, a pearl, and a ball bearing are all roughly spherical, but are certainly different things. Thus a complete semantics of graphic objects should enable one to distinguish among them. However, we are not prepared to formalise a complete catalogue of essential physical properties in our framework, so instead we offer two partial solutions. First, one is not precluded from defining several different classes of spheres, for example, in which the colour of a particular family of spheres is more carefully chosen to model the particular substance desired. This is not a good solution for objects which are translucent or transparent. Second, as stated earlier, a graphics system specifier is free to customise the framework described here to suit particular application requirements. It is certainly advisable to extend the framework to allow objects to be prescribed certain refining attributes—for example, polished brass (or other anisotropic effects), clear crystal, translucent liquid with index of refraction η, opaque plastic, etc. Indeed, this is what will be done later, when we consider interesting illumination models for scenes which could include glossy, translucent, or transparent objects.

1.5. Combining Primitive Graphic Objects

1.5.1. Graphic Objects

While it is possible to define very complicated PGOs, a scene made up of a single typical PGO is unlikely to be very interesting. We require ways of grouping together PGOs which are natural and mathematically precise. Such combinations of PGOs will be called *graphic objects*. We shall insist that every graphic object must ultimately be expressible as a tuple (Z,I), as described above. Thus the semantics of combinatory operations on objects must prescribe such tuples. There are many ways of creating aggregates of PGOs. We shall consider an example of a hierarchic composition mechanism, as well as some basic set-theoretic operations.

Definition 6. A *graphic object* (GO) is a hierarchic aggregation of PGOs. It can be defined recursively:

(a) Any PGO is a GO.

(b) If $O_1, \cdots, O_n$ are GOs, then so is $O = (O_1, \cdots, O_n)$.

As we shall see, it is straightforward to define graphic transformations over these structures. Ultimately, however, a graphics system designer will be obliged to show how these structures are mapped to a single object tuple. One possibility would be to base the mapping on object union. More formally, we shall define a constructor Φ which maps graphic objects to object tuples. We must also define precisely what we mean by the union of n PGOs.

Definition 7. Let O be a graphic object, and let Ψ be a set of PGOs.

(a) If O consists of a single PGO $O' = (Z_{O'}, I_{O'}) \in \Psi$, then $\Phi O =_{df} (Z_{O'}, I_{O'})$.

(b) If $O = (O_1, \cdots, O_n)$, for graphic objects O_i, $i = 1, \cdots, n$, then $\Phi O =_{df} \cup_i \Phi O_i$.

Definition 8. Let $O_1, \cdots, O_n$ be PGOs, where $O_i = (Z_{O_i}, I_{O_i})$. Then

$$\bigcup_i^n O_i =_{df} (Z_O, I_O),$$

where

$$Z_O =_{df} \bigcup_{i=1}^n Z_{O_i},$$

$$I_O(x,y,z) =_{df} \otimes \left[\{ (I_{O_i}(x,y,z),i) : (x,y,z) \in Z_{O_i}, i = 1, \cdots, n \} \right].$$

The function $\otimes$ combines the intensities of all objects sharing a particular point, and is used to define a unique representative colour for each (x,y,z) in the union of these objects. We shall call such a function an *intensity blending function*. Each intensity value is "tagged" with the index of the object to which it corresponds to permit duplicate intensities, or to allow one to give certain objects

priority over others. A simple example of an intensity blending function would be
an averaging function, defined as follows.

$$\otimes\Big[\,\{\,(I_1, 1),\,\cdots,(I_m, m)\,\}\,\Big]\;=_{df}\;\frac{\sum\limits_{i=1}^{m} I_i}{m}\;,\qquad\qquad(10)$$

$$\otimes(\varnothing)\;=_{df}\;0\,.$$

It is easy to define more interesting combining functions such as weighted colour
blending.

Example 8. The segment. A traditional graphic object called the *segment*
[NeSp79] is of the form $(\sigma_1,\,\cdots,\sigma_n)$, where each σ_i is a PGO such as a polygon
or line segment. In other words, a segment is a simple list of PGOs. It is the only
scene-structuring mechanism supported by two proposed graphics standards,
GSPC and GKS [GSPC79; GKS84]. Our formalism is considerably more general
than segmented scenes, since any composite graphic object, itself an aggregate,
may be included within an aggregate. This corresponds to the notion of a "structured" graphic object. Objects similar to this are supported by PHIGS and
PHIGS+ [vanD88].

The above definition of graphic objects embodies the useful view of objects as
conceptual "chunks" of information, the details of which are hierarchically
unveiled. Technically, however, this structuring mechanism adds no power to our
framework, for the class of graphic objects is simply the closure of PGOs with
respect to a general form of set union. Whether a system specifier chooses to
admit structured objects as above, or to allow only simple combinatory operators
such as set union and intersection (see below), is a matter of personal choice.

1.5.2. Object Overlap

It was mentioned earlier that when mapping an object in $\mathbf{R}^n$ to an image in a
discrete subset of $\mathbf{R}^2$, several ambiguities can arise. In fact, this problem is made
more acute when object composition is also considered. Loosely speaking, these
problems arise because objects are not simply "hollow shells" in $\mathbf{R}^n$, so that there
are regions of overlap in their projection onto $\mathbf{R}^2$. We pause briefly from our
development of the framework to consider the conditions under which these overlaps occur, and their resolution:

- an object O might be such that (the relations) $Z_O(x,y)$ and $I_O(x,y)$ are
  many-valued   for   some $(x,y) \in \mathbf{R}^2$.   For   example,   if O is
  Sphere$((0,0,0), i, 1)$, then by definition $Z_O(0,0)$ is the interval $[-1,1]$.
  Cases of this sort are resolved by the semantics of visibility, which, as

will be seen in the next chapter, would choose a distinguished *visible* point to be projected onto each point (x,y) in the image plane.

- when combining two objects of non-empty intersection, there may be a point $Q \in \mathbf{R}^3$ which is assigned colour i_0 by one object and $i_1 \neq i_0$ by the other object. A suitable choice of an intensity combining function removes this problem within an object. However, the problem returns when we consider scenes, which are collections of graphic objects. For example, if two objects interpenetrate or abut so that they share a boundary edge or curve, it is advisable to assign consistently the intensity of one object to that boundary. Once again, this issue will be handled by the visibility semantics of the next chapter.

1.5.3. Other Combinatory Operators on Objects

By far the most common scene construction mechanism is some form of union composition operator as was defined above. However, many other techniques are possible, especially in more specialised areas, solid modelling for example, which use less typical PGOs. The semantics of several interesting combinatory operators will be given in this section.

1.5.3.1. Clipping or Restriction

The operation of restricting an object or scene to a specific region is very important to computer graphics. This operation, which is known as *clipping* in computer graphics, is used, for example, to restrict objects to the screen space or to a specific viewing volume. It is very easy to define a more general operator within our framework. Let $R \subseteq \mathbf{R}^3$ be the desired region of restriction and let $O = (Z_O, I_O)$ be an arbitrary object. Then the *restriction* of O to R, denoted by $O \mid R$, is defined as follows.

$$O \mid R \ =_{df} \ (Z_O \cap R, \ I_O \, \chi_R). \tag{11}$$

It is trivial to extend the restriction operator to dynamic objects.

Remark 1. Any object O can be employed as a clipping region by using Z_O for R.

Remark 2. If O is a GO, then $O \mid Z_O = O$.

1.5.3.2. Set-Theoretic Operators

Set-theoretic operators other than union can defined over objects. Graphics systems containing such operators are required for solid modelling applications which use constructive solid geometry as their basic modelling tool. Let us consider some sample operators. Throughout this section, let $O_1 = (Z_{O_1}, I_{O_1})$,

$O_2 = (Z_{O_2}, I_{O_2})$ be arbitrary objects. The semantics of the following operations, while quite straightforward, is not entirely trivial, because we have to be careful about the colour assigned to the result of a 3-D set-theoretic operation.

Intersection. The *intersection* of two objects, denoted $O_1 \cap O_2$, is defined as

$$O = O_1 \cap O_2 =_{df} (Z_{O_1} \cap Z_{O_2}, I_O),   \tag{12}$$

where

$$I_O =_{df} I_{O_1} \chi_{Z_O} \quad \text{or} \quad I_O =_{df} I_{O_2} \chi_{Z_O}$$

In this case, we have made explicit the requirement that the intensity assigned to any point in the intersection of two objects in 3-space is to come consistently from one object or the other. No preference is given as to *which* object should have this honour.

Symmetric Difference. We define a volume R as follows.

$$R = (Z_{O_1} \cup Z_{O_2}) - (Z_{O_1} \cap Z_{O_2}).   \tag{13}$$

The *symmetric difference* of two objects, denoted $O_1 \oplus O_2$, is defined as

$$O_1 \oplus O_2 =_{df} (O_1 \cup O_2) \mid R.   \tag{14}$$

Exclusion. This operation is the converse of restriction. The idea is that a given volume $R \subseteq \mathbf{R}^3$ is to be "scooped out" of an object $O = (Z_O, I_O)$. Thus we define the *exclusion* of R from O, denoted by $O - R$, as follows.

$$O - R =_{df} (Z_O - R, I_O \chi_{\bar{R}}).   \tag{15}$$

One can imagine using this operation to scoop an appropriately defined tube (see the **Worm** PGO above) out of a cylinder to arrive at something that resembles a screw.

1.6. Graphic Transformations

A *graphic transformation* on an object alters one or more of its properites such as its size, shape, intensity, or orientation. The study of various families of graphic transformations is one of the few areas in computer graphics that has a fairly well-defined semantics, and numerous textbooks deal with them (e.g. [NeSp79; FoDa82]). Our treatment of them will be brief and certainly not exhaustive. The goal is simply to demonstrate how transformations are defined within our framework. Our derivation for viewing transformations differs from that found in the standard textbooks.

1.6.1. Geometric Transformations

Definition 9. A three-dimensional *geometric transformation* α is a bijection $\alpha: \mathbf{R}^3 \rightarrow \mathbf{R}^3$. Its behaviour over an arbitrary set $S \subseteq \mathbf{R}^3$ is defined pointwise as follows:

$$\alpha S =_{df} \{ \alpha p : p \in S \}. \tag{16}$$

This is a perfectly good theoretical definition. However, in practice, it is of some utility to design transformations and PGOs so that PGOs can be transformed to other PGOs rather than directly to point sets.[9] This enables an implementation to maintain a more compact scene representation, deferring the decomposition of a scene into a set of points. As an example, we shall define the semantics of scaling, translating, and rotating a line segment. Since these transformations are affine, line segments are mapped to line segments. Recall the definition of the PGO **LineSeg** above.

Example 9. Scaling a line segment. Suppose $a,b,c \in \mathbf{R}$ are all non-zero. Let $i \in C$, and let $Q_1 = (x_1, y_1, z_1)$, $Q_2 = (x_2, y_2, z_2) \in \mathbf{R}^3$. For brevity, we shall write **L** for **LineSeg**.

$$S_{abc}\,\mathbf{L}(Q_1, Q_2, i) =_{df} \mathbf{L}(S_{abc}\,Q_1, S_{abc}\,Q_2, i) \tag{17}$$

$$= \mathbf{L}((ax_1, by_1, cz_1), (ax_2, by_2, cz_2), i)$$

Example 10. Translating a line segment. Let u, v, $w \in \mathbf{R}^3$.

$$T_{uvw}\,\mathbf{L}(Q_1, Q_2, i) =_{df} \mathbf{L}(T_{uvw}Q_1, T_{uvw}Q_2, i) \tag{18}$$

$$= \mathbf{L}((u+x_1, v+y_1, w+z_1), (u+x_2, v+y_2, w+z_2), i).$$

Example 11. Rotating a line segment. Let $\theta \in \mathbf{R}$ be an angle of rotation. The clockwise rotation of a line segment about the z-axis is expressed by

$$R_\theta^z\,\mathbf{L}(Q_1, Q_2, i) =_{df} \mathbf{L}(R_\theta^z Q_1, R_\theta^z Q_2, i), \tag{19}$$

where

$$R_\theta^z(x,y,z) =_{df} (x\cos\theta - y\sin\theta, \, x\sin\theta + y\cos\theta, \, z). \tag{20}$$

---

[9] In such a case, it is important that, when specifying a set of PGOs, Ψ, and a set of transformations, **T**, consideration be given to whether Ψ is closed with respect to **T**.

Rotations about the other axes can be defined similarly.

Example 12. General affine transformations. Any general affine transformation α has the property of mapping parallel line segments to parallel line segments. Each component of a point $(x,y,z) \in \mathbf{R}^3$ is mapped to an invertible linear combination of x, y, and z as follows.

$$\alpha(x, y, z) =_{df} (Ax+By+Cz+D, \ Ex+Fy+Gz+H, \ Ix+Jy+Kz+L), \qquad (21)$$

for A, B, $\cdots$, $L \in \mathbf{R}$. Scaling, translating, and rotating by specific constants are all affine transformations. We can write the semantics of α over a line segment as

$$\alpha \mathbf{L}(Q_1, Q_2, i) =_{df} \mathbf{L}(\alpha Q_1, \alpha Q_2, i). \qquad (22)$$

A standard and useful way of representing affine (and some non-affine transformations such as perspective) is by the use of matrices. Concatenation of several transformations is then easily implemented as a series of matrix multiplications [NeSp79; FoDa82].

If one chooses to structure graphic objects in a hierarchical manner as described above, it is natural to extend the semantics of a graphic transformation to these structures by a distributivity law: for an arbitrary object O and geometric transformation α, if $O = (O_1, \cdots, O_m)$, then

$$\alpha O =_{df} (\alpha O_1, \cdots, \alpha O_m). \qquad (23)$$

One should also show that for each intensity blending function a system designer wishes to use, that distributivity is well-defined. That is, if

$$O = (O_1, \cdots, O_n) = (O'_1, \cdots, O'_m), \qquad (24)$$

is it true that

$$(\alpha O_1, \cdots, \alpha O_n) = (\alpha O'_1, \cdots, \alpha O'_m)? \qquad (25)$$

An alternative semantics of graphic transformations on graphic objects would be as follows:

$$\alpha O =_{df} \alpha \Phi O, \qquad (26)$$

meaning that the transformation is defined over the (Z,I) tuples induced by applying Φ on graphic objects of the form $O = (O_1, \cdots, O_m)$.

Many other interesting geometric transformations are possible. For instance, A. Barr outlines a useful set of *deformations* of solid graphic primitives (i.e., PGOs) [Barr84]. These deformations include twisting, tapering, bending, and scaling PGOs. Since they have a straightforward mathematical definition, their semantics can be easily expressed in our framework.

1.6.1.1. Viewing Transformations

One important application of affine transformations is to orient objects and to position them within the scene. Any good text on linear algebra will stress another use of these transformations: change of co-ordinate system. In computer graphics, a scene is typically transformed into a left-handed co-ordinate system with respect to a specified eye position and viewing direction. After such a transformation, the scene is oriented such that:

- the viewpoint or eye is placed at the origin.
- the viewing direction is down the positive z axis.
- the screen extent or *window* is embedded in the $z=D$ plane.
- the centre of the window is $(0,0,D)$.

The larger the value of z of a point, the further from the eye it is. This creates a *pyramid of vision* as illustrated in profile by Figure 2. In a traditional graphics framework, the scene may then be clipped to this pyramid. This readies the scene for perspective transformation and for subsequent visible surface determination.

Definition 10. A *viewing transformation* **V** maps points in the initial *world co-ordinate system* into the *eye co-ordinate system*.

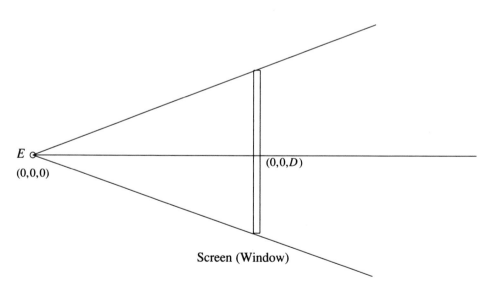

Figure 2. Pyramid of vision: side view.

A viewing transformation is typically redundantly parameterised by:

- a viewing direction vector $\bar{N}$,
- a vector $\bar{V}$ to indicate which way is up,
- an optional vector $\bar{U}$ to denoting which way x increases.
- a viewing position, $E \in \mathbf{R}^3$,

Because the derivation for **V** is overly complicated in the standard textbooks, we shall derive it here using vector calculus rather than analytic geometry. A viewing transformation consists of a change of basis **B** and a translation **T**. The translation **T** simply maps the viewpoint E to the origin. **B** takes the basis vectors of the viewing co-ordinate system, $(\bar{V}, \bar{U}, \bar{N})$, to the standard orthonormal basis $(\bar{e}_x, \bar{e}_y, \bar{e}_z)$ of the world co-ordinate system. More specifically, **B** maps:

- $\bar{N} = (N_x, N_y, N_z)$ to $\bar{e}_z = (0,0,1)$.
- $\bar{U} = (U_x, U_y, U_z)$ to $\bar{e}_x = (1,0,0)$.
- $\bar{V} = (V_x, V_y, V_z)$ to $\bar{e}_y = (0,1,0)$.

We shall assume that all vectors are normalised. If $\bar{U}$ has not been specified, then a suitable candidate would be

$$\bar{U} = \bar{V} \times \bar{N}.$$

Thus $\bar{U}$ would be perpendicular to both $\bar{V}$ and $\bar{N}$. If the specified $\bar{V}$ is not perpendicular to $\bar{N}$, then replace it by

$$\bar{V}' = \bar{N} \times \bar{U}.$$

This would give an orthonormal basis for the viewing co-ordinate system. The matrix transformation to the world co-ordinate system can be written down immediately simply by looking at how each basis vector in the window co-ordinate system is to be mapped. From the above discussion, the following constraints hold when **B** is in matrix form:

$$[U_x \quad U_y \quad U_z] \mathbf{B} = [1 \quad 0 \quad 0]^T,$$

$$[V_x \quad V_y \quad V_z] \mathbf{B} = [0 \quad 1 \quad 0]^T, \tag{27}$$

$$[N_x \quad N_y \quad N_z] \mathbf{B} = [0 \quad 0 \quad 1]^T.$$

Hence **B** has the following matrix representation (in homogeneous form):

$$\mathbf{B} = \begin{bmatrix} U_x & V_x & N_x & 0 \\ U_y & V_y & N_y & 0 \\ U_z & V_z & N_z & 0 \\ 0 & 0 & 0 & 1 \end{bmatrix}. \tag{28}$$

In matrix form the translation $\mathbf{T}$ is

$$\mathbf{T} = \begin{bmatrix} 1 & 0 & 0 & 0 \\ 0 & 1 & 0 & 0 \\ 0 & 0 & 1 & 0 \\ -E_x & -E_y & -E_z & 1 \end{bmatrix}. \tag{29}$$

In matrix form, $\mathbf{V} = \mathbf{T}\,\mathbf{B}$. A point $P(x,y,z) \in \mathbf{R}^3$ in the world co-ordinate system is converted to the viewing co-ordinate system by performing the following operation:

$$[x \quad y \quad z \quad 1]\ \mathbf{V}. \tag{30}$$

A more conventional graphical treatment by analytic geometry can be found in [NeSp78; FoDa82].

1.6.1.2. Perspective Transformation

We now discuss the third important application of geometric transformations: perspective. Intuitively, a perspective transformation preserves depth information but distorts the scene so that when ultimately projected onto the window, objects closer to the eye will be larger than objects further away. More formally, a perspective transformation maps the viewing pyramid into a parallelepiped. This greatly simplifies visibility semantics, as will be seen in the next chapter, and enhances the realism of the rendered image. Perspective is usually applied only to scenes which undergo traditional visibility determination as in the next chapter. If scenes are "ray traced" as described in Chapter 5, then perspective is not normally applied (although it could be applied after illumination calculation).

Again, we stress that this material is covered more thoroughly by the standard textbooks in computer graphics. However, for some semblance of completeness, we shall write down the semantics of a common perspective transformation. Given eye-to-window distance, D, this transformation can be computed by similar triangles as illustrated by Figure 3.

It is readily seen that the desired perspective transformation is

$$\mathbf{P}(x, y, z) =_{df} \left[\frac{D\,x}{z}, \frac{D\,y}{z}, z \right]. \tag{31}$$

Note the division by z to arrive at the transformed x and y values. $\mathbf{P}$ is therefore not affine. However, it shares with the affine transformations the very beneficial property that line segments are always mapped in perspective to line segments. Unlike affine transformations, however, parallel lines are unlikely to remain

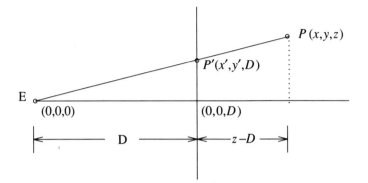

Figure 3. Geometry of the perspective transformation.

parallel in perspective. As will be seen, a perspective transformation is applied to the scene once, after the viewing transformation has been performed.

Observe that for $z > 0$, $\mathbf{P}$ is invertible. Thus for an object $O = (Z_O, I_O)$ we can define the semantics of object perspective as

$$\mathbf{P}O \ =_{df} \ (\mathbf{P}Z_O, I_O \circ \mathbf{P}^{-1}). \tag{32}$$

In practice, the treatment of the z-component in Eq. 31 above is not as straightforward as indicated. When combined with clipping and an image-space visibility algorithm (see Chapter 2), z is often normalised, and sometimes perspective is also applied to it. Given a front clipping plane of $z = hither$ and far clipping plane $z = yon$, $0 < hither < yon$, we may normalise z as follows:

$$z_n \ =_{df} \ \frac{z - hither}{yon - hither} \ \in \ [0,1]. \tag{33}$$

If desired, a perspective distortion may be applied to z_n just as was done for x and y:

$$z' \ =_{df} \ \frac{D z_n}{z} \ = \ \frac{D \, (z - hither)}{z \, (yon - hither)} \ \in \ \left[0, \frac{D}{yon} \right]. \tag{34}$$

The effect of Eq. 34 is to distribute, after conversion to physical device coordinates, the precision of depth values in a nonlinear fashion. In particular, greater precision is applied to z values close to the *hither* clipping plane (see Figure 4). That is, points closer to the eye are given increased depth discrimination.

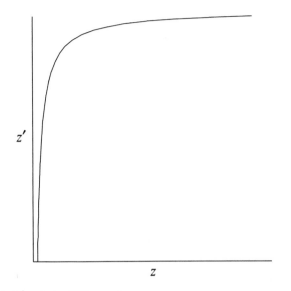

Figure 4. A plot of z' against $z \in [hither, yon]$.

1.6.1.3. Geometric Projections

Definition 11. A 3-dimensional *geometric projection* π is a surjection $\pi: \mathbf{R}^3 \rightarrow \mathbf{R}^d$, $d < 3$.

We shall briefly discuss two geometric projections: perspective projection and orthographic projection. These are often used for viewing line drawings, and their origin certainly precedes computer graphics (as, of course, do most of the transformations discussed in this chapter).

Example 13. Perspective projection. A perspective projection collapses a scene onto the window after perspective transformation. In other words, we simply take a perspective transform of the scene and drop the z component. Let O be an object. Then a *perspective projection* π_P has the following semantics.

$$\pi_P O =_{df} \{ (x,y) \in \mathbf{R}^2 : (x,y,z) \in Z_{\mathbf{PV}O}, z \in \mathbf{R} \}. \tag{35}$$

$\mathbf{V}$ is an optional viewing transformation and $\mathbf{P}$ is the perspective transformation, both defined above, and $Z_{\mathbf{PV}O}$ is the spatial extent of O under these transformations.[10] We shall denote $\pi_P O$ by S_O, and call this set the *screen extent* of O. We shall use this notion when we define the semantics of visibility.

---

[10] $\mathbf{PV}O$ is in functional form here rather than in matrix form.

Example 14. Orthographic projection. An orthographic projection collapses an object in $\mathbf{R}^3$ onto a plane. In particular, after a viewing transformation $\mathbf{V}$ has been applied, we define an *orthographic projection* onto the screen plane as follows.

$$\pi_{Or}\, O =_{df} \{\, (x,y) \in \mathbf{R}^2 : (x,y,z) \in Z_{\mathbf{V}O}, \, z \in \mathbf{R} \,\}. \tag{36}$$

1.6.2. Colour Transformations

One of the most active areas of computer graphipcsconcerns developing ways of defining and altering the colour of an object. Many of the techniques discovered so far have arisen because they are cheap substitutes for physically or computationally complex processes. Some of these techniques are now so sophisticated that they warrant a formalisation in their own right, and certainly deserve a status that is elevated beyond that of "implementation trick".

1.6.2.1. Texture Mapping

Texture mapping is perhaps the most successful "trick" in computer graphics. It, together with colour-mapping described later, is a graphic transformation that can honestly be said to originate from computer graphics. When developed by E. Catmull, texture mapping was seen as a cheap way of wrapping a "texture" around an object [Catm75]. The effect produced is akin to wallpapering a wall or sticking a decal on some object. It was soon realised that this technique had great potential. Most notably, J. Blinn developed many new ways of using texture mapping, and extended the notion of mapping textures onto surfaces to that of perturbing the *normal* of an object's surface at any point [Blin78]. In many illumination models (see below) the shade of the object at a point depends on the direction of the surface normal at that point. The act of perturbing the surface normal at a point by an entry in a *bump map* has the effect, after shading, of making features of an object appear bumpy, wrinkled, raised, or lowered, without actually changing any spatial properties of the object. We shall not discuss bump mapping further, as its semantics is almost identical to texture mapping, except that the latter is a colour transformation, whereas the former is a transformation of an object's surface normal function. Recently, the notion of texture mapping has been extended to 3-D textures to create some very realistic effects such as trees [Grin84], clouds [Gard85] woodgrains, and marble [Peac85; Perl85]. While it took some time for researchers to come up with the notion of a 3-D texture mapping [FoAm84], it will be seen that it is a trivial extension semantically of 2-D texture mapping. See [Heck86] for a very good survey of texture mapping.

In practice, texture mapping consists of two distinct (but often interleaved) parts: the geometric texture-mapping technique itself (which is what we mean by texture mapping in this section), and rendering. A failure to distinguish between these parts can obscure the unique problems that are a consequence of each issue.

The fundamental problem of texture mapping is the choice of a suitable function that maps points from an object into the texture space. The fundamental problem of rendering a textured scene is identical to that of rendering any scene: the choice of a suitable scene sampling mechanism. Our view of texture mapping is thus entirely consistent with our position taken on scene specification: scenes are to be distinguished from images.

2-D Texture Mapping. Let $\tau: \mathbf{TS} \to \mathbf{C}$ be an arbitrary function mapping each point (u,v) in the *texture space* $\mathbf{TS} \subseteq \mathbf{R}^2$ to a colour space $\mathbf{C}$. This texture space is often a closed subset of $\mathbf{R}^2$ such as a unit square. In practice, τ prescribes a texture (i.e., the wallpaper) that is to be mapped onto an object's surface. Recall from a discussion earlier that in addition to defining an object's spatio-temporal semantics, a system specifier may wish to add other attributes to refine its semantics. Suppose we attribute a projection mapping $C_O : Z_O \to \mathbf{TS}$ to each object O. This projection takes points in object O and maps them into the texture space. There is no explicit requirement that C_O be bijective, or even surjective, for that matter. Indeed, neither of these conditions is easy to guarantee, unless, for example, C_O is a *conformal mapping* of object O to $\mathbf{TS}$ (see below).

Definition 12. Given texture function τ and projection C_O, a *2-D texture mapping* is of the form

$$I_O(x,y,z) =_{df} \tau(C_O(x,y,z)), \quad \forall (x,y,z) \in Z_O. \tag{37}$$

A reasonable alternative formulation of the semantics would be as a function which maps an object and a texture to a textured object. The above approach was taken instead because one intuitively thinks of an object as having its colour *defined* by the texture mapping rather than altered by it. The reader may wish to contrast this with colour mapping, described momentarily.

One possible objection to this definition is that the texture is mapped throughout the object, and that normally the texture is mapped only on the object's surface. An alternative definition would be to restrict the domain of the mapping to the set of visible points of the object. This set is defined formally in the next chapter, and the above equation could be rewritten accordingly.

There are some obvious candidates for C_O:

- the perspective projection π_P,

- the orthographic projection π_{Or},

- any conformal mapping from Z_O (or its bounding surface) to $\mathbf{TS}$ (see below).

In the case of the first two projections, care is required to ensure that the range of the projection lies within **TS**.

3-D Texture Mapping. We now show how to extend the above semantics to 3-D textures. It is of course trivial to do so. Let $TS \subseteq \mathbf{R}^3$, and let $\tau : TS \rightarrow C$ prescribe a texture volume (of colour values). Suppose $C_O : Z_O \rightarrow TS$ is an arbitrary projection. Then the semantics of *3-D texture mapping* is exactly as in Eq. 37. Two examples of C_O are:

- the identity map of Z_O to Z_O.
- the perspective transformation, PZ_O.

Spatio-Temporal Textures? It is clear that texture mapping can easily be extended to higher dimensions. What is not obvious is what exactly a "temporal texture" is. It might, for example, describe the motion of an object that is difficult to model—phenomena such as fire, waves, and lightning come to mind. To the author's knowledge, 4-D "texture" mapping has never been tried.

Common Examples of Textures. Textures used in practice include digitised photographs of natural scenes, procedural textures such as fractal terrains, probabilistic texture models, clouds, characters, wood grain, veins in rock, and tree bark.

1.6.2.2. Colour Mapping and Quantisation

Colour mapping is a very popular technique in raster graphics. It has been used for a wide variety of applications, ranging from its original technical uses such as compensation for non-linearities in display screens to more creative uses such as providing some crude animation. The basic idea of colour mapping is similar to texture-mapping, except that instead of using an object's spatial position to determine a colour, the *current colour i* of an object at point (x, y, z) is mapped to the point's ultimate colour i'. Normally, colour-mapping is performed *after* rendering (i.e., on images), but since it is a colour transformation, we present its semantics here, noting that the technique can be applied formally to either a scene or an image. In practice, it is performed on images because colour mapping functions are often built into the hardware of raster graphics systems. Moreover, an index into a colour map (alternatively called a *look-up table*) is normally a value in a prefix of the natural numbers.

The formal view of colour mapping we shall adopt is that it is a transformation from one colour space to another. Let C_0 and C_1 be two arbitrary colour spaces, and let $m : C_0 \rightarrow C_1$ be a total function. Typically, C_0 and C_1 are both finite prefixes of the natural numbers:

$$C_0 =_{df} I^d, d \in N, d \geq 1, \qquad (38)$$

where $I = \{ 0, \cdots, n \} \subseteq N$ for some $n > 0$. Common choices for n and d are $n = 255$ and $d = 3$. We define the semantics of a *colour mapping*, M, of object $O = (Z_O, I_O)$ to be

$$M O =_{df} (Z_O, m \circ I_O). \qquad (39)$$

A colour-mapping, therefore, has the effect of transforming an object space containing C_0 to an object space containing C_1. A colour-mapped scene is defined by distributing the colour-mapping operator over all objects in the scene. Recall that all graphic transformations are defined to distribute over objects in this manner. A similar colour-mapping operator can be applied to images. Observe that if the mapping M is extended to a temporal dimension, then colour-mapping can be used as an animation tool. See [Shou79] for many practical applications of this technique, which is often called *colour-table animation*.

We observed in Eq. 38 that colour mappings are usually defined over discrete intensity spaces. An important operation that can be applied to either scenes or images is *quantisation*, which is a transformation from a continuous to a discrete colour space. At some point, a quantisation step is required in virtually every graphics system. Formally, the semantics of quantisation is as in Eq. 39.

Example 15. Suppose $C_0 = [0, 1]$ and $C_1 = \{ 0, 1, \cdots, 255 \}$. Define a mapping function $m : C_0 \rightarrow C_1$ as follows

$$m(x) =_{df} \langle 255x \rangle. \qquad (40)$$

The notation $\langle a \rangle$ denotes rounding $a \in R$ up to the nearest integer. The resulting colour mapping, M, is a common quantisation.

1.6.2.3. Other Colour Transformations

The above transformations constitute some of the more popular mechanisms which alter or define the colour field of an object. However, these are by no means all possible colour transformations. We note in passing, for example, two other possibilities which have an easily-expressed semantics.

Filtering. One may wish to condition a colour field before attempting to render a scene. This might include enhancing edges or certain features, or perhaps blurring others. The typical way to perform such operations is to apply a filter to the colour field. Several filters are defined in the next chapter on rendering. An image processing textbook such as [Prat78] is a very good introduction to these filters, most of which have an analytic definition, and consequently are easily incorporated into our framework. See also Chapter 3 for a discussion of filtering.

Blending. We saw above that it is a simple matter to blend uniformly the intensity functions of overlapping objects or scenes. Alternatively, if several objects coincide spatially, one can define a mechanism for blending their colours together in a non-uniform fashion, or taking their maximum, etc. This technique is called *compositing*, and it has a semantics which is expressible by intensity blending functions defined above. See also [MaSh78; Mall82a,b; PoDu84] for several other approaches.

1.6.3. Conformal Mappings

Conformal maps are geometric transformations in the complex plane. Their effect can therefore easily be considered over R^2. We are discussing them here rather than in the above section on geometric transformations because their most obvious application is texture mapping. As is evident from its semantics, there are two critical steps in the texture-mapping process. The first step is choosing a texture. The second step is choosing the manner in which points on an object are mapped into the texture space (or conversely). An interesting question to ask, therefore, is whether there exist "nice" mappings from a PGO into a texture space, or more generally, to another PGO. Here, "nice" might mean continuous, differentiable, and practical. To begin to solve this problem, we can turn to the theory of conformal maps. It turns out that there exist continuous differentiable mappings between almost any two reasonable subsets of the complex plane (and thus R^2). We briefly explore this topic in this section, and we shall discuss the practical progress we have made. Since the notion of conformal maps in texture mapping is entirely novel to computer graphics, we shall focus on intuition. A completely rigorous development would take us too far afield, but the interested reader is encouraged to consult a book on complex analysis for inspiration (e.g., [Mars73; Poly74]).

Definition 13. A *conformal map*, f, in the complex plane is a function that is analytic with a non-zero derivative at every point $z \in C$.

An amazing result by Riemann states that there exists a bijective conformal map between any two simply-connected complex regions [Mars73]. With some minor constraints, a conformal mapping is unique. A *simply-connected* region is, loosely speaking, a subset of the complex plane that contains no holes. Unfortunately, Riemann's mapping theorem establishes the existence of such maps, but does not offer a prescription for their construction. Indeed, determining a conformal map between two sets can be extremely challenging. In this light, we suggest the following new research area within computer graphics: *to determine practical conformal mappings among basic graphic shapes.* This problem appears not to have been suggested in the computer graphics literature before, but it is clearly of interest. In the remainder of this section, we shall show that the problem is highly nontrivial.

Consider how we might go about mapping an equilateral triangle to a unit square. This choice of shapes is not arbitrary. First, squares and triangles are very simple shapes. Second, all polygonal objects can be decomposed into triangles, which remain triangles after perspective transformation. Third, texture spaces are typically square. Unfortunately, even for intuitively simple mappings, the mathematics is complicated. We divide the task into the composition of two conformal maps: from a triangle to the upper-half complex plane, and from the upper-half complex plane to a square.

Mapping a Triangle to the Upper-Half Complex Plane. Graphically, we wish to perform the mapping depicted in Figure 5.

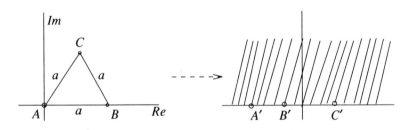

Figure 5. Conformal mapping from an equilateral triangle to the upper-half plane.

A', B', and C' can be chosen arbitrarily, so we shall define $A' = -1$, $B' = 0$, $C' = 1$ to keep the equations simple. As proven in [Poly74], a powerful theorem known as the *Schwarz-Christoffel Formulae* shows how to contruct a conformal map from an arbitrary simple polygon to the upper-half complex plane. The inverse formula is presented in [Mars73]. The mapping we want turns out to be:

$$w_1(z) = -a + C \int_{-1}^{z} (\zeta+1)^{-2/3} - \zeta^{-2/3} (1-\zeta)^{-2/3} \, d\zeta, \qquad (41)$$

where

$$C = \frac{4a\sqrt{\pi}}{\Gamma(\frac{1}{6})\,\Gamma(\frac{1}{3})} \ ,$$

and Γ is Euler's gamma function, which takes on the value $(n-1)!$ for integral n:

$$\Gamma(x) =_{df} \int_0^\infty t^{x-1} e^{-t} dt.$$

Eq. 41 is not a particularly pleasant-looking integral, but observe that C is a constant which can be pre-computed. The mapping $w_1(z)$ can be computed by numerical means. The form of w_1 for more general triangles is very similar to the above, except that the exponents in its definition reflect the interior angles of the triangle (divided by π radians), and C is slightly more complicated.

Mapping the Upper-Half Complex Plane to a Unit Square. By a direct application of the Schwarz-Christoffel Formula as given in [Mars73], it is straightforward but tedious to show that the mapping from the upper-half plane to a rectangle as in Figure 6 is given by

$$w(z) = \int_0^z \frac{d\zeta}{\sqrt{\zeta(\zeta-1)(\zeta-c)}} \ . \tag{42}$$

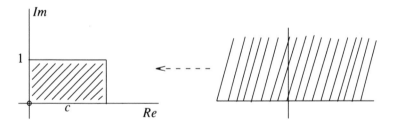

Figure 6. Conformal mapping from the upper-half plane to a rectangle.

Eq. 42 is an elliptic integral which does not have a closed-form solution for arbitrary $c > 0$. In our case, $c = 1$, so our mapping simplifies slightly to

$$w(z) = \int_0^z \frac{d\zeta}{(\zeta-1)\sqrt{\zeta}} \tag{43}$$

$$= \frac{1}{2} \log\left[\frac{\sqrt{z}-1}{\sqrt{z}+1}\right] - i\pi$$

by a straightforward substitution argument (the straightforwardness of which the author is still verifying!). The map from an equilateral triangle to unit square is therefore

$$w(z) = w_2(w_1(z)).$$

The practical computation of this map is a somewhat daunting task, and we pose the development of techniques to approximate such maps as a challenging problem in computer graphics. We have recently implemented a system that computes conformal texture maps between polygonal figures. A summary of this work appears in [FiFC87]. Figure 7 depicts conformal mappings from a square to a dodecagon and to a concave polygon, using the technique described in [FiFC87], severely deforming a poor primate in the process.

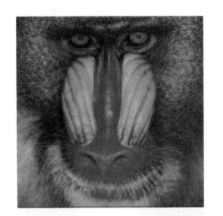

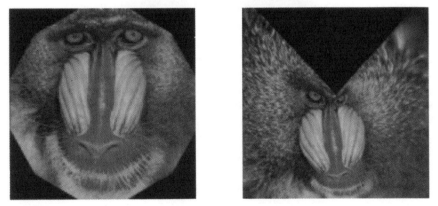

Figure 7. Conformal map between a square (above) and two polygons (below).

1.7. Scenes and Scene Semantics

Definition 14. A *scene* is a sequence $S = (O'_1, \cdots, O'_n)$ of graphic objects.

Definition 15. Let **V** and **P** be optional viewing and perspective transformations, and let $R \subseteq \mathbf{R}^3$ be an optional clipping region. Then the *scene semantics* of S, ($[S]$)

is

$$\langle\!\langle S \rangle\!\rangle =_{df} (\mathbf{P}\,\mathbf{V}\,S) \mid R \;=\; \left[(\mathbf{P}\,\mathbf{V}\,O_i') \mid R : i=1, \cdots, n \right] \qquad (44)$$

$$=\; \left[(S_{O_i}, Z_{O_i}, I_{O_i}) : i=1, \cdots, n \right],$$

where $O_i = (\mathbf{P}\,\mathbf{V}\,O_i') \mid R$.

Thus the semantics of the scene is precisely the sequence of objects in the scene after viewing, perspective and clipping operations. The scene is oriented in the eye co-ordinate system as described above. Since the semantics of the scene is so structurally similar to the scene itself, we shall simply assume, unless stated otherwise, that a scene has undergone these operations, and shall thus drop the bracket notation. This assumption will be in effect when we define the semantics of visibility and the semantics of an image corresponding to a scene in later chapters.

1.8. Summary

This chapter has presented a scene specification framework. Objects are built up by combining primitive elements. Scenes are composed of a collection of these objects. Various transformations were also defined over scenes and objects. Ultimately, the notion of a scene semantics was defined, which gives the semantics of each object in the scene after orientation into the desired field of view.

One useful extension to the framework would be to define the semantics of temporal transformations. A *temporal transformation* is a sequence of graphic transformations which prescribes the evolution of a scene over a period of time. One interesting application of temporal transformations is *keyframe* animation. Using this technique, two still (key) frames of animation are used to bracket an animation sequence. A temporal transformation from the first frame to the second would be given, which then defines a set of "in-between" frames to accomplish a smooth transition from one to the other. Developing a suitable notation for temporal transformations is an interesting and challenging research area in itself. A related topic would be to develop a notation and semantics of colour-table animation (see above). We defer these topics to future investigation.

2   Visibility

The moral: a good proof is one which makes us wiser.

−Y.I. Manin[1]

Synopsis. A problem fundamental to computer graphics is that of determining the visible points of a scene from a specific viewpoint. In this chapter, a semantics of visibility is presented. A formal definition of the visible surface problem (VSP) based on this semantics is then given. This foundation for the VSP facilitates the derivation of its computational complexity with respect to several familiar models of graphic computation. It is shown that in either case, one or both of the problems of sorting or finding the minimum distance between a set of numbers reduce to simple instances of the VSP. However, the complexity of the VSP in more general cases is greater than that for sorting, since a large number of visible objects may be produced with respect to a given set of input objects. The complexity of the VSP thus depends on both the input and output size of the problem instance. Some basic upper and lower bounds will be proven for these more complex cases. The results are of both theoretical and practical interest, particularly for our frame buffer models, in that the models differ from one another by the addition of a single, feasible, primitive operation, and yet the complexity results are substantially different.

---

[1] Y.I. Manin, *A Course in Mathematical Logic* (Springer-Verlag: New York, NY), N. Koblitz: trans., 1977.

2.1. Introduction

The *visible surface problem* (VSP) is that of determining the *visible* points of a scene with respect to a given viewpoint.[2] The notion of visibility has received some formal treatment in the computer graphics literature [FoFu88; FoDa82; Nayl81; Gilo78]. Our formalism is inspired by these efforts, but our analysis of the visible surface problem, particularly of interpenetrating surfaces, is somewhat more precise. The first objective of this chapter is to present a mathematical semantics of visibility and the VSP. Such an effort is a prerequisite to proving interesting properties of the problem. As such, our second objective is to analyse the computational complexity of the VSP. As a formally-defined problem, standard reduction techniques and known results from complexity theory can be exploited to establish nontrivial complexity bounds for the VSP. The main contribution of this chapter is that the complexity results are bound to realistic, but abstract, *graphical models of computation*. The complexity results are themselves actually fairly simple to prove. Their import is that, unlike many results in theoretical computer science, they are related to familiar models that say something about real graphics systems.

It has long been known that there is a fundamental relationship between sorting and the VSP [SuSS74]. We shall show that this intuition has a basis in theory: the problem of sorting a list of natural numbers reduces to a simple instance of the visible surface problem. However, as pointed out in [NeSp79], the visibility problem seems to be more difficult than that of sorting. Again, we shall show that this is formally true: the visibility problem for geometrically complex scenes has a greater computational complexity than sorting. Several upper and lower bounds for the VSP acting on complex scenes will be proven. The next section presents basic formal definitions and motivates the use of realistic models of computation.

2.2. Definitions and Semantics

As in the last chapter, we shall define a scene S as a sequence of objects $(O_1, \cdots, O_N)$. S is assumed to have undergone viewing and perspective transformations. Each object O in S is a tuple (Z'_O, I'_O), where Z'_O is the spatial extent of O in $\mathbf{R}^3$, and I'_O attaches an intensity value to each point in Z'_O. Also recall that $S_O \subseteq \mathbf{R}^2$ is the screen extent of O. Observe that both the depth and intensity relations can be many-valued for a given $(x,y) \in S_O$. We transform these relations

---

[2] It is traditional to use the word *surface* in connection with determining visible points, since regardless of the extent of the object in three-space, only its bounding surface plays a part in visibility determination. On the other hand, a definition of the *intensity* of each point on a visible surface may require knowledge of the interior of the object as well as other scene information (see the discussion of illumination models, Chapter 5).

into single-valued functions as follows:

$$Z_O(x,y) \quad =_{df} \quad \min Z'_O(x,y), \quad (x,y) \in S_O, \tag{1}$$

$$I_O(x,y) \quad =_{df} \quad I'_O(x,y, Z_O(x,y)), \quad (x,y) \in S_O.$$

The point $(x,y,Z_O(x,y))$ for $(x,y) \in S_O$ is the point in O closest to the viewpoint. $I_O(x,y)$ gives the intensity of this point. The set of all such points over S_O defines the surface of O that is potentially visible from the viewpoint.

Definition 1. Let $P = (x_p, y_p, z_p)$ and $Q = (x_q, y_q, z_q)$ be arbitrary points in $\mathbf{R}^3$. We define the relation P *obscures* Q, denoted by $P \bullet Q$, as

$$P \bullet Q \quad =_{df} \quad x_p = x_q \; \wedge \; y_p = y_q \; \wedge \; z_p \leq z_q. \tag{2}$$

Remark 1. A strict inequality is used by Fournier and Fussell in their *hides* relation, which ensures that a point cannot hide itself [FoFu88]. However, the gain in the use of "$\leq$" in the above definition is that we can handle surface interpenetration easily, which is a somewhat neglected issue in the literature. As observed by Fournier and Fussell, the *obscures* relation induces a partial order on $\mathbf{R}^3$.

The *obscures* relation will be used to define a visibility predicate, denoted by $V_S(x,y,O)$. Informally, the visibility predicate is true if and only if (x,y) is a visible point of object O in the sense that it is not obscured by any other object in the scene. Formally, for each object O_i present in scene S,

$$V_S(x,y,O_i) =_{df} (x,y) \in S_{O_i} \wedge \forall j \neq i [\, (x,y) \in S_{O_j} \Rightarrow (x,y,Z_{O_i}(x,y)) \bullet (x,y,Z_{O_j}(x,y)) \,]. \tag{3}$$

This predicate captures the meaning of visibility to some extent. However, explaining precisely what is meant by the "visible portion" of an object is complicated by the fact that objects may interpenetrate, thus possibly sharing a common subset of visible points. On the other hand, it seems reasonable to insist that visible portions of objects should be mutually disjoint.

Definition 2. The *visible portion* of object O_i, denoted by $Vis_S(O_i)$, is defined formally as follows.

$$Vis_S(O_i) =_{df} Disj_S(O_i) \cup Int_S(O_i), \tag{4}$$

where

$$Disj_S(O_i) =_{df} \{ \, (x,y) \in \mathbf{R}^2 : V_S(x,y,O_i) \wedge \forall j \neq i [\sim V_S(x,y,O_j)] \, \}, \tag{5a}$$

and

$$Int_S(O_i) =_{df} \{ \, (x,y) \in \mathbf{R}^2 - Disj_S(O_i) : V_S(x,y,O_i) \wedge \forall j < i [\sim V_S(x,y,O_j)] \, \}. \tag{5b}$$

The semantics of visibility is captured by two rules; one rule, Eq. 5(a), provides a semantics of visibility over the portions of the scene in which objects are disjoint (*Disj*), and Eq. 5(b) provides a uniqueness rule that arbitrates in the case of interpenetration (*Int*). Other rules for interpenetration are possible, but what is required is that all of the interpenetrating points be consistently given to a single object. In this manner, the interpenetration set may be consistently assigned intensity values from a single object.

It is worthwhile to review the basic order notations. From [Knut76],

$$O(f(n)) =_{df} \{ g(n) : \exists c, n_0 > 0 \ni |g(n)| \leq cf(n), \forall n > n_0 \}.$$

$$\Omega(f(n)) =_{df} \{ g(n) : \exists c, n_0 > 0 \ni g(n) \geq cf(n), \forall n > n_0 \}.$$

$$\Theta(f(n)) =_{df} \{ g(n) : \exists c_0, c_1, n_0 > 0 \ni c_0 f(n) \leq |g(n)| \leq c_1 f(n), \forall n > n_0 \}.$$

Loosely speaking, $O(f(n))$ means "at most $cf(n)$ for some $c > 0$ and sufficiently large n"; $\Omega(f(n))$ means "at least $cf(n)$ for some $c > 0$ and sufficiently large n"; $\Theta(f(n))$ means "both $O(f(n))$ and $\Omega(f(n))$".

2.3. On Lower Bounds for the Visible Surface Problem

After formally defining the visible surface problem, we shall derive some very basic lower bounds for it. We shall be relying on two familiar problems in our reductions.

Sorting Problem (SORT)

INPUT: A list $N = \langle N_1, N_2, \cdots, N_n \rangle$ of distinct, positive natural numbers, such that $N_i \in O(n^d)$, for $i = 1, \cdots, n$, and constant $d \in \mathbf{N}$.
OUTPUT: A list $\langle S_1, S_2, \cdots, S_n \rangle$ which is a permutation of N, such that $\forall 1 \leq i < n. [S_i < S_{i+1}]$.

Minimum Distance Problem (MINDIST)

INPUT: A list $N = \langle N_1, N_2, \cdots, N_n \rangle$ of distinct, positive natural numbers, such that $N_i \in O(n^d)$, for $i = 1, \cdots, n$, and constant $d \in \mathbf{N}$.
OUTPUT: $\min\limits_{i \neq j} \{ | N_i - N_j | \}$.

Several models of computation will be considered in this chapter. All are derived from the well-known RAM model, which has unit-cost $+$, $-$, $*$, **div**, **mod**, and indirect addressing operations [AhHU74]. Memory cells in the RAM are assumed to contain $O(\log n)$ bits on n inputs.

Conjecture 1. *Given n input values* $N_1, \cdots, N_n$, *suppose M is a RAM which solves SORT. Then M has worst-case time complexity of* $\Omega(n \log n)$.

Conjecture 2. *Given n input values* $N_1, \cdots, N_n$, *suppose M is a RAM which solves MINDIST. Then M has worst-case time complexity of* $\Omega(n \log n)$.

Remark 2. As formulated above, SORT is known to be $\Omega(n \log n)$ under the comparison (decision-tree) model of computation [AhHU74; DoLR76; Sham78; PrSh85].[3] However, the RAM model is a more realistic one for the visible surface problem. Unfortunately $\Omega(n \log n)$ lower bounds under the RAM model for these problems when input values are of "moderate" size, have not been established. While the above conjectures are plausible, it is important to note that changes to them could result in changes to the theorems below.

The basic "surfaces" we shall deal with in this chapter are polygons. A k-gon P is denoted by a sequence $\langle p_1, \cdots, p_k \rangle$ of points defining a clockwise tour of P. Thus the "inside" of P is always to the right of the polygon edge being traversed. Associated with every input or output polygon P is a depth value Z_P which defines a constant depth of each point in P. So that our results remain as general as possible we shall restrict input to any visible surface algorithm to be a set of rectangles. Clearly any lower bound derived for this restricted set of polygons applies to any visible surface algorithm handling more sophisticated surfaces (if they include rectangles as a special case).

We shall be establishing lower bounds for very simple versions of the VSP with respect to two models of graphic output. Both of these models are well known in computer graphics. We shall call one the *output list model* (OLM), in that the output of a visible surface algorithm is assumed to be a list of polygons whose insides specify the visible points of the scene and their intensities. The second output model is called the *image store model* (ISM). The output of a visible surface algorithm under an image store model is a rectangular store of intensity and depth values. Each entry in the image store contains information about a single *picture element* or *pixel* in a raster display. The intensity information in an image store is a representation of a raster display screen such as that in a television set.[4] The depth information corresponds to the depth of the object closest to the viewpoint at each pixel. An image store is commonly known as a *frame buffer*.

---

[3] Since MINDIST reduces to SORT, it would also be $\Omega(n \log n)$ if it were formulated as a decision problem.

[4] The image store model is a precursor to the *bit-mapped image* model which is considered in Chapter 4. The difference between an image store and a bit-map is that the former also contains depth information, whereas a bit-mapped image only deals with bi-level intensity values.

2.3.1. VSP Complexity under the Output List Model

The main problem we shall be considering in this section is as follows.

Rectangular Visible Surface Problem (RVSP) (Output List Model)

INPUT: A list $S = \langle R_1, R_2, \cdots, R_n \rangle$ of rectangles, where each $R \in S$ is a triple (S_R, Z_R, I_R). The screen extent, S_R, of each rectangle R is denoted by a sequence of four vertices $\langle p_1, \cdots, p_4 \rangle$, with p_1 corresponding to the bottom-left corner of the rectangle. The left and right sides of each rectangle must be parallel to the y-axis, and the bottom and top sides must be parallel to the x-axis. The depth function, Z_R, and the intensity function, I_R, over rectangle R are both constant values that are bounded by a polynomial in n.

OUTPUT: A list $P = \langle (P_1, j_1), \cdots, (P_m, j_m) \rangle$, where P_i is a polygon, and $j_i \in \mathbf{N}$. Each polygon P_i has extent S_{P_i} denoted by a sequence $\langle p_1, \cdots, p_{k_i} \rangle$ such that

$$\forall i \left[S_{P_i} \subseteq Vis_S(R_{j_i}) \wedge \forall (x,y) \in S_{P_i} [Z_{P_i}(x,y) = Z_{R_{j_i}}(x,y) \wedge I_{P_i}(x,y) = I_{R_{j_i}}(x,y)] \right], \quad (6a)$$

and

$$\forall i . \ Vis_S(R_i) = \bigcup_k S_{P_k} \cap S_{R_i}. \quad (6b)$$

For completeness, we define the visible surface problem for general polygons as follows.

Polygonal Visible Surface Problem (VSP) (Output List Model)

INPUT: A list S of polygons, with possibly variable depth and intensity functions.

OUTPUT: As in RVSP.

The first output criterion, Eq. 6(a), states that each output polygon P_i is a piece of the visible portion of a single input polygon R_{j_i}. Since the geometry of the output is usually more complex to describe in terms of a set of basic geometric shapes like polygons, it is often the case that the visible portion of an input polygon must be described by several output polygons. The second criterion, Eq. 6(b), states that the visible portion of each input polygon is covered by the output polygons. Together, these criteria state that the output polygons must cover all visible points of the scene and no others, and that each output polygon is a portion of a single input polygon. A sample instance of the RVSP is given in Figure 1. Suppose $Z_1 > Z_2 > Z_3$. Then polygon 3 is entirely visible and the other two are partially obscured. Figure 2 gives two ways of satisfying the RVSP as defined.

At the moment we shall only be concerned with cases in which the number of output polygons equals the number of input polygons. In particular, we wish the

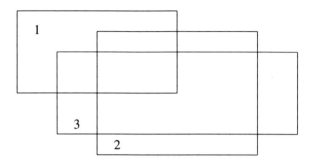

Figure 1. Input to visible surface algorithm.

following to hold:

$$S_{P_i} = Vis_S(R_i). \tag{7}$$

As was alluded to earlier, and as will be shown later, this is not always possible in more complex scenes. In fact, Eq. (7) expresses the simplest possible instance of the RVSP: when the problem input size plus the output size is still $O(n)$.

Theorem 1. *Any instance of MINDIST on n inputs can be transformed in linear time to an instance of an output list model RVSP containing $O(n)$ outputs.*

Data Structures. Each polygon will be described as a record:

> Polygon: **record**
>   Z: **integer**   {depth}
>   I: **integer**   {intensity}
>   BotLeft, TopLeft, BotRight, TopRight: **Point**   {corner points}

> Point: **record**
>   X,Y: **integer**

Thus each polygon requires ten registers for storage. It will be seen that no values larger than the largest input value are required for any reduction in this chapter. The empty set (i.e., a completely obscured object) is denoted by a rectangle whose lower right hand corner (p_4) is to the left of the lower "left" hand corner (p_1). Fields within a given polygon are assumed to be accessed at unit cost using the familiar "dot" notation as in, for example, $P_3.TopLeft$.

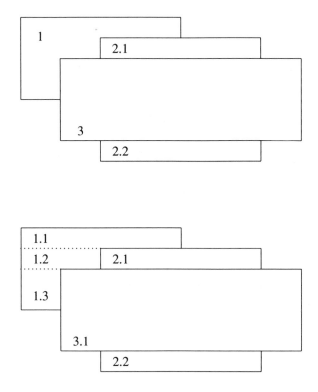

Figure 2. Two possible output configurations with $Z_1 > Z_2 > Z_3$.

Proof of Theorem. Given an instance $N = \langle N_1, N_2, \cdots, N_n \rangle$ of MINDIST construct an instance $S = \langle R_1, R_2, \cdots, R_n \rangle$ of the RVSP with

$R_i . Z = N_i,$
$R_i . I = arbitrary,$
$R_i . BotLeft = (0,0),$
$R_i . TopLeft = (0,1),$
$R_i . BotRight = (N_i, 0),$
$R_i . TopRight = (N_i, 1).$

The construction is illustrated in Figure 3.

It is clear that S can be generated by making a single pass of N. This transformation requires only $O(n)$ time and space. It is important that all input rectangles be of the same height, for otherwise each of the n output polygons could contain $\Omega(n)$ vertices. In any case, each input polygon R_i is a rectangular strip of unit

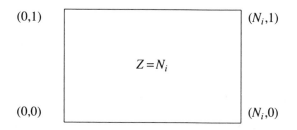

Figure 3. Transformation of MINDIST to RVSP.

height, with length and depth N_i, and with lower-left corner at the origin. The output P_i after visible surface determination is described by the following values.

$$P_i . Z = N_i,$$
$$P_i . I = arbitrary,$$
$$P_i . BotLeft = (pred, 0),$$
$$P_i . TopLeft = (pred, 1),$$
$$P_i . BotRight = (N_i, 0),$$
$$P_i . TopRight = (N_i, 1),$$

where *pred* is the predecessor of N_i in the sorted list of N (see Figure 4).

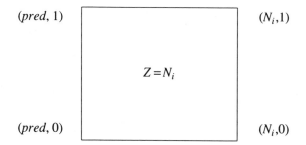

Figure 4. Output of visible surface algorithm.

It is clear that to find the minimum distance among the input values, we need only make a single pass of the output list, printing

$$\min_{2 \le i \le n} \{ P_i . BotRight . X - P_i . BotLeft . X \}. \tag{8}$$

The theorem follows.

Corollary 1. Assuming Conjecture 2, the output list RVSP requires $\Omega(n \log n)$ time under the RAM model even when the output size of the RVSP is $O(n)$ rectangles.

2.3.2. VSP Complexity under the Image Store Model

A traditional and natural way of viewing the output of a visible surface algorithm is as an actual array of pixels representing an image. In such a basic *image store model*, each pixel read and write operation would be charged unit cost. Thus if the dimensions of an image store were $n_1 \times n_2$, then the RVSP under this model would be $\Omega(n_1 n_2)$. Clearly, this can be expensive in practice, for a typical image store would be on the order of $1\,024 \times 1\,024$ pixels. It is reasonable, therefore, to imagine operations which can very quickly operate on large portions of the image store. Indeed, many modern image stores contain hardware for doing just this. For example, the *bitblt* or *rasterop* is a pixel-manipulation facility that is espcially well suited to operations over arbitrary rectangular regions in an image store. When implemented in hardware, such operations are not much slower than a single pixel access. In fact, there now exist architectures which can set all pixels within an n-sided convex polygon in $O(n)$ steps. Thus an arbitrary rectangle can be set in $O(1)$ steps.

In view of these hardware possibilities, it would be of interest to define image store models containing instructions which, in constant time, would perform simple operations on arbitrary rectangles of pixels. Subsequently, their effect on the RVSP on an image store can be assessed.

2.3.2.1. Description of Image Store Model

Definition 3. An *image store model* (ISM) is a standard RAM equipped with a 2-dimensional random-access store rather than a 1-dimensional store. Each memory cell P_{ij} in the ISM is called a *pixel*. A read or write operation on any pixel is charged unit cost. We shall adopt the following input/output conventions for an ISM. Input to an ISM is a sequence of natural numbers as before. An ISM has two output "media": an output tape, and the 2-D RAM store itself. When an ISM finishes its computation, the output tape must contain four natural numbers (x_1, y_1) and (x_2, y_2) which give the bottom-left and top-right corners respectively of the rectangular region in the 2-D RAM store representing the output image.

Remark 3. Once we define unit-cost operations over rectangular portions of the image store, this output convention will allow us to "output" considerably more values than the actual time that would otherwise be required to write each pixel separately.

Remark 4. Whenever the term *pixel* is used in this chapter, it refers to a cell in an ISM. In subsequent chapters, the notion of a pixel will not be bound to an ISM.

Definition 4. A *weak-blit image store model* (WISM) is an ISM with an additional unit-cost operation: **Blit**. The semantics of **Blit** is: for v, $x_1, x_2, y_1, y_2 \in \mathbf{N}$, $0 \le x_1 \le x_2, 0 \le y_1 \le y_2$

$$\mathbf{Blit}(v, (x_1,y_1), (x_2,y_2)) =_{df} \forall (i,j) \in \mathbf{N}^2, x_1 \le i \le x_2, y_1 \le j \le y_2 : P_{ij} \leftarrow v. \quad (9)$$

All other image store pixels are unchanged. The input/output conventions for a WISM are the same as those for an ISM.

Remark 5. A WISM allows one to set simultaneously all the pixels within an arbitrarily large rectangular subset of the image store to a specific value.

Definition 5. A *strong-blit image store model* (SISM) is a WISM with an additional unit-cost operation: **RepMin**. The semantics of **RepMin** is: for v, $x_1, x_2, y_1, y_2 \in \mathbf{N}$, $0 \le x_1 \le x_2, 0 \le y_1 \le y_2$

$$\mathbf{RepMin}(v, (x_1,y_1), (x_2,y_2)) =_{df} \quad (10)$$

$$\forall (i,j) \in \mathbf{N}^2, x_1 \le i \le x_2, y_1 \le j \le y_2 : \text{ if } v < P_{ij} \text{ then } P_{ij} \leftarrow v.$$

All other image store pixels are unchanged. The input/output conventions for a SISM are the same as those for an ISM.

Remark 6. A parallel version of **RepMin** was first considered by Fiume, Fournier, and Rudolph in [FiFR83]. It is not obvious that a **Blit** can always be replaced by **RepMin**.

Coding Convention. For the purposes of defining the RVSP under the ISM, we introduce the convention that each pixel P_{ij} in an image store can encode a pair of values (Z, I). Where required, $P_{ij} . Z \in \mathbf{N}$ is the depth value and $P_{ij} . I \in \mathbf{N}$ is the intensity value encoded in pixel P_{ij}. Since the definition of the RVSP below places polynomial bounds on the size of depth and intensity values, encoding and decoding these values can be performed quickly.

Output Convention for SORT. The output of an algorithm to sort a list of n numbers under an ISM consists of the specification of a 1 by n rectangle on the output tape, which denotes an n-pixel row of the image store. Successive pixel values in this row give the sorted list.

Rectangular Visible Surface Problem (RVSP) (ISM)

INPUT: A list $S = \langle x_1, y_1, x_2, y_2, R_1, R_2, \cdots, R_n \rangle$, where $x_1, y_1, x_2, y_2 \in \mathbf{N}$, $x_1 \leq x_2$, $y_1 \leq y_2$, and each $R \in S$ is a rectangle represented by a triple (S_R, Z_R, I_R). The screen extent, S_R, of each rectangle R is denoted by a sequence of four vertices $\langle p_1, \cdots, p_4 \rangle$, with p_1 corresponding to the bottom-left corner of the rectangle. The depth function, Z_R, and the intensity function, I_R, over rectangle R are both constant values that are bounded by a polynomial in n. The pairs (x_1, y_1) and (x_2, y_2) define the bottom-left and top-right corners of the 2-D RAM store in the ISM to be viewed as the output image. We shall assume that the input polygons together cover the screen (i.e., output image). If this is not so, then add a "background" polygon which covers the screen and which lies behind all other polygons.

OUTPUT: The output tape contains (x_1, y_1), (x_2, y_2), and the image store contains a set of values satisfying

$$\forall x_1 \leq i \leq x_2, y_1 \leq j \leq y_2. \exists! k :$$

$$[(i,j) \in Vis_S(R_k) \ \wedge \ P_{ij}.I = I_{R_k}(i,j) \ \wedge \ P_{ij}.Z = Z_{R_k}(i,j)].$$

This definition states that each pixel (i,j) is assigned a depth and intensity according to the visible surface containing it (see Figure 5).

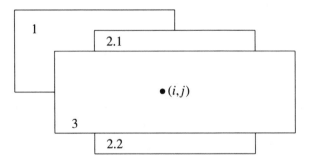

Figure 5. Pixel value assignment: P_{ij} is assigned the depth and intensity of polygon 3.

2.3.2.2. On Lower Bounds for the RVSP under the WISM

Theorem 2. *If the RVSP under the WISM is solvable in $O(n)$ time, then SORT under the WISM is solvable in $O(n)$ time.*

Proof. The RVSP under the WISM will be used to sort n natural numbers. We shall place the sorted output in the first n pixels of row 1 of the image store. As above, given an instance $N = \langle N_1, N_2, \cdots, N_n \rangle$ of SORT, we construct an instance $S = \langle 0, 0, M, 1, R_1, R_2, \cdots, R_n \rangle$ of the RVSP where $M = \max\{N_i\}$, and

$$R_i \cdot Z = N_i,$$
$$R_i \cdot I = N_i,$$
$$R_i \cdot BotLeft = (0,0),$$
$$R_i \cdot TopLeft = (0,1),$$
$$R_i \cdot BotRight = (N_i, 0),$$
$$R_i \cdot TopRight = (N_i, 1).$$

The sorted list can be generated by the following algorithm.

```
x := j := 0
loop exit when j ≥ n
    P_{j1} . (Z,I) := P_{x0} . (0,I)
    x := P_{x0} . I
    j := j + 1
print (on output tape) (0,1),(n−1,1)
```

Only $2n$ pixel accesses are required to generate the sorted list. The theorem follows.

Remark 7. The above proof is actually a reduction from sorting to the RVSP under the WISM. The reduction itself does not need **Blit**, and could be accomplished in linear time on a simpler model.

Theorem 3. *SORT can be solved in linear time under the SISM.*

Proof. Transform an instance of SORT to unit-height rectangles as in Theorem 1. Perform a **RepMin** of each rectangle into the image store. Generate the sorted list as in Theorem 1.

Remark 8. The previous two theorems introduce an interesting issue regarding the power of WISM and SISM for sorting. Clearly, the SISM is a powerful model, for it allows us to sort in $O(n)$ time, so that by Conjecture 1 it is stronger than a RAM for sorting. Whether or not the same is true of a WISM is not obvious. In fact, since a **Blit** operation seems to provide no way of doing some type of comparison, the following conjecture is plausible.

Conjecture 2. *Suppose M is a WISM which solves SORT. Then M has worst-case time complexity $\Omega(n \log n)$.*

From Theorem 2, this conjecture gives rise to the following corollary.

Corollary 2. *Assuming Conjecture 2, the RVSP is of time complexity* $\Omega(n \log n)$ *under the WISM.*

Remark 9. As we discuss in the conclusions, there may exist problems other than sorting which are solvable only in $\Theta(n \log n)$ time on a RAM, but which are provably solvable in $O(n)$ time on a WISM. This would suggest either that the WISM/SISM models cut across the complexity structure induced by a RAM, or that the WISM is of equal power to the SISM. The latter seems to be less likely, although this opinion may not be shared by the reader.

2.3.2.3. Upper Bounds for the RVSP under the WISM

Any algorithm that solves the RVSP for the output list model can be used to solve the problem for the image store model. However, such an algorithm would run in $\Omega(n^2)$ time (see Section 2.4). In this section it is shown that we can get a better upper bound if we take advantage of the power of a WISM.

Theorem 4. *The RVSP under the WISM can be solved in time* $O(n \log n)$.

Corollary 3. *Assuming Conjecture 2, the RVSP under the WISM runs in time* $\Theta(n \log n)$.

Proof of Theorem. Given an instance $S = \langle R_1, \cdots, R_n \rangle$ of the RVSP, we use a simple "painter's algorithm" [NeSp79] to paint the rectangles into the image store from back to front:

$S' := S$ sorted in descending z order
for each rectangle $R \in S'$ in order
$\quad \forall (i,j) \in S_R \, . \, P_{ij}(I,Z) := (I_R(i,j), Z_R(i,j))$
print (on output tape) appropriate image store dimensions

The final values in the image store correctly solve the RVSP for this instance. Observe that under the WISM, the inner loop is actually a unit cost operation for each rectangle. Since we can sort in $O(n \log n)$ time, the above algorithm would run in $O(n \log n + n)$, or $O(n \log n)$ time. This proves the theorem.

Theorem 5. *The RVSP under the SISM can be solved in time* $O(n)$.
Proof. First **Blit** the entire image store to a higher value than the maximum depth value in the input. Then **RepMin** each input rectangle.

2.4. A Lower Bound for the VSP on More Complex Scenes

The previous section demonstrated that some well-known problems which are conjectured to be $\Omega(n\log n)$ reduce to simple instances of the RVSP. This establishes a basic lower bound for the VSP of $\Omega(n\log n)$ time subject to these conjectures. Such instances have an input and output size of $O(n)$. However, it is very easy (in hindsight) to invent an instance of the VSP that has n input rectangles, each of constant depth, but has $\Omega(n^2)$ output rectangles. In these cases, therefore, it is clear that $\Omega(n^2)$ time is a lower bound, since it takes that much time just to output the list of output rectangles.[5] Consider n thin rectangular strips arranged in a criss-cross pattern. One half of the strips are oriented horizontally and are disjoint. The other half of the strips are oriented vertically, again disjoint, and placed on top of the horizontal strips. Only two depth values are required: set each vertical strip to depth Z_v and each horizontal strip to Z_h, with $Z_v < Z_h$. Figure 6 provides some graphic intuition.

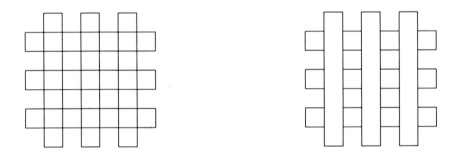

Figure 6. Placement of n=6 rectangular strips and resulting visible surfaces.

With this figure in mind, let us now consider the minimum number of polygons (rectangles in this case) that must be generated to specify all visible regions in the scene. Clearly each vertical strip is entirely visible. However, each horizontal strip is broken up into $n/2+1$ visible rectangles. Therefore, the total number of visible rectangles is:

$$Output\ Size\ =\ \frac{n}{2} + \frac{n}{2}\left\lceil \frac{n}{2}+1 \right\rceil$$

$$=\ \frac{n}{2}\left\lceil \frac{n}{2}+2 \right\rceil\ ,$$

---

[5] We shall be using the output list model of the VSP for the remainder of the chapter.

which is $\Omega(n^2)$ rectangles. We have therefore established the following theorem.

Theorem 6. *The RVSP requires* $\Omega(n^2)$ *time on the output list model.*

Remark 10. The VSP therefore requires $\Omega(n^2)$ time on the output list model.

2.5. Upper Bounds for the RVSP under the Output List Model

We saw earlier that the RVSP for the image store model can be solved in time $O(n \log n)$. As was observed earlier, an output list retains significantly more scene information than does a set of image store values. Thus it is not surprising that the obvious upper bounds for the output list model are somewhat larger than those for the image store model. In this section, some basic upper bounds will be discussed for the former.

Upper bounds for the RVSP are less important than lower bounds, since most practical graphics applications support more sophisticated geometric primitives than rectangles. Thus any visible surface algorithm in practice is likely to run much more slowly than any upper bound we develop for rectangles. However, a good upper bound for the RVSP has some practical applications. For example, the problem of determining the covered or uncovered portions of rectangular "windows" in bit-mapped workstations is very similar to the RVSP. Moreover, it will be seen that the same lower bound applies to the visibility problem for a list of trapezoids. Since any simple polygon can be transformed into a set of trapezoids, this brings us closer to a realistic upper bound on the visibility problem for general polygons.

Very little work has been done in formally deriving and analysing the complexity of efficient visible surface algorithms. Some literature exists on a related problem: the visible *line* problem.[6] The goal of this problem is to output a list of the visible edges of input polygons, rather than a description of the visible surface covered by each input polygon. Schmitt claims to have an $O((n+k) \log n)$ time and O(n+k) space algorithm [Schm81], where k is the number of edge intersections (which is $O(n^2)$).[7] Ottmann *et al.* have an $O((n+k) \log^2 n)$ time and $O(n \log n)$ space algorithm [OtWW82]. Both of these algorithms therefore have a behaviour of something approaching $O(n^2 \log n)$ time. However, it is unclear that a list of visible output polygons can be reconstructed from a list of visible edges in this time. Therefore these results may not be sufficient to demonstrate a

---

[6] The *visible surface (line) problem* is synonymous with a less-descriptive term, the *hidden surface (line) problem.* One can only hope that the latter term becomes obscured by the former in time.

[7] The author has not seen this technical report, the result of which is reported in [OtWW82].

$O(n^2 \log n)$ time upper bound for the VSP, particularly if interpenetrating polygons are to be handled. We shall demonstrate that this bound holds for the RVSP. A straightforward algorithm will be presented in support of this claim. The basic intuition behind the algorithm is to sweep across the scene, determining the visible portions of the scene from top to bottom. Visible portions will be output as rectangles. There will be at most $O(n^2)$ such rectangles, each of which requiring at most $O(\log n)$ processing.

In a recent paper, McKenna reports an $O(n^2)$ algorithm to solve the visible surface problem for arbitrary polygons, which represents a significant advance over the results cited above [McKe87]. However, it is not clear how feasible the algorithm will be in practice, both in the sense that the data structures are quite complicated, and in the sense that the assumptions regarding numerical precision may not be valid on real computers. It also appears that the algorithm *always* runs in $O(n^2)$ time, even when the number of intersections among edges of the polygon is small. This may account for the careful wording of the paper's title, in that the algorithm is optimal when handling worst-case problems, but is not optimal otherwise. Nevertheless, in light of this result, the algorithm below should be viewed essentially as an introduction to the more complex techniques required to achieve good upper bounds for the visibility problem.

The algorithm is a so-called "plane-sweep" algorithm as is often used in computational geometry (but was invented for computer graphics). More accurately, it is based on Watkins' visible surface algorithm which "sweeps" the plane scanline by scanline (i.e. row of image store) [Watk70; NeSp79]. Our algorithm will instead sweep out larger areas at a time. As an example, recall Figures 1-2. Assume that in Figure 7, $Z_1 > Z_2 > Z_3$, where the subscript refers to the polygon number. Figure 8 gives the visible surfaces resulting from this configuration, and Figure 9 illustrates the output of our algorithm.

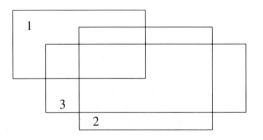

Figure 7. The input scene, with $Z_1 > Z_2 > Z_3$.

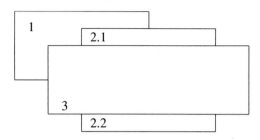

Figure 8. Visible surfaces.

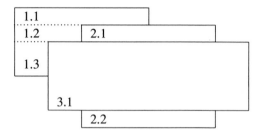

Figure 9. Output rectangles.

Outline of Data Structures. We shall use one data structure, a *Y-Bucket* that is similar in intent but more sophisticated than that used by Watkins, since we wish the algorithm to have good worst-case performance. Another data structure, the so-called *active edge (polygon) list*, will not be required.

The Y-Bucket has the following form and function. Each element of the bucket points to the collection of rectangles whose top (i.e., maximal *y* value) begins at this value of *y*. The data structure holding the rectangles for a given Y-bucket must permit fast search/insert operations and must be ordered in ascending *x* (i.e. left to right--obviously one could also go from right to left). A balanced binary tree, or a 2-3 tree data structure would give O(log *n*) time per operation performance in the worst case [AhHU74]. The Y-bucket itself must be sorted in descending *y* value, so that the next *y*-value in the bucket denotes the top of the set of rectangles immediately below the current *y*. Each rectangle will be represented by a record containing a top-left origin, its length (in *x*), its height (in *y*), and its depth and intensity.

Outline of Algorithm. The algorithm is quite straightforward. The scene is swept from top to bottom by visiting each Y-bucket successively. Within each bucket, the algorithm sweeps left to right. Because the rectangles in each bucket are sorted in x, determining the visible portion of one rectangle only involves checking it against rectangles to its right. With every comparison, a rectangle is eliminated (the one which is obscured), and a visible rectangle is begun (or continued if one visible rectangle overlaps with several rectangles). The algorithm thus has $O(n^2 \log n)$ worst-case behaviour, because each of the $O(n^2)$ rectangle comparisions can be performed in constant time, and it takes $O(\log n)$ time to do the appropriate manipulations of the data structures. Let us consider the algorithm in slightly more detail.

(0) Sort input rectangles from top to bottom, and from left to right.

(1) Create Y-Bucket from sorted input list. Sort Y-bucket entries so that scanning can proceed from top to bottom.

(2) For each y in Y-Bucket:

   Starting with the leftmost rectangle in the Y-bucket, compare its depth to the rectangle to its right. Do an obscurity test and output the resulting visible rectangle(s) (there are several cases to consider here, but they are all easily performed). Continue the intersection test with the current visible rectangle and next rectangle in the Y-bucket. The height of the rectangles output only extends down to the value of the next y in the Y-bucket. Since new rectangles begin at that value, the visible portions of the input rectangles may change. Once through the current Y-bucket, merge all unprocessed portions of rectangles (i.e., those portions of rectangles extending beyond the next lower y value) into the next lower Y-bucket.[8]

   Advance to next y in Y-Bucket.

End of Algorithm.

The above algorithm decomposes the visible portions of the scene into visible rectangles, although the number of rectangles produced is not necessarily minimal. The visibility check is very simple, since one need only test adjacent rectangles for overlap.

Complexity. At first blush, it may seem that too many rectangles are generated by this algorithm for it to have good worst-case behaviour. Notice, however, that any horizontal line can intersect with the scene at most $O(n)$ times. Since we split

---

[8] This is a slight oversimplification. Since the current Y-bucket will likely contain many more rectangles than the next lower bucket, it is more efficient if the lower bucket is merged into the current bucket, the result of which then replaces the lower bucket.

the scene up into at most $O(n)$ pieces (one piece for each distinct y value which is the top of some rectangle in the scene), we never process more than $O(n^2)$ rectangles. Since all intersection and output steps require only constant time for each rectangle, the complexity of processing a single rectangle is dominated by searching and inserting the rectangle into the Y-Bucket. This requires time $O(\log n^2) = O(\log n)$ for each rectangle. We have therefore established the following.

Theorem 7. *The RVSP can be solved in time* $O(n^2 \log n)$.

Remark 11. This result relies on the fact that input polygons have top and bottom edges that are both parallel to the x-axis. However, we have not relied on the fact that the vertical sides of rectangles are also parallel. Therefore the algorithm and the complexity result extend to the visible surface problem for trapezoids.

Remark 12. An arbitrary convex k-gon can be decomposed into at most $k-1$ trapezoids in time $O(k)$ [FoMo84].

Corollary 4. *The visible surface problem for scenes composed of n convex k-gons with k less than a fixed constant K can be solved in time* $O(Kn^2 \log n)$.

Proof. From Theorem 5 and the above two remarks.

2.6. Summary

The first goal of this chapter was to capture formally the meaning of visibility and the visible surface problem. We were then able to make use of this formalism to prove a variety of interesting complexity results for the visible surface problem under two abstract (and realistic) graphic output models. The results of our complexity investigation can be summarised by Table 1. See also [McKe87] for a better upper bounds for the VSP under the OLM.

Model	Input Size	Output Size	Lower Bound	Upper Bound
WISM	n	–	$\Omega(n \log n)$*	$O(n \log n)$
SISM	n	–	$\Omega(n)$	$O(n)$
Output List	n	$O(n)$	$\Omega(n \log n)$*	$O(n \log n)$
Output List	n	$O(n^2)$	$\Omega(n^2)$	$O(n^2 \log n)$

Table 0. RVSP Complexity Summary. Asterisked entries are subject to conjectures.

This chapter leaves open a particularly interesting problem: to determine whether or not the WISM is stronger than a RAM for sorting. Recently, the author has found an $O(n)$ algorithm under the WISM for the problem of determining the measure (i.e., "area") of the union of intervals on the real line. That is, given intervals $[a_1, b_1], \cdots ,[a_n, b_n]$ what is

$$\mu\left[\cup [a_i, b_i] \right] ? \tag{11}$$

If the intervals are disjoint, then the measure is just a simple summation. In general, the intervals are not disjoint, and the problem has been shown to be $\Theta(n \log n)$ under a variety of models [PrSh85]. If it is indeed true that there is an $O(n)$ algorithm under the WISM for this problem, then we have an interesting situation, in that it is possible that the WISM is capable of solving some problems as quickly as a SISM, but there are others that are in the same complexity class under a RAM for which quick solutions may not exist under a WISM.

3 Rendering

There are limits to my tolerance of tolerance. I admire the statesman tolerant of divergent political opinions, and the person tolerant of racial and educational differences; but I do not admire the accountant who is tolerant about his addition, the logician who is tolerant about his proofs, or the musician who is tolerant about his tone. In every activity, satisfactory performance requires meticulous care in some matters.

—N. Goodman[1]

Synopsis. The immense variety of ways in which a scene can be mapped onto a set of pixels for viewing necessitates an examination into precisely what is meant by the process of *rendering*. This chapter develops a mathematical semantics of rendering using the very basic notion of measure. All known rendering techniques are concisely captured within this framework, and it is sufficiently powerful and expressive to facilitate experimentation with novel rendering approaches.

3.1. Introduction

Let us recall the basic graphics paradigm introduced in Chapter 0. Suppose we have a picture in mind that we wish to see displayed. A *scene* is a mathematical representation of this picture, and an image is a manifestation of the scene on a display screen. The most basic problem of computer graphics is the mapping of a

---

[1] N. Goodman, "A World of Individuals", in *The Problem of Universals*, University of Notre Dame Press, Notre Dame, IN, 1956.

scene to an image. This process is called *rendering*. Within the domain of raster graphics, rendering amounts to choosing a suitable intensity value for each pixel in a raster display, given a scene specification. Figure 1 illustrates that different rendering techniques can exhibit striking differences in the resulting image. It is not at all clear that the notion of a "suitable rendering" can be formalised. On the other hand, this chapter will demonstrate that an extremely large class of mappings from scenes to images can be formalised. This class certainly includes all those we consider intuitively reasonable.

It is important to account for the ingredients common to all rendering techniques for several reasons.

(0)   To examine properties of renderings, such as when two renderings agree, what the computational complexity or feasibility of a rendering is, etc.

(1)   To allow the direct specification of the rendering techniques to be supported by a graphics standard or graphical programming language without resorting to side-effects or undue assumptions about the implementation.

(2)   To facilitate proofs of implementations of graphics systems and programs.

(3)   To develop, specify, prove, and assess computationally-attractive approximations to ideal or inherently impractical rendering techniques.

Our goal is a semantic one: to unify into a single framework all rendering techniques that could possibly be performed in a graphics system. We shall assume that many of the basic transformations in the "graphics pipeline" have already been performed, in order to isolate the issues related to rendering that have not yet been formally specified from those that have been(or are within easy reach of being) specified. As with any effort to develop a semantics, we shall first develop a "language" of rendering. The components of our language will be pixels, images, illumination, colours, scenes, and so on. The fundamental mechanism that will give meaning to rendering in terms of these components is measure theory. We shall then characterise several rendering techniques, some of which are familiar, and others of which are not. The choice of a measure-theoretic method provides a new perspective from which to view issues such as anti-aliasing, as the framework makes no reference to frequency domain in the definition of filters. The goal is *not* to replace frequency-domain analysis, but to provide a notation that casts the problem in a different light. Following this, we shall put our approach to good use by transforming ideal (and computationally infeasible) rendering techniques into approximate (and tractable) rendering techniques, all the while remaining within the measure-theoretic framework.

Figure 1. Two possible renderings for a simple scene. The left half of the image was computed using a combination of jitter and stratified sampling. The right half of the image was computed by taking a single point sample for each pixel.

The framework presented in this chapter does not embody a perceptually-based semantics. It is intended to capture rigorously the rendering processes that can be performed by graphics systems—that is, up to and including the display screen. It does not account for the perceptual differences among renderings except that it can be used to predict that they do or do not differ. However, it can be used as one of the main steps in a perceptually-based semantics of rendering.

3.2. The Rendering Framework

The idea of exploiting measures in the formalisation of rendering was first discussed by Fiume and Fournier in [FiFo84]. The framework to be described in this chapter is somewhat richer, more comprehensive and unified than our earlier proposal. Chapter 1 made the notion of a scene precise. Our first task will be to impose a similarly precise mathematical structure on images. We shall then go on to describe a measure-theoretic rendering framework.

3.2.1. Images

The intuition behind the following definitions is that an image is thought of as an arrangement of pixels over some subset of the cartesian plane. Each pixel is an instance of a basic pixel prototype, and each is assigned a colour from a colour space.

Definition 1. A *pixel P* is a tuple (S_P, I_P), where $S_P \subseteq \mathbf{R}^2$ is the extent of P in the screen plane, and $I_P \in \mathbf{C}$ is its colour intensity, for colour space $\mathbf{C}$.

Definition 2. A *pixel prototype* $\mathbf{P} \subseteq \mathbf{R}^2$ is a prototypical pixel extent. A pixel prototype defines the domain of the scene (when projected onto the screen plane) that is to be considered for determining the intensity of a given pixel.

Example 1. Pixel Prototypes.

(0) $\mathbf{P}_0 = [-\frac{1}{2}, +\frac{1}{2}] \times [-\frac{1}{2}, +\frac{1}{2}]$, namely the unit square with centre (0,0).

(1) $\mathbf{P}_1 = \{ (x,y) \in \mathbf{R}^2 : x^2 + y^2 \leq 1 \}$, or the unit circle with centre (0,0).

(2) $\mathbf{P}_2 = \mathbf{R}^2$, or the entire cartesian plane. This model of a pixel is used when the entire scene is used to determine the intensity of each pixel. As will be seen, a *filter* often operates over the entire scene for each pixel.

(3) $\mathbf{P}_3 = \{ (0,0) \}$. A pixel "shape" consisting of a single point is plausible, if somewhat degenerate.

Definition 3. An *index set* $\mathbf{IS} \subseteq \mathbf{Z}^2$ is a set of ordered pairs of integers.

Definition 4. Let $\mathbf{IS}$ be an index set, and let $\alpha_{ij} : \mathbf{P} \rightarrow \mathbf{R}^2$, $(i,j) \in \mathbf{IS}$ be a family of isometries[2] such that for each pixel (i,j), α_{ij} transforms a pixel prototile $\mathbf{P}$ to the desired location and orientation in $\mathbf{R}^2$. We call the set $\mathbf{A} = \{ \alpha_{ij} \mathbf{P} : (i,j) \in \mathbf{IS} \}$ a *pixel arrangement*.

Definition 5. Let $\mathbf{IS} \subseteq \mathbf{Z}^2$ be an index set, let $\mathbf{P} \subseteq \mathbf{R}^2$ be a pixel prototype, let $\mathbf{A} = \{ \alpha_{ij} \mathbf{P} : (i,j) \in \mathbf{IS} \}$ be a pixel arrangement, and let $\mathbf{C}$ be a colour space. Then an *image* over $\mathbf{IS}, \mathbf{P}, \mathbf{A}$, and $\mathbf{C}$ is of the form

$$R = \{ P_{ij} = (S_{ij}, I_{ij}) : (i,j) \in \mathbf{IS}, I_{ij} \in \mathbf{C}, S_{ij} = \alpha_{ij} \mathbf{P} \}. \tag{1}$$

---

[2] An *isometry* is an invertible transformation that preserves distance. See §4.6.1 in Chapter 4.

Example 2. A rectangular image over a unit square pixel prototype. In this example, we define a class of images that very frequently occur in practice. A *rectangular image* of *resolution* $n_1 \times n_2$ is an image such that the index set **IS** is of the form

$$\mathbf{IS} = \{ (i,j) \in \mathbf{Z}^2 : 0 \le i < n_1, 0 \le j < n_2 \}. \tag{2}$$

The pixel prototype is a unit square:

$$\mathbf{P} = [0,1] \times [0,1]. \tag{3}$$

In many commercial image displays, the pixel prototype is a rectangle that is 4 units wide by 3 units high, giving the traditional television *aspect ratio* of 4/3. In fact, in many graphics systems, two or more pixel prototypes are supported. As one would expect, our rendering semantics will distinguish between otherwise identical rendering techniques, which differ in only the pixel prototype used. Without an explicit pixel model, the ability to make such an obvious distinction would not be possible.

The pixel arrangement **A** is

$$\mathbf{A} = \{ T_{ij} \mathbf{P} : (i,j) \in \mathbf{IS} \}, \tag{4}$$

where T_{ij} is a translation as defined in Chapter 1 such that $T_{ij}(x,y) = (x+i, y+j)$.

Lastly, the colour space **C** is $C \times C \times C$, where $C = \{ 0, 1, \cdots, 255 \}$. Any colour in the image is described by an ordered triple of values (r,g,b), indicating, respectively, the intensity or amount of red, green and blue making up the colour. These values are subsequently used to determine the voltage to be applied to each of the red, green and blue electron guns as the electron beam passes over the appropriate area on the display screen. This area need not match the shape of the pixel prototype.

Observe that the arrangement of pixels in the above rectangular images form a *tiling* of the first quadrant of the cartesian plane, if n_1 and n_2 are allowed to go to infinity. When images are discussed within the context of bit-mapped graphics, we shall consider tilings in more detail.

Convention. We shall restrict our discussion to rectangular images, since any image can be embedded in a rectangular image of sufficient size. For convenience, we shall refer to the elements of a pixel $P_{ij} = (S_{ij}, I_{ij}) \in R$, where R is a rectangular image, by $R.S_{ij}$ and $R.I_{ij}$.

Definition 6. An *image space* over index set **IS**, colour space **C**, pixel prototype **P**, and pixel arrangement **A** is the set of all images of the form given in Eq. 1.

Remark 1. The space of rectangular images of resolution $n \times m$ described above is of cardinality $(2^{24})^{nm}$.

3.2.2. Mathematical Preliminaries

Several mathematical concepts in this chapter are taken from the area of measure and integration theory. However, our use of these concepts should be entirely accessible to anyone familiar with undergraduate calculus or real analysis (at the level of [Mars74] for example). Because the notions of measure and integration are critical to the understanding of our framework, we shall briefly outline some basic mathematical concepts here. Most of the definitions to follow are derived from Halmos [Halm70] or Craven [Crav82]. The mathematically-advanced reader is warned that the presentation of this material sacrifices rigour for intuition.

Definition 7. A *ring* of sets is a non-empty class $\mathbf{R}$ of sets such that if $A, B \in \mathbf{R}$, then $A \cup B \in \mathbf{R}$ and $A - B \in \mathbf{R}$.

A ring is a non-empty class of sets which is closed under (finite) unions and differences. The empty set belongs to any ring $\mathbf{D}$, since if $A \in \mathbf{D}$, then $A - A = \varnothing \in \mathbf{D}$. Rings are closed under intersection, since $A \cap B = (A \cup B) - (A - B) - (B - A)$.

Definition 8. A σ-*ring* is a non-empty class of $\mathbf{S}$ sets such that

   (a) If $A, B \in \mathbf{S}$, then $A - B \in \mathbf{S}$.
   (b) If $A_1, A_2, \cdots \in \mathbf{S}$, then $\cup_{i=1}^{\infty} A_i \in \mathbf{S}$.

By definition, a σ-ring is a ring closed under countable union and difference operations. We note that a σ-ring is also closed under countable intersections: if we let $A_1, A_2, \cdots \in \mathbf{S}$, and let $A = \cup_i A_i$, then observe that $\cap_i A_i = A - \cup_i (A - A_i)$.

Example 3. Borel sets. We shall define a special class of σ-rings to which we shall subsequently restrict our attention. Let $\mathbf{D}$ be the set of all semi-closed blocks of the form $[a, b) \times [c, d)$. The set $\mathbf{S}$ generated by countable unions and differences (and intersections) of elements of $\mathbf{D}$ is a σ-ring, and the elements of $\mathbf{S}$ are called the *Borel sets* over $\mathbf{R}^2$. In [Halm70], it is shown that the class of Borel sets is equivalent to the σ-ring generated by the open sets of $\mathbf{R}^2$. That is, any element of $\mathbf{S}$ can be formed by the countable union, intersection, and complementation of open sets. Classes of Borel sets can be formed over a variety of domains Ω. In our work, $\Omega = \mathbf{R}^2$ or some closed subset of $\mathbf{R}^2$. We shall denote the Borel sets over a *domain* Ω by $\mathbf{B}(\Omega)$. Observe that $\Omega \in \mathbf{B}(\Omega)$.

We shall restrict our attention to Borel sets over $\mathbf{R}^2$ because we shall be defining measures over visible surfaces (projected onto the screen plane). It is instructive to note that defining our measures over the Borel sets is sufficient. Intuitively, this is clear because the visible surfaces of an object can be formed by countable intersection and union operations with the other objects in the scene (see Chapter 2). Thus the visible surfaces are Borel sets if the original objects are. Our semantics does not depend on this fact; we are simply restricting ourselves to a large but natural class of sets.

We are now in a position to define the notion of a measure over a class of Borel sets (or more generally, over a σ-ring [Halm70]). Intuitively, a measure is a flexible way of defining the "size" of a set.

Definition 9. A *measure* $\mu : \mathbf{S} \rightarrow \mathbf{R}$ is a real-valued set function over a class of Borel sets $\mathbf{S} = \mathbf{B}(\Omega)$ such that

   (a) $\mu(\varnothing) = 0$.

   (b) $S \in \mathbf{S} \Rightarrow \mu(S) \geq 0$.

   (c) *Countable additivity*: if $S_1, S_2, \cdots$ are pairwise disjoint sets, then

$$\mu(\bigcup_i S_i) = \sum_i \mu(S_i). \tag{5}$$

If a measure μ also satisfies the constraint that $\mu(\Omega) = 1$, then μ is called a *probability measure*. Furthermore, it is straightforward to extend our discussion to *signed* measures, so that a measure may be negative for some sets. The customary way to deal with this is to define a signed measure μ as

$$\mu(E) = \mu_1(E) - \mu_2(E), \tag{6}$$

where both μ_1 and μ_2 are positive-valued measures.

Example 4. Lebesgue measure.

   (a) In $\mathbf{R}$, take $\mu([a,b)) = b - a$.

   (b) In $\mathbf{R}^2$, take $\mu([a,b) \times [c,d)) = (b-a)(d-c)$.

These measures as applied to their respective classes of Borel sets are called *Lebesgue measures*. The elements of $\mathbf{B}(\Omega)$ are called the *Lebesgue-measurable* (or just *measurable*) sets of Ω. There exist Lebesgue-measurable sets that are not Borel sets, but as we discussed earlier, Borel sets are sufficient for our purposes.

Our work will generally only require measures to be *finitely* additive. It will be seen that measures nicely capture the intuitive notions in computer graphics of "weight" or "fractional coverage". We shall also require them for their more traditional use of extending the notion of integral. For a much more thorough (and necessarily less intuitive) development of the general Lebesgue integral than will be given here, see Craven [Crav82] and Halmos [Halm70].

Definition 10.   A real-valued function f is *measurable* if the set $N_a = \{ x \in \mathbf{R}^n : f(x) > a \}$ is measurable for each $a \in \mathbf{R}$ [Crav82].

Definition 11. The *integral*, *I*, of an almost everywhere finite-valued, measurable function $f : \mathbf{R}^n \to \mathbf{R}$, over a measurable set $A \subseteq \mathbf{R}^n$ with respect to measure μ, is written as

$$I f = \int_A f \, d\mu \tag{7}$$

and is related to the area of *ordinate set* $O \subseteq \mathbf{R}^{n+1}$:

$$O =_{df} \{ (x,y) : x \in A, \; 0 \leq y \leq f(x) \}. \tag{8}$$

For arbitrary measure μ, define the function

$$g_f(y) =_{df} \mu\{ x \in A : f(x) > y \}. \tag{9}$$

Let $Y = \{ y_i : 0 \leq i \leq n \}$ be a finite set such that $0 = y_0 < y_1 < \cdots < y_n < \infty$. An approximation to If is then the following sum:

$$\sum_{j=1}^{n} g_f(y_{j-1})(y_j - y_{j-1}). \tag{10}$$

This approximation is illustrated in Figure 2.

The integral of f with respect to measure μ is defined as a limit

$$I f = \int_A f \, d\mu =_{df} \lim_Y \sum_{j=1}^{n} g_f(y_{j-1})(y_j - y_{j-1}), \tag{11}$$

where the limit, if it exists, is taken to mean that the cardinality of $Y \to \infty$ and $\max(y_j - y_{j-1}) \to 0$.

When μ is taken to be a Lebesgue measure, Eq. 11 is called the *Lebesgue integral* of f over A, and is precisely the area of the ordinate set O as defined in Eq. 8. The approach naturally extends to cases in which μ is an arbitrary probability measure. This powerful integral is called the *Lebesgue-Stieltjes integral* of f over A with respect to μ. It generalises the Lebesgue integral. The examples we shall see below of this integral should aid intuition.

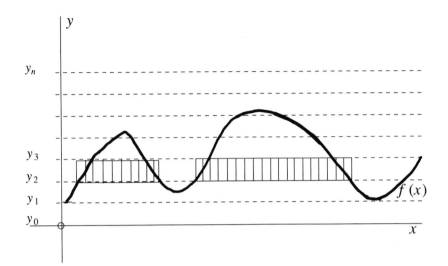

Figure 2. An approximation to the Lebesgue integral. The shaded region corresponds to $g_f(y_2)(y_3 - y_2)$.

A measure-theoretic basis for integration admits a much richer class of *integrable* functions. This class is captured by the following definition [Halm70].

Definition 12. An almost everywhere finite-valued measurable function f on $\mathbf{B}(\Omega)$ with respect to measure μ is *integrable* if there exists a mean fundamental sequence $\langle f_n \rangle$ which converges in measure to f. An alternative way of defining the integral of f is

$$\int f \, d\mu =_{df} \lim_{n \to \infty} \int f_n \, d\mu. \tag{12}$$

Remark 2. More mathematical machinery is required to define precisely the notions of "mean fundamental sequences", and "convergence in measure" (and indeed the notion of measure itself, which is normally rigorously defined in terms of limits). For our purposes, it suffices to say that a function is integrable if it is almost everywhere approximated by a converging sequence of functions. We require this definition because some of our sampling measures are most easily described in terms of sequences of functions.

Remark 3. The Lebesgue integral will allow us to interchange limit and integration opertions under the conditions of Definition 12. That is,

$$\lim_{n\to\infty} \int f_n \, d\mu = \int \lim_{n\to\infty} f_n \, d\mu. \tag{13}$$

From Chapter 1, we recall a definition.

Definition 13. The *characteristic function* of a set $S \subseteq \mathbf{R}^n$ is a function $\chi_S : \mathbf{R}^n \to \{\,0,1\,\}$, such that

$$\chi_S(p) = \begin{cases} 1 & \text{if } p \in S. \\ 0 & \text{if } p \in \mathbf{R}^n - S. \end{cases} \tag{14}$$

Thus $S = \{\, p \in \mathbf{R}^n : \chi_S(p) = 1 \,\}$. Recall that for any two sets $A,B \subseteq \mathbf{R}^n$ having characteristic functions χ_A and χ_B, respectively,

$$\chi_{A \cap B} = \min(\chi_A, \chi_B) = \chi_A \, \chi_B$$
$$\chi_{A \cup B} = \max(\chi_A, \chi_B) \tag{15}$$
$$\chi_{\bar{A}} = 1 - \chi_A.$$

One particularly useful property of a characteristic function is that it can be used to restrict the range of an arbitrary function f by simple multiplication:

$$\chi_A(p) f(p) = \begin{cases} f(p) & \text{if } p \in A. \\ 0 & \text{otherwise.} \end{cases} \tag{16}$$

If $A \subseteq \mathbf{R}^n$ is measurable and f is integrable, then Eq. 7 can be usefully rewritten:

$$I f = \int_A f \, d\mu = \int_{\mathbf{R}^n} \chi_A f \, d\mu. \tag{17}$$

Theorem 1. *If A is a measurable set, then χ_A is a measurable function.*

Proof. Recall N_a from Def. 10 above. If $a \geq 1$, then $N_a = \varnothing$, which is measurable. Likewise, $N_a = \Omega$ and measurable if $a < 0$. Observe that N_a is precisely A when $a \in [0,1)$, and since A is measurable, the theorem follows.

The following theorem is of great importance, in that it establishes a general way of determining the measure of any set in $\mathbf{B}(\Omega)$, given a measure μ defined on the basic blocks or intervals in Ω.

Theorem 2. *Let μ be an arbitrary measure. If $A \in \mathbf{B}(\Omega)$, then the measure of A is*

$$\mu(A) = \int_{\Omega} \chi_A \, d\mu. \tag{18}$$

Definition 14. Let $A \subseteq \mathbf{R}^n$ be measurable and let s be integrable on $\mathbf{R}^n$. Then $\mu_s(A)$, the *Lebesgue-Stieltjes measure of A induced by s*, is

$$\mu_s(A) =_{df} \int_A s \, d\mu. \tag{19}$$

It is easy to verify that μ_s is indeed a measure.

Theorem 3. *If s is an integrable function, then for any measurable function* $f : \mathbf{R}^n \to \mathbf{R}$ *and measurable set* $A \subseteq \mathbf{R}^n$,

$$\int_A f \, d\mu_s = \int_A f s \, d\mu, \tag{20}$$

in the sense that if one integral exists, then so does the other, and the two are equal.

We shall often make use of this equivalence. We hasten to point out, however, that there are perfectly intuitive and well-defined Lebesgue-Stieltjes integrals that are not expressible as Riemann, or even Lebesgue, integrals. For this chapter, the symbol μ will always denote Lebesgue measure. The symbol μ_s will be used to denote Lebesgue-Stieltjes measure. Another common practice adopted is that "$d\mu$" will be written as "dx" in an integral expression when the integrand is explicitly written as a function of x.

We are now in a position to exploit the power and elegance of the Lebesgue-Stieltjes integral to define the semantics of rendering. In fact, its use leads to a very practical methodology for defining new rendering techniques and constructing approximations to them. This is due to the fact that this integral enables us to do a "top-down" design of rendering techniques.

3.2.3. Intensity Measure

From other chapters in this book, we shall assume that a scene S has the following properties (relevant chapters are given in parenthesis).

- It is composed of a sequence $(O_1, \cdots, O_N)$ of objects (Chapter 1).
- It is properly oriented and in perspective (Chapter 1).
- Only the visible portions of each object are included (Chapter 2).
- A scene illumination function $I : \mathbf{R}^2 \to \mathbf{C}$ has been defined over the entire screen plane, for colour space $\mathbf{C}$ (Chapter 5).

Taking these properties into account, for the purposes of this chapter, we make the following definition.

Definition 15. A *scene* S is a sequence of objects $(O_1, \cdots, O_N)$, together with a scene illumination function $I : \mathbf{R}^2 \to \mathbf{C}$. Each object O_i is a pair (V_i, Z_i), where V_i denotes the Borel set (or sets) of visible points of O_i in the screen plane, and $Z_i(x,y)$ gives the depth of $(x,y) \in V_i$ after perspective. The depth function $Z_i(x,y)$ is single valued for each $(x,y) \in V_i$. It is assumed that V_i is defined implicitly in terms of its characteristic function χ_{V_i}. We note that by definition the visible surfaces in a scene are disjoint, and are assumed to be measurable.[3]

Definition 16. Let **Image** be an image space induced by index set **IS**, measurable pixel prototype **P**, pixel arrangement **A**, and colour space **C**. A *rendering* is a function $\rho : O^* \to$ **Image**. That is, a rendering maps any sequence of objects (i.e., any scene) to an image $R \in$ **Image**. Since the arrangement of pixels for any image in **Image** is already given, we adopt the convention that a rendering must prescribe an intensity function $\hat{I} : \mathbf{Z}^2 \to \mathbf{C}$ such that

$$\hat{I}(i,j) = \begin{cases} R.I_{ij} & \text{if } (i,j) \in \mathbf{IS} \\ 0 & \text{otherwise} \end{cases} \tag{21}$$

A rendering semantics provides a prescription for the intensity of each pixel. On what factors does this intensity depend? The answer is that the image intensity should depend on the visible surfaces overlapping with that pixel (see Figure 3).

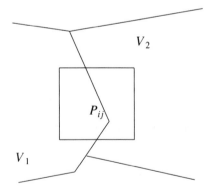

Figure 3. Objects V_1 and V_2 contribute to $\hat{I}(i,j)$.

---

[3] Observe from Chapter 2 that the visible surfaces of a scene are formed by set intersections, unions, and perhaps differences. Therefore, visible surfaces are measurable if their parent objects are.

It is important to remark that even if a surface is transparent, it formally *is* the visible surface (see Chapter 2). The onus of handling issues such as transparency, translucency, reflectivity, and so on, lies with the *illumination model* one chooses to employ (Chapter 5). In order to define a scene illumination function, an illumination model is certainly entitled to consider the objects behind a transparent surface, and in so doing it would be defining the illumination across that surface. To define the semantics of rendering, on the other hand, we must describe how to sample the scene illumination function to determine the contribution of each object within a pixel to the pixel's colour. To do this, it is sufficient for a rendering semantics to consider only the visible surfaces of the object, regardless of the illumination model employed. Note that the mechanisms used to define a *semantics* of a rendering do not need to be imposed on an *implementation*. We do not insist that visible surfaces be explicitly determined, nor do we require that an illumination function be computed for all $(x,y) \in \mathbf{R}^2$. Our semantics simply defines the outcome that any implementation is expected to achieve, and it does so using a basic set of abstractions such as visible surfaces, measure, and illumination functions. An implementation is welcome to achieve the defined result in any manner desired.

The basic observation of this chapter is that this process is completely and concisely described by the notion of an *intensity measure*. Given a scene S with integrable scene illumination function I, we define the image intensity of a pixel P_{ij} under a particular rendering in terms of an intensity measure μ_{ij}^I:

$$\hat{I}(i,j) =_{df} \mu_{ij}^I \left[\bigcup_{k=1}^{N} V_k \right], \quad (i,j) \in \mathbf{Z}^2. \tag{22a}$$

The general form of an intensity measure will be presented momentarily. Since visible surfaces are disjoint (see Chapter 2) and measurable, and since measures are additive for disjoint sets, we can rewrite this equation as:

$$\hat{I}(i,j) = \sum_{k=1}^{N} \mu_{ij}^I (V_k). \tag{22b}$$

Equation 22(a) means that the intensity of P_{ij} is a function of all the visible surfaces about P_{ij}. Equation 22(b) states that since visible objects are disjoint, one may consider the contribution of each independently. Note, moreover, that every pixel in an image can also be computed independently.

To summarise, we claim that the semantics of any desired rendering can be captured by a family of intensity measures { $\mu_{ij}^I : (i,j) \in \mathbf{IS}$ }. Each intensity measure prescribes the semantics of rendering a single pixel. Normally, the same rendering technique is employed on each pixel; however, we shall see that this is not always true.

3.2.3.1. General Form of Intensity Measures

Our strategy in formalising rendering mechanisms is to separate *what* is used to determine a pixel intensity from *how* it is used. This separation is precisely captured by the use of a Lebesgue-Stieltjes integral, which we present over the next two definitions, and subsequently discuss.

Definition 17. Let s be an integrable function on $\mathbf{R}^2$, let μ_s be the Lebesgue-Stieltjes measure induced by s, and let $\mathbf{P}$ be the (measurable) pixel prototype of the image space in question. If μ_s is also a probability measure over $\mathbf{B}(\mathbf{P})$, that is, if $\mu_s(\mathbf{P}) = 1$, then μ_s is a *sampling process* with *basis s*.

Definition 18. Let $V \subseteq \mathbf{R}^2$, let S_{ij} be the extent of pixel P_{ij} in an image space (see above), and let μ_s be a sampling process with integrable basis s. An *intensity measure*, μ_{ij}^I, over integrable scene illumination function I and pixel P_{ij} is of the form

$$\mu_{ij}^I(V) = \int_{S_{ij} \cap V} I \, d\mu_s. \qquad (23a)$$

If V is a visible surface in a scene, the value defined by $\mu_{ij}^I(V)$ is the *intensity contribution* of visible surface V to pixel P_{ij}.

Recall that S_{ij} defines the extent of the scene which can contribute to $\hat{I}(i,j)$, the intensity of pixel P_{ij}. Once again, it is assumed that S_{ij} is defined implicitly by its characteristic function $\chi_{S_{ij}}$. The scene illumination function $I(x,y)$ over domain $S_{ij} \cap V$ defines *what* is to be sampled, and a sampling process μ_s defines *how*. Note that we have made no assumptions about $I(x,y)$ except that it must be measurable. In particular, it can be discontinuous or otherwise badly behaved. This is an important observation (and one that is not often made in computer graphics), since in practice $I(x,y)$ is usually discontinuous along the edges of visible surfaces.

Intuitively, the basis of a sampling process indicates how the sampled intensity points (or areas) are weighted. An important and satisfying aspect of our formal rendering model is that specifying a basis completely defines a particular intensity measure and hence the semantics of a specific rendering technique. This insight yields simple specifications of nontrivial rendering techniques. It is noteworthy that a similar approach was taken long ago in probability theory to unify continuous and discrete stochastic processes into a single formalism (see [Fell66; Rose74]). Indeed, readers familiar with probability theory may choose to view Eq. 23(a) as the *expected value* of I over $S_{ij} \cap V$ with respect to probability distribution s. For future reference, let us rewrite Equation 23(a) as

$$\mu_{ij}^l(V) = \int_{\mathbf{R}^2} \chi_{S_{ij}} \chi_V I \, d\mu_s \,. \tag{23b}$$

It is clear from either equation that the region of integration can be arbitrarily large (or small).

Theorem 4. *If μ_s is a sampling process with integrable basis s, then μ_{ij}^l is a measure on* $\mathbf{B}(\mathbf{P})$.

Proof. Since S_{ij} is measurable and I is integrable,

$$\mu_{ij}^l(\varnothing) = \int_{\mathbf{R}^2} \chi_\varnothing(x,y) \chi_{S_{ij}}(x,y) \, d\mu_s = \int_{\mathbf{R}^2} 0 \cdot \chi_{S_{ij}}(x,y) \, d\mu_s = 0.$$

Let $V_1, V_2, \cdots \subseteq S_{ij}$ be a countable collection of mutually disjoint, measurable sets. Any point (x,y) is thus in at most one V_k. Therefore, by the definition of the characteristic function of $\cup V_k$,

$$\chi_{\cup V_k} = \max_k \{ \chi_{V_k} \} = \sum_k \chi_{V_k} \,.$$

From this observation, the theorem follows easily, since

$$\mu_{ij}^l \left(\bigcup_k V_k \right) = \int_{\mathbf{R}^2} \chi_{\cup V_k} \chi_{S_{ij}} I \, d\mu_s$$

$$= \int_{\mathbf{R}^2} \sum_k \chi_{V_k} \chi_{S_{ij}} I \, d\mu_s$$

$$= \sum_k \int_{\mathbf{R}^2} \chi_{V_k} \chi_{S_{ij}} I \, d\mu_s$$

$$= \sum_k \mu_{ij}^l(V_k).$$

As will be seen, sampling processes can express, as a subcase, all *anti-aliasing* techniques found in the computer graphics literature [Crow77]. This term originates from digital signal processing and typically refers to any technique in which an illumination signal, or what we call the scene illumination function, is filtered to remove or attenuate its "high-frequency" components, that is, to soften its areas of high contrast. It must be said that there is more to rendering than anti-aliasing. All rendering techniques, however, are based on some kind of *sampling* of the scene illumination function. It is for this reason that we have based our semantics on this notion. We shall now see how sampling processes can be used to express a variety of rendering techniques.

3.2.4. Rendering Techniques as Sampling Processes

To define a rendering technique, one simply indicates how scene illumination function samples are to be used to prescribe an image intensity. We shall see that this reduces to inventing an appropriate basis function s for a sampling process. A rendering technique fits into one of two broad categories. It obtains an image intensity value either:

- by sampling the scene illumination function over an area, or
- by sampling at one or more distinct points.[4]

We shall call such rendering techniques *area-sampling* and *point-sampling* processes, respectively.

3.2.4.1. Area-Sampling Processes

Definition 19. A sampling process μ_s is an *area-sampling process* if its basis, s, is non-zero almost everywhere (i.e., except on a set of measure zero over $\mathbf{R}^2$).

Informally, an area-sampling process is such that almost all of the points of a visible surface are used towards the sampling of the scene illumination function. These samples all "count" in the sense that they are given non-zero weight in their contribution to the image intensity.

3.2.4.1.1. Exact-Area Sampling

Let us assume for this technique that each pixel P_{ij} has finite area; often, the area of each pixel is 1 (i.e., $\mu(S_{ij}) = 1$), but we shall not insist on such a restriction. In an exact-area sampling rendering, every point of a visible surface V over a pixel P_{ij} is to be used as a sample point. Moreover, the contribution of each sample point to the intensity of P_{ij} is the same. Clearly, exact-area sampling corresponds to a measure with basis

$$s(x,y) =_{df} \frac{1}{\mu(S_{ij})}, \tag{24}$$

since all sample points have equal weight, and since the cumulative weight must be 1. This completely specifies the exact-area sampling process. Observe the importance of the requirement that $\mu(S_{ij})$ be finite. If $S_{ij} = \mathbf{R}^2$, for example, then $\mu(S_{ij}) = \infty$, and hence $s(x,y) = 0$ for any $(x,y) \in S_{ij}$.

---

[4] The set of point samples should be countable, or more generally, a set of measure zero.

As a straight-forward exercise, let us derive the intensity measure induced by this basis. From Eq. 19, the sampling process μ_s over an arbitrary measurable set A is defined as

$$\mu_s(A) =_{df} \int_A s \, d\mu \tag{25}$$

$$= \frac{1}{\mu(S_{ij})} \int_A d\mu$$

$$= \frac{1}{\mu(S_{ij})} \int_{\mathbf{R}^2} \chi_A \, d\mu$$

$$= \frac{\mu(A)}{\mu(S_{ij})} \,.$$

When expressed as a family of intensity measures, therefore, the semantics of exact-area sampling can be written as

$$\mu_{ij}^I(V) = \frac{1}{\mu(S_{ij})} \int_{S_{ij} \cap V} I \, d\mu, \quad (i,j) \in \mathbf{Z}^2. \tag{26}$$

Observe that if the scene illumination function I is a constant, I_V, across visible surface V, then the contribution of V to the intensity of P_{ij} is exactly

$$\mu_{ij}^I(V) = I_V \int_{\mathbf{R}^2} \chi_{S_{ij}} \chi_V \, d\mu = I_V \frac{\mu(S_{ij} \cap V)}{\mu(S_{ij})} \,. \tag{27}$$

Thus V contributes exactly in proportion to its coverage of pixel (i,j), as expected.

Example 5. From Figure 3 (on page 78), suppose V_1 covers $1/3$ of P_{ij}, and V_2 covers the remainder. Suppose further that V_1 and V_2 are of constant colours, I_1 and I_2, respectively. Then

$$\hat{I}(i,j) = \frac{1}{3} I_1 + \frac{2}{3} I_2 \,. \tag{28}$$

3.2.4.1.2. Filtering as a Continuous Sampling Process

As stated earlier, the classical approach to anti-aliasing is to convolve a filter with the scene illumination function. In this case, our notion of a pixel extent (i.e., the S_{ij}'s) corresponds to the notion of a filter *kernel*, that is, the domain of the filter function. From a signal-theoretic point of view, the effect of the filter should be to attenuate the "high-frequency" components of the illumination signal, and to *pass* the "low-frequency" components without distortion.[5] Naturally, such a filter

---

[5] The notions of "high" and "low" frequencies as applied to signals is with respect to the set of fre-

is called a *low-pass filter*. The practical result of a low-pass filtering operation is typically a softening or blurring of sharp-edged, high-contrast regions. A low-pass filter can be thought of as a (probability) function $h : \mathbf{R}^2 \to \mathbf{R}$ centred at the origin such that

$$\int_{\mathbf{R}^2} h \, d\mu = 1. \tag{29}$$

What does a filtering operation mean intuitively in terms of a sampling process? The answer is that unlike exact-area sampling, which gives every visible point the same weight, a filtering operation gives each visible point a weight as defined by a probability function.

It is very easy to write down a measure which characterises a filtering operation. Since we wish the effect of the filter to be centred over the pixel in question, we define the basis for the intensity measure to translate h appropriately. Let (x_c, y_c) denote the centre of pixel P_{ij}. Then the basis function s on pixel (i, j) is

$$s(x, y) =_{df} h(x_c - x, y_c - y). \tag{30}$$

As above, let us derive the rendering semantics induced by s. In this case, the sampling process μ_s is the *distribution function* of h centred at (x_c, y_c):

$$\mu_s(A) = \int_A h(x_c - x, y_c - y) \, dx \, dy. \tag{31}$$

Assuming h is integrable, we can rewrite the semantics of the filtering operation as:

$$\mu^I_{ij}(V) = \int_{S_{ij} \cap V} I(x, y) h(x_c - x, y_c - y) \, dx \, dy. \tag{32}$$

This exactly corresponds to the formula for classical scene filtering ([Crow77; Prat78]). From a rather novel viewpoint, namely that of specifying a sampling process from a basis function which indicates how samples are weighted, we have arrived at the classical filtering model as a special case. This is not a surprising result, in that measures obviously subsume all linear filtering schemes. The main point is that the same notation can express other kinds of rendering approaches such as point sampling, stochastic sampling, "strange" renderings, as well as a diverse range of approximations to these schemes. We shall first consider some simple examples of filters expressed as measures; subsequently, we shall consider some nonstandard rendering techniques.

---

quencies present in the Fourier spectrum of the signal (see [Prat78]).

3.2.4.1.3. Examples of Filters

In this section, we shall give the semantics of several filtering techniques. The ease with which they are specified should be apparent.

Example 6. A box filter. A *box filter* is precisely the exact-area sampling basis over a rectangular pixel prototype. Suppose our "box" **P** is as in Figure 4.

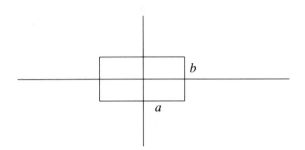

Figure 4. A box pixel prototype with half-width *a*, and half-height *b*.

From the semantics of exact-area sampling above, we see that $\mu(\mathbf{P}) = 4ab$. Therefore,

$$s(x,y) = h(x,y) = \frac{1}{4ab} . \tag{33}$$

Example 7. A gaussian filter. A commonly advocated (but rarely implemented) filter is based on a *gaussian probability distribution* of the form

$$N(x,y;\sigma) =_{df} \frac{1}{2\pi\sigma^2} \exp\left[-\frac{x^2+y^2}{2\sigma^2} \right] . \tag{34}$$

A gaussian distribution is depicted in Figure 5. Note that a gaussian is radially symmetric about the origin.[6] The *standard deviation*, σ, of h, models the desired light spread of the pixel [Prat78]. This is often set to between one and two pixel units, assuming pixel centres are one unit apart. Under this abstraction, the pixel prototype is $\mathbf{P} = \mathbf{R}^2$. It is assumed that each pixel P_{ij} in an image is centred at $(i,j) \in \mathbf{Z}^2$. The basis, s, for the intensity measure about P_{ij} is

$$s(x,y) =_{df} N(i-x, j-y;\sigma). \tag{35}$$

---

[6] A function $f(x,y)$ is *radially symmetric* about a point P if for any circle C centred at P, $f(x,y)$ is the same value for every point on C.

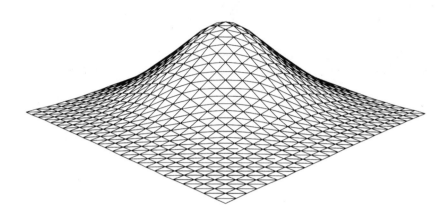

Figure 5. Gaussian distribution.

Since the resulting sampling process involves an integral over $\mathbf{R}^2$, a practical implementation may wish to truncate the filter to within a circular region centred by the pixel centre, (i,j). This is easily specified by changing the definition of $\mathbf{P}$. The following pixel prototype restricts the distribution to a circular region with radius one standard deviation:

$$\mathbf{P} =_{df} \{ (x,y) \in \mathbf{R}^2 : x^2 + y^2 \le \sigma^2 \}. \tag{36}$$

It is advisable to scale s appropriately so that μ_s is indeed a sampling process.

Example 8. A Hamming filter. A Hamming filter has a slightly more efficient implementation than a gaussian, and is of the form

$$H(x,y\,;r) =_{df} k \left[0.56 + 0.44 \cos \frac{\pi \sqrt{x^2 + y^2}}{r} \right] \tag{37}$$

about a circular region $\mathbf{P} =_{df} \{ (x,y) \in \mathbf{R}^2 : x^2 + y^2 \le r \}$. The constant k is chosen so that

$$\int_{\mathbf{P}} h = 1. \tag{38}$$

Typically the radius r is between 1 and 2.

Example 9. A cylindrical filter. This filter is simply a version of exact-area sampling over a circular pixel extent rather than a box. Let the pixel prototype be

$$\mathbf{P} =_{df} \{ (x,y) \in \mathbf{R}^2 : x^2 + y^2 \le r^2 \}, \tag{39}$$

where $r > 0$. Then the basis is defined by:

$$Cy(x,y;r) =_{df} \frac{1}{2\pi r} . \tag{40}$$

Example 10. A conical filter. A slightly more interesting filter than the cylinder is conical filter defined over $\mathbf{P}$ as in the cylinder, with basis function

$$Co(x,y;r) =_{df} \frac{3}{\pi r^2} \left[1 - \frac{\sqrt{x^2+y^2}}{r} \right] . \tag{41}$$

We have only specified a few of the many well-known filters, but the method should be clear. As can be seen, their manner of specification is at heart not far removed from their traditional specification. The difference lies in the fact that any filter specified in terms of basis functions immediately "snaps into" the framework we have developed, and inherits its semantics.

3.2.4.2. Strange Rendering Techniques

The main goal of this chapter is to express traditional ideal rendering techniques within a single framework. As we saw above, the classical filtering model is entirely subsumed by our rendering semantics, and it will be seen below that the same happens for point sampling models. On the other hand, one of the benefits of a uniform notation is that it invites experimentation: we can express novel rendering techniques that do not typically appear in graphics systems (but which might appear in future systems). Let us briefly consider some possibilities in this section. For clarity, we shall assume that the centre of each pixel (i,j) is simply (i,j). The computation of the figures in this section is described in [FoFi88].

3.2.4.2.1. Difference of Gaussians

This "rendering technique" is well known in computer vision and can be defined as $s(x,y) =_{df} dog(i-x, j-y; \sigma_1, \sigma_2)$ about each pixel (i,j), where

$$dog(x,y; \sigma_1,\sigma_2) =_{df} k \left[N(x, y;\sigma_1) - N(x, y;\sigma_2) \right] . \tag{42}$$

$N(x, y;\sigma)$ is the gaussian (i.e., normal) distribution defined above, and k is a normalisation coefficient. Observe that a *dog* is a good example of a signed measure (see Eq. 6). Figure 6 depicts a *dog*, and its effect on a familiar texture.

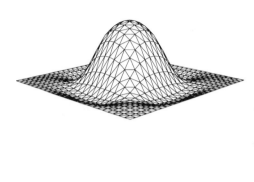

Figure 6. A plot of $dog(x,y; 0.5, 1.0)$ and its effect on a primate.

3.2.4.2.2. Motion Blur

Suppose we wish to model the effect of moving a camera across the scene while the shutter remains open [KoBa83]. A simple example would be to define a "stretched" gaussian as follows:

$$SN(x,y;a,b,\sigma) =_{df} \frac{1}{2\pi\sigma^2} \exp\left[-\frac{ax^2 + by^2}{2\sigma^2} \right] \tag{43}$$

subject to $a^2 + b^2 = 1$. Unlike the standard gaussian, this distribution is not radially symmetric, as the Figure 7 illustrates. A texture has been chosen for illustration because it is the simplest possible "scene", allowing us to ignore the fact that, for example, different parts of the scene become visible as the camera (or scene) moves.

In this case, the sampling process is identical for each pixel. A more sophisticated example would be to take an arbitrary filter and rotate it about some axis that is perpendicular to the screen. For example, imagine a circular arc γ_{ij} formed by rotating the centre of pixel (i,j) about the screen centre by some angle θ. Then further imagine dragging a gaussian along γ_{ij}. Close to the centre of the rotation, the gaussian would be largely undistorted because γ_{ij} is short arc. As the distance from the centre increases, the the cross-section of gaussian about σ becomes sickle shaped, as Figure 8 depicts. Let $(a',b') = R((a,b), (c,d), \theta)$ denote a rotation of θ radians of point (a,b) about (c,d) in the screen plane. The basis function for each pixel (i,j) for this rendering technique is then

$$s_{ij}(x,y;\theta,\sigma) =_{df} \int_0^1 N[\, R((i,j),(r_x, r_y), t\theta) - (x,y); \sigma\,]\, dt, \tag{44}$$

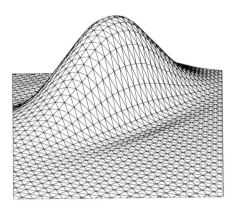

Figure 7. Stretched gaussian with $a = 0.1$.

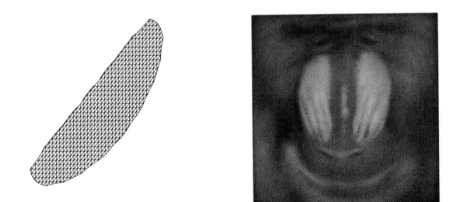

Figure 8. Cross-section of rotated gaussian and its effect on a texture.

where θ is the overall angle of rotation, and (r_x, r_y) is the centre of the rotation.

The above sampling process is somewhat involved, but it illustrates two fundamental points: that nontrivial rendering techniques may be specified in this framework, and that intensity measures which differ in behaviour for every pixel can be defined. Such intensity measures are called *space variant* [FoFi88]. Like the stretched gaussian, it is also radially asymmetric.

3.2.4.3. Point-Sampling Processes

Definition 20. A measure μ_s is a *point-sampling process* if its basis, s, is zero almost everywhere.

Unlike an area-sampling process, a point-sampling process ignores all but a countable set of points to define the intensity of a pixel. Typically, only a small finite set of point samples is used. Figure 1 above illustrates the typical effect of using two varieties of point sampling.

A convenient tool for expressing point-sampling processes is the so-called Dirac δ-function, which is used in mathematics, physics, and in image processing [Prat78]. In order to use it in our framework, we have to be slightly careful, since we have to justify that sampling processes based on δ-functions can behave as measures.

Definition 21. The function $\delta : \mathbf{R} \to \mathbf{R}$ has the following properties:

$$\delta(x) = \begin{cases} 0 & \text{if } x \neq 0 \\ \infty & \text{if } x = 0 \end{cases} \qquad (45a)$$

and

$$\forall \, \varepsilon > 0 \; \int_{-\varepsilon}^{+\varepsilon} \delta(x)\,dx \; = \; 1 \,. \qquad (45b)$$

The behaviour of this function is illustrated in Figure 9.

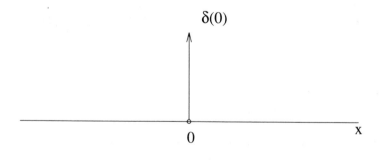

Figure 9. The delta function.

Clearly, $\delta(x)$ is not continuous on $\mathbf{R}$. However, when expressed as a functional (a map from functions to functions), it in fact is continuous, linear, and differentiable on the space of all real-valued functions that are locally continuous around the origin [Mars74; Hosk79]. This is due to the extremely useful *sifting property* of the δ-functional:

$$\delta(f) =_{df} \int_{\mathbf{R}} \delta(x) f(x) \, dx = f(0), \qquad (46)$$

for any continuous function $f: \mathbf{R} \to \mathbf{R}$. Under the Lebesgue integral, the functional be applied to an even richer function space. For reasons of mathematical purity and aesthetics, it is preferable to view the "δ-function" as a functional that maps a real-valued function to a real-valued constant function.[7] We shall nevertheless remain consistent with traditional use by saying "δ-function" when we mean $\delta(x)$, and "δ-functional" when we mean $\delta(f)$. In any case, it is straightforward to extend the definition of the δ-functional to functions over $\mathbf{R}^n$, as we shall see.

Another pertinent fact about the δ-function is that it can be defined as the limit of a sequence of continuous probability distributions. That is, there exist sequences of probability distributions of the form $\langle h_n \rangle_{n=0}^{\infty}$ such that

$$\delta(x) = \lim_{n \to \infty} h_n(x), \qquad (47)$$

In particular, the sequence of gaussian distributions

$$\langle \sqrt{n/\pi} \, \exp(-nx^2) \rangle_{n=0}^{\infty}, \qquad (48)$$

converges in a "good" way to $\delta(x)$. While convergence is not uniform [Mars74], it is stronger than simple pointwise convergence in that that it will later allow us to interchange the Lebesgue-integration and summation operations (see above) [Jone82]. The behaviour of this sequence as n increases is depicted in Figure 10.

3.2.4.3.1. *Single Point Sampling Processes*

Suppose we wish the intensity of pixel (i,j) to be the value of the scene intensity for exactly one point in S_{ij}. That is, we shall insist that $\hat{I}(i,j) = I(x_0, y_0)$. Note that since all visible surfaces across S_{ij} are disjoint, (x_0, y_0) belongs to at most one visible surface V. From the properties of the δ-function, it is natural to define the basis function for single point sampling as

$$s(x,y) = \delta(x_0 - x, \, y_0 - y). \qquad (49)$$

Intuitively, the sampling process induced by s "pulses" at exactly one point within the pixel, ignoring all other points. See Figure 11 for a 1-D analogue. Let us

---

[7] Indeed, an alternative formulation of rendering would be to view every sampling process as a linear functional. This approach was rejected because the measure-theoretic formulation more closely captures our intuitions about the rendering process.

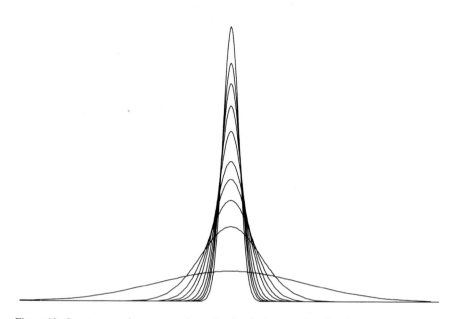

Figure 10. Convergence of a sequence of gaussian distributions to a delta function.

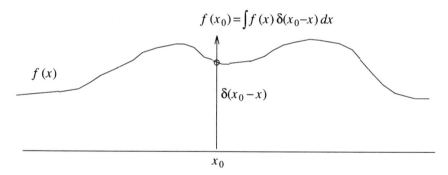

$$f(x_0) = \int f(x)\, \delta(x_0 - x)\, dx$$

$f(x)$

$\delta(x_0 - x)$

x_0

Figure 11. Point-sampling using a δ-function.

verify that this intuition yields a reasonable intensity measure. First, we must show that δ induces a probability measure.

Lemma 1. *The following function is a probability measure:*

$$\mu_s(A) = \int_A \delta(x_0 - x, y_0 - y)\, dx\, dy .$$

Remark 4. In fact, μ_s is a *step function*. For example, let $A_1, A_2, \cdots$ be a sequence of circles of increasing radius, centred at the origin. Suppose A_n is the smallest circle such that $(x_0, y_0) \in A_n$. Then $\mu_s(A_i) = 0$ if $i < n$ and 1 otherwise. This function is depicted in Figure 12.

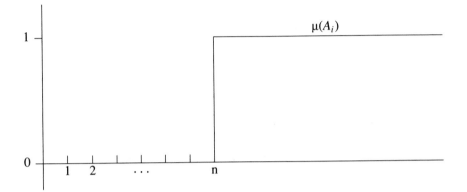

Figure 12. The step function $\mu_s(A_i)$.

Therefore, a (perhaps unintuitive) way to define $\delta(x)$ is as the derivative of the unit step function. This observation is helpful in our proof of the theorem following this lemma.

Proof of Lemma. We verify the properties of probability measures from Section 1.1, exploiting the sifting property of $\delta(x)$ and various properties of characteristic functions (see Eq. 17). Observe that if we are measuring the empty set,

$$\mu_s(\varnothing) = \int_{\mathbf{R}^2} \chi_\varnothing(x,y)\, \delta(x_0-x, y_0-y)\, dx\, dy = \chi_\varnothing(x_0, y_0) = 0.$$

Let $S_1, S_2, \cdots \subseteq S_{ij}$ be a countable collection of mutually disjoint, measurable sets. Then

$$\mu_s(\bigcup_i S_i) = \int_{\mathbf{R}^2} \max_i \{\, \chi_{S_i}(x,y)\, \}\, \delta(x_0-x, y_0-y)\, dx\, dy = \max_i \{\, \chi_{S_i}(x_0, y_0)\, \}.$$

Moreover, $\chi_{S_i}(x_0, y_0) = 1$ for at most one S_i. Hence

$$\sum_i \mu_s(S_i) = \sum_i \int_{\mathbf{R}^2} \chi_{S_i}(x,y)\, \delta(x_0-x, y_0-y)\, dx\, dy$$

$$= \sum_i \chi_{S_i}(x_0, y_0)$$

$$= \max_i \{\, \chi_{S_i}(x_0, y_0)\, \}.$$

Therefore, $\mu_s(\cup_i S_i) = \sum_i \mu_s(S_i)$, which establishes that μ_s is a measure. The fact that it is a probability measure follows from the second property of the δ-function, Eq. 45(b). The lemma follows.

Next, we shall show that $\delta(x)$ can be written as in Eq. 20.

Theorem 5. *Let I be an integrable scene illumination function, and let S_{ij} be measurable. If $s(x,y) = \delta(x_0 - x, y_0 - y)$, then*

$$\int_{S_{ij}} I \, d\mu_s = \int_{S_{ij}} I s \, d\mu.$$

Proof. First, note that the integral on the left-hand side is well-defined, since by the above lemma, μ_s is a probability measure. An intuitive argument would run as follows. By the remark earlier, we can write $\mu_s(X)$ for measurable X as

$$\mu_s(X) = \int_X s \, d\mu = \begin{cases} 1 & \text{if } (x_0, y_0) \in X. \\ 0 & \text{otherwise.} \end{cases}$$

Therefore,

$$\int_{S_{ij} \cap V} I \, d\mu_s = \begin{cases} I(x_0, y_0) & \text{if } (x_0, y_0) \in V \cap S_{ij}. \\ 0 & \text{otherwise.} \end{cases}$$

$$= \int_{S_{ij} \cap V} I(x,y) \, \delta(x_0 - x, y_0 - y) \, dx \, dy,$$

as required. This argument is based on the fact that as a basis function, $\delta(x)$ applies zero weight to every point but the centre of its distribution.

A more rigorous proof requires a limit argument. Recall that $\delta(x)$ can be defined as the limit of a convergent series of probability distributions $\langle h_n \rangle$. The nature of convergence allows us to interchange limit and differentiation/integration operations (see above and [Jone82]). For measurable X,

$$\mu_s(X) = \int_X \lim_{n \to \infty} h_n \, d\mu = \lim_{n \to \infty} \int_X h_n \, d\mu.$$

Substituting into the general form of an intensity measure,

$$\int_{S_{ij}} I \, d\mu_s = \int_{S_{ij}} I \, d\left[\lim_{n \to \infty} \int h_n \, d\mu \right]$$

$$= \int_{S_{ij}} I \left[\lim_{n \to \infty} d\left(\int h_n \, d\mu \right) \right]$$

$$= \int\limits_{S_{ij}} I \left[\lim_{n \to \infty} h_n \right] d\mu$$

$$= \int\limits_{S_{ij}} I \, s \, d\mu.$$

The theorem follows.

3.2.4.3.2. Super-Sampling

The simplest and most common anti-aliasing technique used in computer graphics involves sampling the scene illumination at several points within a pixel, and averaging the sampled values to arrive at a single image intensity value. This approach, called *super-sampling*, is easy to express as an extension of single point sampling. Let $\Phi = \{ (x_1, y_1), \cdots, (x_M, y_M) \} \subset S_{ij}$ be a finite set of sample points. We define the basis function as:

$$s(x,y) =_{df} \frac{1}{M} \sum_{k=1}^{M} \delta(x_k - x, \, y_k - y). \tag{50}$$

Then

$$\mu_s(A) = \frac{1}{M} \int\limits_A \sum_{k=1}^{M} \delta(x_k - x, \, y_k - y) \, dx \, dy \tag{51}$$

$$= \frac{1}{M} \sum_{k=1}^{M} \int\limits_A \delta(x_k - x, \, y_k - y) \, dx \, dy$$

By the above theorem,

$$\mu_{ij}^I(V) = \int\limits_{S_{ij} \cap V} I \, d\mu_s \tag{52}$$

$$= \frac{1}{M} \sum_{k=1}^{M} \int\limits_{S_{ij} \cap V} I(x,y) \, \delta(x_k - x, \, y_k - y) \, dx \, dy$$

$$= \frac{1}{M} \sum_{p \in \Phi \cap V} I(p).$$

Observe that if $I(x,y)$ is a constant, I_V, across V, then

$$\mu_{ij}^I(V) = I_V \frac{| \Phi \cap V |}{M} \tag{53}$$

There is a precise relationship between super-sampling and exact-area sampling.

Theorem 6. *If the sample points in Φ are uniformly distributed across S_{ij}, then*

$$\lim_{M \to \infty} \left[\frac{1}{M} \sum_{(x,y) \in P \cap V} I(x,y) \right] = \frac{1}{\mu(S_{ij})} \int_{S_{ij} \cap V} I \, d\mu, \tag{54}$$

almost everywhere (abbreviated "a.e.").

Proof. This is in effect a Monte Carlo process convergence theorem and the result can be proven in this light (see [HaHo64]). However, we shall prove a more general result below of which this is a corollary.

Thus the relationship between exact-area sampling and super-sampling is that the latter approximates the former.

3.2.4.3.3. Weighted Super-Sampling

The set of sample points in super-sampling all contributed uniformly to the image intensity value. It is certainly reasonable to apply a non-uniform set of weights to the intensity samples. This approach then becomes a discrete version of filtering as discussed in Section 1.4.1.2. Let $\Phi = \{ (x_1,y_1), \cdots, (x_M,y_M) \} \subset S_{ij}$ be a finite set of uniformly-distributed sample points, and let h be a probability distribution centred at $(0,0)$ as above. The basis function for discrete filtering is

$$s(x,y) =_{df} \frac{1}{X} \sum_{k=1}^{M} \delta(x_k - x, y_k - y) \, h(x_c - x_k, y_c - y_k), \tag{55}$$

where

$$X = \sum_{i} h(x_c - x_i, y_c - y_i).$$

Obviously, setting $h(x,y)=1$ gives rise to equally-weighted super-sampling, Eq. 50, so this technique certainly generalises super-sampling. By a similar analysis to the previous section,

$$\mu_s(A) = \frac{1}{X} \sum_{k=1}^{M} \int_A \delta(x_k - x, y_k - y) \, h(x_c - x_k, y_c - y_k) \, dx \, dy. \tag{56}$$

Moreover, the induced intensity measure is

$$\mu_{ij}^I(V) = \frac{1}{X} \sum_{(x,y) \in \Phi \cap V} I(x,y) \, h(x_c - x, y_c - y). \tag{57}$$

3.2.4.3.4. Stochastic Point Sampling

When we discussed super-sampling, we noted that the image intensity is a function of the scene intensity sampled at a set of distinguished points, but we did not say how these points are chosen. It was remarked above that there may be other ways of choosing sample points. It is useful to give the semantics of this process, for it will allow us to prove an important relationship between point-sampling and area-sampling processes. First we provide some intuitive grounds for our general approach.

Let us view a point-sampling process as "tracing out" or monitoring a scene illumination function by periodically pulsing to take a sample intensity value. There are of course uncountably many possible scene samplings, and thus uncountably many different instances of a sampling process. However, a particular point-sampling strategy places some constraints on the nature of the point-sample sets which are reasonable. These constraints can be captured by a probability function, which provides a measure of the "reasonableness" of a particular sample set, or collection of such sets. We can therefore model different strategies for choosing sets of samples by viewing each strategy as inducing a distinguishing probability space.

The intuition behind the formalism is quite simple. Suppose we allow the set of sample points Φ to be the outcome of a *stochastic process* with probability distribution s. In the case of super-sampling, for example, sample points assume a uniform distribution across a pixel. However, our formalism certainly allows for more interesting processes, many of which are worth exploring.

The following two definitions, taken from [Rose74], are standard notions in probability theory.

Definition 22. A *probability space* is a triple (Ω, F, P), where Ω is the space of all possible sample points (in our case, $\Omega = S_{ij}$), F is a collection of Borel sets of Ω, and P is a probability function defined on the sets of F. The sets of F are called *events*. A sample point is typically written as $\omega \in \Omega$.

Definition 23. A *random variable* $\mathbf{X}(\omega)$ is a measurable real-valued function which generates events in F.

In our case, random variables will be used to generate ordered pairs of points within extent S_{ij} of a pixel. Each random variable generates a single point. Thus $F = \Omega$. In the next section, this formalism will be employed to specify jitter sampling.

Definition 24. A set Φ of *stochastic sample points* is a finite set of mutually-independent random variables

$$\Phi = \{ X_1(\omega), X_2(\omega), \cdots, X_M(\omega) \} = \{ (x_i, y_i) : i = 1, \cdots, M \} \tag{58}$$

for a particular $\omega \in \Omega$.

An alternative way of saying this is that Φ is the outcome of a *stochastic process* with probability distribution P. In the case of super-sampling, for example, events assume a uniform distribution across a pixel. However, our formalism certainly allows for more interesting processes, many of which are worth exploring.

The following result is very satisfying and, thanks to the strong law of large numbers, not difficult. It states that the choice of point-samples according to a given probability distribution will converge to the analogous area-sampling process. This result is very similar to theorems regarding convergence of "estimators" in probability theory and is by no means surprising. A recent paper also makes a similar claim with an informal proof [LeRU85]. Our result is somewhat more precise and general, and is consistent with our formal framework for rendering.

Theorem 7. Let μ_s be a probability measure induced by basis function s. Let $\Phi = \{ (x_1, y_1), \cdots, (x_M, y_M) \}$ be a set of mutually-independent random variables with probability distribution s. Then

$$\lim_{M \to \infty} \left[\frac{1}{M} \sum_{(x,y) \in \Phi \cap V} I(x,y) \right] = \frac{1}{\mu(S_{ij})} \int_{S_{ij} \cap V} I \, d\mu_s \quad \text{a.e.} \tag{59}$$

for integrable I and measurable S_{ij} and V.

Remark 5. Theorem 4 follows from Theorem 5 by replacing s with the uniform distribution over S_{ij}.[8]

Proof. Let us rewrite a general intensity measure defined in Eq. 23(a) as

$$\mu_{ij}^I(V) = \int_{S_{ij} \cap V} I \, d\mu_s = \int_{S_{ij}} I_V \, d\mu_s, \tag{60}$$

---

[8] *A Note on Terminology.* In probability theory, what we call a "basis function", s, would be called either a *probability density function* or a *probability distribution* [Fell66]. This is not to be confused with the Lebesgue-Stieltjes measure induced by s, μ_s, which is called a *distribution function* in functional analysis, an unfortunate coincidence (see Eq. 31). The same object is called a *cumulative* distribution function in probability theory.

where $I_V = \chi_V I$ simply restricts the scene illumination function to V. Let $\Phi = \{ (x_1, y_1), \cdots, (x_M, y_M) \}$ be a set of mutually independent random variables with probability distribution s. Then

$$I = \{ I_i : I_i = I_V(x_i, y_i), \ 1 \le i \le M \} \tag{61}$$

is also a random variable of independent values with probability distribution s. By definition [Fell68], the *expected value* of this set is

$$E(I) = \int_{S_{ij}} I_V \, d\mu_s. \tag{62}$$

Put $S_M =_{df} \sum_{i=1}^{M} I_i$. The value $m = S_M / M$ is an approximation for E. In fact, it is a very good approximation, for the *(strong) law of large numbers* states that if E exists and the elements of $\{ I_i \}$ are identically distributed, then $\forall \, \varepsilon > 0$,

$$\lim_{M \to \infty} \left| \frac{S_M}{M} - E(I) \right| < \varepsilon \quad \text{a.e.}$$

(see [Fell68; Halm70:p205]). Clearly this law applies in our case. Now it is just a simple matter of seeing that m and E actually are the expressions in the statement of the theorem. Note that

$$m = \frac{S_M}{M} = \frac{1}{M} \sum_{i=1}^{M} I_i \tag{63}$$

$$= \frac{1}{M} \sum_{i=1}^{M} I_V(x_i, y_i)$$

$$= \frac{1}{M} \sum_{(x,y) \in \Phi \cap V} I(x,y),$$

since $I_V(x,y) = 0$, $\forall (x,y) \notin P \cap V$. Combining the above results, we find that $\forall \, \varepsilon > 0$,

$$\lim_{M \to \infty} \left| \frac{1}{M} \sum_{i=1}^{M} I_V(x_i, y_i) - \int_{S_{ij}} I_V(x,y) \, d\mu_s \right| < \varepsilon \quad \text{a.e.}$$

This establishes the theorem.

While Theorem 7 is satisfying in that it says that a point-sampling technique converges to an area-sampling technique, it does not say how many samples must be taken for each ε. Unfortunately, the general result is not optimistic, as we now briefly discuss.

Definition 25. The *variance* of a random variable X with an arbitrary distribution is defined as

$$\sigma^2(\mathbf{X}) =_{df} E((\mathbf{X}-E(\mathbf{X}))^2), \qquad (64)$$

which provides a measure of the dispersion of a random variable about the expected value of the distribution.

Just as Theorem 7 demonstrated that $E(\{I_i\}) = E(I_V)$, it can be shown that

$$\sigma^2(\{I_i\}) = \frac{\sigma^2(I_V)}{M}. \qquad (65)$$

Definition 26. The *standard deviation* of $\mathbf{X}$ is $\sqrt{\sigma^2(\mathbf{X})}$.

Therefore, in our case, the standard deviation is

$$\sigma(\{I_i\}) = \frac{\sigma(I_V)}{\sqrt{M}}. \qquad (66)$$

An important point to note here is the inverse square property of Eq. 66: to *halve* the error, one should expect to take *four* times as many samples. Thus it is important to develop sampling techniques that converge more quickly in practice, and which prevent the introduction of undue noise or distortion in the image intensity.[9] This is a new, exciting area of raster graphics that appears to be inspiring considerable interest (see [DiWo85; LeRU85; Cook86; Mitc87]).

Example 11. Jitter sampling. The notion of "jitter" sampling has recently been advocated as a useful sampling technique for computer graphics (although it is well known in other areas) [DiWo85; Cook86]. The basic sampling strategy is to take a set of uniformly-spaced samples and perturb them according to some probability distribution. More formally, over each pixel extent S in an image, we define a set of uniformly-spaced samples

$$U = \{(x_1, y_1), \cdots, (x_M, y_M) : (x_i, y_i) \in S\}. \qquad (67)$$

We also define a stochastic process $\mathbf{X}(\omega)$, $\omega \in S$, as follows.

---

[9] Aliasing, a problem which we alluded to earlier, is one particularly annoying form of noise that can occur in an image [Crow77]. It is thought that the effect of aliasing is so annoying because it is *coherent* noise, in the sense that as a result of point-sampling the original intensity signal, and subsequently *reconstructing* an image signal from these point samples, a Fourier spectrum of the reconstructed signal would reveal regularly occurring distortions and deviations from the original signal throughout the frequency domain. On the other hand, stochastic sampling typically results in much less regular noise patterns, which usually takes on the appearance of "snow" in an image. Psychophysical studies have shown that such *incoherent* noise can be less annoying than coherent noise (see [Prat78; DiWo85]).

$$\mathbf{X}\Big[(x,y)\Big] =_{df} (x+\delta_x, y+\delta_y), \tag{68}$$

where δ_x and δ_y are chosen independently for each (x,y) according to a probability distribution h. The set of samples to be used in determining the intensity of the pixel with extent S is

$$\Phi =_{df} \{ \mathbf{X}(\omega) \in S : \omega \in U \}. \tag{69}$$

If S is a unit square with bottom-left corner at (i,j), and s_x, s_y denote the number of samples to be taken in the x and y directions, respectively, then

$$U =_{df} \left\{ \left[i+\frac{a+0.5}{s_x}, \; j+\frac{b+0.5}{s_y} \right] \; : \; 0 \le a < s_x, \, 0 \le b < s_y \right\}. \tag{70}$$

3.2.5. Summary

This section has presented a formal model of rendering which allows for the specification of all known rendering techniques in a completely uniform and simple manner. Since it also offers a considerable degree of generality, there is strong justification that it will facilitate the discovery of new techniques. Certainly none of the above rendering techniques have ever been specified to this level of precision and abstraction.

A particularly gratifying aspect of the framework is that as it was being developed, several papers on stochastic sampling referenced above were published, and were immediately expressible within the existing framework. We were also able to prove a simple but important inverse-square error property of these approaches. This provides some evidence that our framework is robust, and will provide a good tool for analysing new developments as they arise.

The semantics of a rendering technique is given by an intensity measure which defines the contribution each visible object makes to the intensity of a pixel. By specifying a basis function characterising how a scene intensity is sampled, the formal semantics of the rendering technique is easily induced. The precision of our formalism has allowed us to investigate various relationships among well-known and practised techniques in raster graphics that were previously only informally understood.

One particular advantage of developing a semantics of rendering based on measure theory is the fact that measures can be defined over very general sets. Thus it is a simple matter to extend the rendering framework presented above to many more dimensions, if desired. Certainly one extra dimension worth incorporating is time. Measures defining sampling processes over both space and time are by no means inconceivable and would be useful for defining the semantics of so-called *temporal anti-aliasing* [KoBa83].

3.3. Discrete Approximations to Continuous Intensity Measures

In the last section, we saw that for each area-sampling rendering, there exists an almost everywhere approximating point-sampling rendering. However, we also saw the drawback of this approximation strategy: a very large number of point samples may be required. In this section, we shall consider other approaches to approximating area-sampling processes.

It is important to find approximations to area-sampling for several reasons. First, while area-sampling yields the mathematically precise result, exact integration may be analytically impossible and/or computationally intractable. Second, even if integration is easy, an illumination model may make the scene illumination function, $I(x,y)$, very expensive to compute.[10] We therefore would like to minimise the number of samples required of I.

It is not only important to find approximations, but also to specify formally their semantics. First, approximations are employed throughout every graphics system implementation. A formal specification of, and the relationship between, approximate and exact approaches is required to have a clear understanding of an implementation's behaviour. Second, if the semantics of an approximation is given, an implementor has a prescription of what must be achieved and can prove that the implementation satisfies the specification of the approximation. If the approximation itself is a good one, then such a proof constitutes realistic certification that the implementation and the exact technique are in close correspondence. Third, it is crucial to the analysis and evaluation of approximations.

As in the previous section, the semantic framework developed in this section is built from some basic integration theory. Specifically, the behaviour of an intensity measure over a pixel will be approximated discretely by dividing the pixel into rectangular blocks and examining its behaviour over each block. These blocks will be called *subpixels*, in keeping with a generally-used term in the computer graphics community. We shall still employ various types of measures, which will be defined over a discrete, and usually finite, space. As in the previous section, the formal framework we develop will allow us to prove some interesting results about the approximations described. Of particular interest in this section is that the generality of this framework is exploited to derive families of recursive intensity measures which converge to their continuous analogues.

---

[10] Indeed, we shall see below that under the common global illumination model called *ray tracing*, the computation of the scene intensity for a single point is a PSPACE-hard problem.

3.3.1. Discrete Intensity Measures

Definition 27. Let $\Pi_{ij} = \{ B_k : 1 \leq k \leq M \}$ be a (finite) collection of *blocks* which partition an arbitrary pixel P_{ij} with rectangular extent S_{ij}. Each block B_k is a closed rectangle $[a_k, b_k] \times [c_k, d_k]$. Blocks are disjoint except on their boundaries and

$$\bigcup_{B \in \Pi_{ij}} B = S_{ij}. \tag{71}$$

Remark 6. It is slightly preferable to define blocks as semi-closed, entirely-disjoint rectangles, but this would cause some notation below to be more cumbersome. As it stands, overlaps among adjacent blocks are sets of measure zero and are therefore negligible.[11]

Typically, all blocks are of equal measure and there is some computationally-efficient number of them; for example, there may be $M = n^2$ blocks, where n is a power of 2. We shall also call these blocks *subpixels*. The notion of a discrete intensity measure and discrete sampling process will now be motivated. These will be approximations for the continuous measures μ_{ij}^I and μ_s respectively.

Informally, a *discrete intensity measure* is distinguished from a continuous intensity measure in that the former is defined over a finite partition of a pixel, whereas the latter is defined over an uncountable partition. Unlike point-sampling, each element of the partition is viewed as having non-zero area.

Definition 28. A *discrete intensity measure* over pixel P_{ij}, scene illumination function I, and partition Π of S_{ij}, is denoted by $\mu_{ij}^I(V; \Pi)$, and is of the form

$$\mu_{ij}^I(V; \Pi) = \sum_{B \in \Pi} f(I, V, B)\, \mu_s(V \cap B). \tag{72}$$

Figure 13 depicts the geometry of the situation. A discrete intensity measure defines the contribution of a visible surface V to the intensity of pixel P_{ij} with respect to a partition Π of S_{ij}. The intensity contribution of V is defined as the sum of an approximating function f over each subpixel B in the partition. An intensity value for each subpixel is defined by the function f and is weighted by discrete sampling measure μ_s. As before, μ_s is a probability measure. The partition Π is a parameter to the measures and will be exploited when we consider

---

[11] Any line in $\mathbf{R}^2$ is a set of measure zero [Mars74]. It follows directly from the definition of measure that any countable collection of lines is also a set of measure zero.

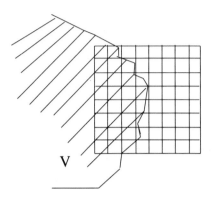

Figure 13. Surface V makes an intensity contribution to the shaded subpixels.

recursive measures. Recall from Eq. 23(a) that a general intensity measure with respect to basis function s is of the form

$$\mu_{ij}^I(V) = \int_{S_{ij} \cap V} I \, d\mu_s. \tag{73}$$

In effect, Eq. 72 replaces the integral of Eq. 73 by a summation over a coarse refinement of S_{ij}.

3.3.2. Discrete Area-Sampling Approximations

3.3.2.1. General Framework

The strategy of all the area sampling approximations we shall be presenting is to approximate the ideal area sampling integral of Eq. 73 by a series of area estimates over each subpixel "covered" by a visible surface (see above figure). There are many useful ways to define "coverage", and each way will provide a potentially different approximation.

The following assumptions are necessary to the success of these approximations.

(1) Each pixel occupies a finite area. That is, for each P_{ij}, $\mu(S_{ij}) < \infty$.

(2) The scene illumination function does not vary greatly over each portion of a subpixel covered by a particular visible surface. That is, $I(x,y)$ is nearly constant $\forall (x,y) \in V \cap B$.

Assumption 2 essentially means that the set of subpixels is a sufficient refinement of S_{ij} so that the illumination function does not vary greatly over each visible object within a subpixel. Later, we shall consider ways of dealing with cases in which this assumption is false. This is a similar but weaker assumption than that for point-sampling discussed earlier, in that a point-sampling technique generally requires $I(x,y)$ to be well-behaved throughout the entire pixel for each visible surface.

If I is nearly constant across $V \cap B$, $B \in \Pi$, then clearly

$$\int_{V \cap B} I \, d\mu_s \sim I(p)\mu_s(V \cap B), \tag{74}$$

for any point $p \in V \cap B$. Under these assumptions, area sampling can be accurately approximated. Note, however, that the measure μ_s in the above approximation may itself be rather difficult to compute. We shall discuss approximations to it shortly.

In our first area-sampling approximation, we shall define the intensity of a pixel in terms of the contribution made by each visible surface to the intensity of each subpixel. Recall from Eq. 72 that to define such an approximation, it suffices to define a discrete intensity measure in terms of a basis function s and a subpixel intensity approximation f.

Definition 29. Let $\Pi = \{ B_1, \cdots, B_M \}$ be a partition of S_{ij}, the (finite) extent of pixel P_{ij}. For convenience, we define a *choice function* $\beta(V, B)$ which chooses, for a specific visible surface V and subpixel B, a distinguished point $p \in V \cap B$. If $V \cap B = \varnothing$, then $\beta(V, B)$ can be arbitrary. Suppose $X \subseteq \mathbf{R}^2$ is measurable. Then a *discrete area sampling* with respect to basis function s is characterised by the subpixel intensity approximation

$$f(I, V, B) =_{df} I(\beta(V, B)). \tag{75}$$

Later on, with a simple change of the partitioning scheme, we shall be able to accommodate recursive pixel subdivision (thereby weakening Assumption 2). Taking into account the above definition and Eq. 72, the discrete intensity measure induced by s and f is

$$\mu_{ij}^I(V; \Pi) = \sum_{B \in \Pi} I(\beta(V, B))\mu_s(V \cap B). \tag{76}$$

There are two significant shortcomings of this approximation. First, as long as $\mu_s(V \cap B) \neq 0$, visible surface V makes a contribution to the intensity of subpixel B. Thus an implementation may devote extensive computational effort for negligible improvements in the approximation. Second, an exact Lebesgue measure calculation, $\mu_s(V \cap B)$ is required for each visible object V and subpixel B. It is certainly possible to use Monte-Carlo techniques on each subpixel to approximate this area. However, since we are trying to develop simple approximations over subpixels, this again seems overly expensive. On the other hand, it is often possible to estimate very accurately some properties of each $V \cap B$, exploiting, for example, the geometry of the subpixels and the visible objects. For example, it is easy to determine if a subpixel is more than one-half covered by a convex polygonal set (see below). This could be used to provide an estimate of how much of a pixel is covered by a visible surface. One estimate would be to take the measure of all covered subpixels divided by the measure of all subpixels. In fact, the development to follow will lead to a very useful way of representing the coverage of each visible object V over all subpixels with respect to any coverage thresholding criterion that obeys certain rules. We shall call this representation a *coverage mask*, and will consider it in some detail later. Let us first develop an axiomatic definition of *coverage predicates*.

Definition 30. Let $A, A_1, A_2 \subseteq S_{ij}$ be disjoint, and let $B \in \Pi$. A *coverage predicate* is any $\{0,1\}$-valued function $C(A,B)$, read "A *covers* B" satisfying the following axioms.

$$C(\bar{A}, B) = 1 - C(A, B). \tag{77a}$$

$$C(S_{ij}, B) = 1. \tag{77b}$$

$$C(A_1, B) = 1 \lor C(A_2, B) = 1 \Rightarrow C(A_1 \cup A_2, B) = 1. \tag{77c}$$

$$C(A_1, B) = 1 \Rightarrow C(A_2, B) = 0. \tag{77d}$$

Axioms (77a) and (77b) imply that $C(\varnothing, B) = 0$. A coverage predicate combines aspects of a measure and of a characteristic function which respects weak versions of the basic set operations. Axiom (77c) allows one to infer coverage information about the union of two sets given separate coverage information of each. Despite the appealing symmetry that would result, we do not expect the converse of (77c) to hold, for, as we shall see, it is easy to defeat natural area-coverage thresholds (such as half-coverage) by splitting sets up into arbitrarily small pieces. Property (77d) says that no two disjoint sets can both cover a subpixel.

Two natural coverage predicates come to mind immediately. We shall present their formal semantics later. First, define $C(A,B) = 1$ iff A more than one-half covers B. It is clear that this definition satisfies the four axioms above. Notice, however, that this predicate would violate axiom (77c) if it were an "iff": let both A_1 and A_2 occupy $1/3$ of a subpixel each, but let their union be greater than $1/2$. Second, define $C(A,B) = 1$ iff A covers B iff the centre of B is in A. In this case, not only does this predicate satisfy the above axioms, but it would also satisfy (77c) if it were an "iff".

Let us now develop a semantics of discrete area sampling with respect to an arbitrary coverage predicate, C. Each subpixel will be "owned" by at most one visible surface as defined by the predicate.

Definition 31. Let C be a coverage predicate, let Π be a partition of S_{ij}, and let $X \subseteq S_{ij}$. The notation $S_C(X;\Pi)$ denotes the set of subpixels covered by X over pixel P_{ij}. Formally,

$$S_C(X;\Pi) =_{df} \{ B \in \Pi : C(X,B) \}. \tag{78}$$

Definition 32. The *discrete sampling process induced by* basis function s, coverage predicate C, and partition Π is

$$\mu_s(X;\Pi,C) =_{df} \mu_s\left(\bigcup_{B \in S_C(X;\Pi)} B \right). \tag{79}$$

Because subpixel interiors are disjoint,

$$\mu_s(X;\Pi,C) = \sum_{B \in S_C(X;\Pi)} \mu_s(B) = \sum_{B \in \Pi} C(X,B)\mu_s(B). \tag{80}$$

It is usually the case that all subpixels have the same area (i.e., if there are M subpixels, then $\mu(B)=\mu(S_{ij})/M$). However, this does not necessarily mean that all $\mu_s(B)$ are the same, nor are they necessarily easy to compute, since they in general require the integration of a probability density function over a rectangular region. In cases in which $\mu_s(B)$ is known beforehand (e.g., for exact-area sampling), or is easily computable, then Eq. 80 is already an efficient approximation to exact area sampling. The cases in which it is not easily computable will be dealt with shortly. Clearly, Eq. 80 converges to $\mu_s(X)$ with successive refinement of the pixel partition Π.

It is important to note that, due to the weakness of the coverage axioms, a discrete μ_s may not be a measure as defined. It satisfies most of the properties of a probability measure except that it may fail on the countable additivity rule. The obvious example for which μ_s fails to be countably additive arises when $C(A,B)$ is the half-coverage rule: define a countable sequence of disjoint sets whose union has coverage greater than $1/2$ with each set having coverage less than $1/2$. Eq. 80 is therefore a *defective measure* in the following sense.

Theorem 8. *Let $A_1, A_2, \cdots \subseteq S_{ij}$ be measurable, mutually disjoint sets. Then*

$$\sum_i \mu_s(A_i;\Pi) \leq \mu_s(\bigcup_i A_i;\Pi). \tag{81}$$

Proof. From axiom 77(c), if $C(A_i,B)=1$ then $C(\cup A_i,B)=1$. Hence $S_C(A_i;\Pi) \subseteq S_C(\cup A_i;\Pi)$. Therefore,

$$\cup S_C(A_i;\Pi) \subseteq S_C(\cup A_i;\Pi), \tag{82}$$

which implies that

$$\mu(\cup S_C(A_i; \Pi)) \leq \mu(S_C(\cup A_i; \Pi)). \tag{83}$$

Since $A_1, A_2, \cdots$ are disjoint, by axiom 77(d) for any subpixel B, $C(A,B)$ can be true for at most one A. Therefore, the sets $S_C(A_i; \Pi)$, $i = 1, 2, \cdots$ are disjoint. Thus

$$\mu(\cup S(A_i; \Pi)) = \sum_i \mu(S(A_i; \Pi)) \leq \mu(S(\cup A_i; \Pi)).$$

The theorem follows.

Despite the fact that μ_s may be defective, it is reasonable to think of it as a measure for two reasons. First, it is a useful approximate measure. Second, the definition can be modified slightly to ensure equality in Eq. 81 (in some cases): for any scene $\{O_1, \cdots, O_N\}$, we introduce a "background" object, O_0, which acts as a sink for any subpixel that is not covered by one of the other objects. This is a useful concept which goes beyond the present discussion of defective sampling measures.

Definition 33. Given scene $\{O_1, \cdots, O_N\}$, and arbitrary coverage predicate C. A *background object* $O_0 = (V_0, I_0)$ over pixel P_{ij} is an object of arbitrary (background) colour I_0, with visible points

$$V_0 =_{df} S_{ij} - \bigcup_{i=1}^{N} V_i. \tag{84}$$

The semantics of a coverage predicate is extended to this background object as follows.

$$C(V_0, B) = 1 \iff \forall 1 \leq i \leq N : C(V_i, B) = 0. \tag{85}$$

Remark 7. V_0 is measurable if both S_{ij} and V_i are.

Remark 8. Equality is ensured in Eq. 81 if a background object is always involved in the measure computation.

From Eqs. 80 and 72, the discrete intensity measure induced by discrete sampling process $\mu_s(X; \Pi, C)$ is

$$\mu_{ij}^I(V; \Pi, C) = \sum_{B \in \Pi} f(I, V, B) \, \mu_s(V \cap B; \Pi, C) \tag{86}$$

$$= \sum_{B \in \Pi} I(\beta(V, B)) \, C(V, B) \, \mu_s(B).$$

Depending on whether or not V covers a given subpixel B, V either makes *the* intensity contribution to B or it does not. If it does, then this contribution is exactly in proportion to the size of B. This provides us with a computationally-tractable approximation to Eq. 72. Let us consider two additional simplifications and their effect on this approximation.

Assumption 1. If $I(x,y)$ is a constant, I_V, across $V \cap S_{ij}$ (see Eqs. 27, 78, and 80), then

$$\mu_{ij}^I(V;\Pi,C) = I_V \sum_{B \in \Pi} C(V,B)\,\mu(B). \tag{87}$$

Assumption 2. If, in addition to Assumption 1, $\mu(S_{ij}) = 1$, each of the M subpixels have measure $1/M$, and we employ exact-area sampling, then

$$\mu_{ij}^I(V;\Pi,C) = I_V \frac{|S_C(V;\Pi)|}{M} = I_V \frac{M'}{M} \tag{88}$$

where $M' = |S_C(V;\Pi)|$ is the number of subpixels covered by V. Thus the measure essentially reduces to weighting the intensity of V by the ratio between the subpixels covered and the total number of subpixels.

3.3.2.2. Examples of Coverage Predicates

Some useful coverage predicates were informally described earlier. We formally define several predicates in this section. The reader is encouraged to verify that they satisfy the axioms listed in Eq. 77.

Example 12. Half-coverage. Our first example is the half-coverage rule: $C(A,B) = 1$ iff A more than one-half covers B. Formally,

$$C_0(A,B) = 1 \iff \frac{\mu(A \cap B)}{\mu(B)} > \frac{1}{2}. \tag{89a}$$

To avoid a division, the predicate could be rewritten as

$$C_0(A,B) = 1 \iff 2\mu(A \cap B) > \mu(B). \tag{89b}$$

In an early paper to employ coverage masks, Fiume, Fournier and Rudolph used a half-coverage rule, although its semantics was not carefully defined [FiFR83].

Example 13. Centre-coverage. Another plausible coverage predicate was also mentioned earlier. In this case, $C(A,B) = 1$ iff A contains the centre of B. Since subpixels are assumed to be rectangular, the centre of B is a well-defined point.[12]

---

[12] For more general subpixel shapes, the notion of a subpixel centre may be more subtle. For regular shapes such as squares, triangles and hexagons, the definition of a centre is straightforward.

Let $c_B \in B$ be its centre. This coverage predicate can then be defined formally as

$$C_1(A,B) =_{df} \chi_A(c_B).$$ (90)

This predicate has the advantage of being very simple to compute. However it is certainly very easy to defeat in the sense that a set may cover a substantial portion of a pixel without containing its centre. It is also obvious that the half-coverage and centre-containment predicates will differ on many sets, since it is easy to come up with sets that more than one-half cover a subpixel without containing its centre. However, for suitably constrained sets, connected convex sets, for example, the predicates are more likely to agree. In fact, it is easy to see that if A is a connected convex set, then $C_0(A,B) = 1 \Rightarrow C_1(A,B) = 1$. The converse is not true.

Example 14. Monte-Carlo half-coverage. The last coverage predicate we shall discuss combines the previous two concepts. Let $\Phi = \{ p_1, \cdots, p_n : p_i \in B \}$ be a set of points. One could either distribute the points of Φ uniformly (or according to some other probability distribution), or these points could be distinguished "sentinel" points. One might, for example, place the corners and centre of B in Φ to allow the coverage predicate to work over less well-behaved sets. We define $C(A,B) = 1$ iff A contains more than one-half of the points of Φ. The formal definition of this coverage predicate is easy:

$$C_2(A,B) \iff \frac{|A \cap \Phi|}{|\Phi|} > \frac{1}{2}.$$ (91)

$$\iff \frac{\sum_{p \in \Phi} \chi_A(p)}{n} > \frac{1}{2}.$$

Observe that for uniformly distributed Φ, as $|\Phi| \to \infty$, $C_2(A,B) \to C_0(A,B)$ a.e., by Theorem 6 above.

3.3.2.3. Coverage Masks

The idea of employing a boolean matrix to approximate area coverage for the purposes of anti-aliasing has been known in computer graphics for some time [FiFR83; Carp84; AbWW85], and has also been employed in several hardware implementations. In this section, we present coverage masks in a general setting, and later use them to approximate convolutions.

The notion of a coverage predicate leads naturally to a representation for the coverage of every visible surface over a pixel. We shall assume that each pixel is rectangular, and that it is partitioned as an $m \times n$ grid of rectangular subpixels. Thus

$$\Pi = \{ B_{ab} : 1 \le a \le m, \ 1 \le b \le n \ \}. \tag{92}$$

Definition 34. A *coverage mask* $\chi(X;\Pi)$ of a set X with respect to partition Π is an $m \times n$ boolean matrix indicating the value of the coverage predicate on each subpixel. We shall use subscripts to denote elements of the coverage mask. Formally,

$$\chi(X;\Pi)_{ab} =_{df} C(X,B_{ab}). \tag{93}$$

A coverage mask is illustrated in Figure 14.

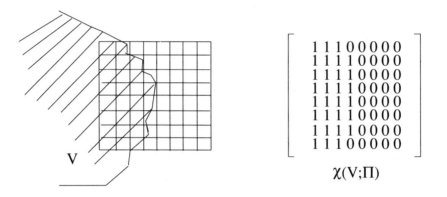

$$
\begin{bmatrix}
1 & 1 & 1 & 0 & 0 & 0 & 0 & 0 \\
1 & 1 & 1 & 1 & 0 & 0 & 0 & 0 \\
1 & 1 & 1 & 1 & 0 & 0 & 0 & 0 \\
1 & 1 & 1 & 1 & 0 & 0 & 0 & 0 \\
1 & 1 & 1 & 1 & 0 & 0 & 0 & 0 \\
1 & 1 & 1 & 1 & 0 & 0 & 0 & 0 \\
1 & 1 & 1 & 1 & 0 & 0 & 0 & 0 \\
1 & 1 & 1 & 0 & 0 & 0 & 0 & 0
\end{bmatrix}
$$

$$\chi(V;\Pi)$$

Figure 14. Example of a coverage mask.

As noted in [FiFR83], coverage masks are useful in approximating set operations. The following identities can be used:

$$\chi(X \cup Y;\Pi) = \max\{ \chi(X;\Pi), \chi(Y;\Pi) \} \tag{94a}$$

$$\chi(X \cap Y;\Pi) = \min\{ \chi(X;\Pi), \chi(Y;\Pi) \} \tag{94b}$$

$$\chi(\overline{X};\Pi) = \mathbf{1} - \chi(X;\Pi). \tag{94c}$$

The operations on the right hand side of each identity are component-wise matrix operations. The symbol $\mathbf{1}$ stands for an $m \times n$ matrix of ones. Identities (a) and (b) are exact only if axiom (77c) above is an iff for the coverage predicate used. A proof of this fact is trivial. Otherwise, they are only approximations.

Another use of coverage masks is that we can approximate the exact coverage of V over a pixel P_{ij} as follows:

$$\mu(V \cap S_{ij}) \ \sim \ \frac{\displaystyle\sum_{a,\,b} \chi(V;\Pi)_{ab}}{m \times n} \ = \ \frac{M'}{M} \tag{95}$$

as in Eq. 88 above. A final remark is that, as is evident from the above figure, coverage masks do more than simply group together a set of bit values. They provide a discrete structure that approximates the coverage behaviour of a set. Indeed, for some kinds of sets, it is almost as easy to determine an entire coverage mask analytically or by look-up table than to compute a coverage predicate for a single subpixel [FiFR83; Carp84].

3.3.3. Discrete Non-Uniform Area Sampling

3.3.3.1. Derivation

In the previous section, we presented some discrete approximations for intensity and sampling measures, but commented that the approximation is still not fast if the quantity $\mu_s(B)$ is not easily computable. For example, Eq. 80 requires the evaluation of an exact Lebesgue-Stieltjes integral over a set of small subpixels. The exact integral of many probability distributions is difficult to compute, even over simple rectangular regions.

We shall approximate $\mu_s(B)$ for subpixel $B \in \Pi$ using β to choose a distinguished point $p_B(x_B, y_B)$ for each B, and sampling the distribution at that point to derive an estimate. If the subpixels are sufficiently small, or if the basis function is smooth, the approximation is good. To capture this line of thought mathematically,

$$\mu_s(B) \sim \int_B h(x_c - x_B, y_c - y_B)\, d\mu \qquad (96)$$

$$= h(x_c - x_B, y_c - y_B) \int_B d\mu$$

$$= h(x_c - x_B, y_c - y_B)\, \mu(B).$$

Thus we have reduced the evaluation of a Lebesgue-Stieltjes measure over a small (finite) area to a single evaluation of $h(x,y)$ and a multiplication. Both $\mu(B)$ and (x_B, y_B) can be pre-computed in an implementation. We can therefore approximate a general discrete intensity measure by

$$\mu_{ij}^I(V; \Pi, C) = \sum_{B \in \Pi} I(\beta(V, B)) h(x_c - x_B, y_c - y_B)\, \mu(B)\, C(V, B). \qquad (97)$$

Note that we could instead sample I at (x_B, y_B). This has the disadvantage of possibly being outside the visible region of the object deemed to cover the pixel. On the other hand, it might be useful as a fast approximation, the merits of which would require some experimental substantiation.

3.3.3.2. Convolution Tables[13]

In this section we shall manipulate the discrete intensity measure in Eq. 97 into a form that facilitates a table look-up implementation. Let us assume that the scene illumination function, $I(x,y)$, is almost constant across each visible object within a pixel. Denote this constant value by I_V for each V. This allows us to simplify Eq. 97:

$$\mu_{ij}^l(V;\Pi,C) = I_V \sum_{B\in\Pi} h(x_c-x_B, y_c-y_B)\mu(B)C(V,B). \tag{98}$$

Observe that $C(V,B)$ across every subpixel $B \in \Pi$ is simply the coverage mask of V, $\chi(V;\Pi)$. as stated earlier, since (x_B,y_B), (x_c,y_c), and $\mu(B)$ are known beforehand, the values

$$H_B = h(x_c-x_B, y_c-y_B)\mu(B) \tag{99}$$

for each B can be precomputed and stored in a table. This reduces Eq. 98 to

$$\mu_{ij}^l(V;\Pi,C) = I_V \sum_{B\in\Pi} C(V,B)H_B. \tag{100}$$

Thus if $|\Pi|=n^2$, then to compute $\mu_s(V;\Pi,C)$ requires $O(n^2)$ additions (and one multiplication). However, we can do much better than this if we use coverage masks in our table look-up. As used in the above summation, $C(V,B)$ simply indicates whether or not to add a certain value to the measure. What we shall do instead is to exploit the fact that a coverage mask can be represented as a bit string, and use *rows* of the mask as an index into a look-up table. If the number of bits in each row is chosen to be a computer-friendly figure, such as 8, 16, or 32, then look-ups can be performed very quickly. More formally, we view each row of coverage mask $\chi(V;\Pi)$ as an n-bit word $m_{n-1} \cdots m_0$. Define a table $H[r,m]$, where $0 \leq r < n$ is the subpixel row, and m is an n-bit row value of the coverage mask. The idea is that $H[r,m]$ contains the sum of H_B for each subpixel B across row r, given coverage row mask m. That is,

$$H[r,m] = \sum_{k=0}^{n-1} m_{n-k-1} h(x_c-x_{B_{rk}}, y_c-y_{B_{rk}})\,\mu(B_{rk}) \tag{101}$$

This strategy is depicted in Figure 15. The table H need only be computed once if the same filter is to be used over all pixels (as is common). Thus Eq. 100 becomes:

$$\mu_{ij}^l(V;\Pi,C) = I_V \sum_{r=0}^{n-1} H[r, M_r], \tag{102}$$

where each M_r is an n-bit word $m_{n-1} \cdots m_0$ with $m_k = \chi(V;\Pi)_{rk} = C(V,B_{rk})$.

---

[13] This section may be omitted without loss of continuity.

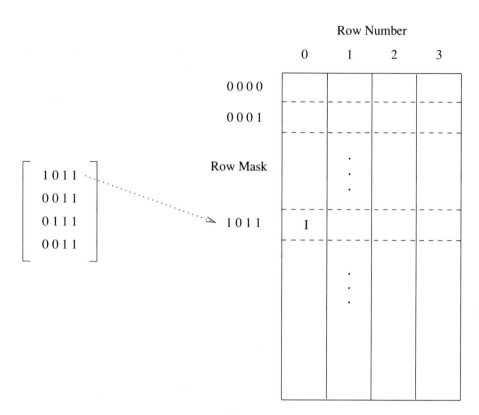

Figure 15. Look-up table at position $(0,11)$ gives $\sum h\mu(B)$ for row mask $(1011)_2$.

Clearly only O(n) additions are required if each M_r is easily computable. These values can be computed in O(n) time beforehand if the visible objects over a pixel are restricted to a fixed set of polygons [FiFR83; Carp84]. Look-up tables can be used to compute these values quickly.

3.3.4. Recursive Discrete Sampling Schemes

We have been careful throughout this section to parameterise our measures by the partition Π. The reason for this is that it would be useful to be able to partition a pixel adaptively and to an arbitrary level of detail. In pixels over which the scene illumination varies little, and where few visible surfaces intersect with the pixel, only a coarse pixel refinement is needed. The converse is true for more complex cases. We would like to treat these cases uniformly. To accomplish this, we shall define and exploit *recursive intensity measures*.

3.3.4.1. Recursive Pixel Subdivision

Recursive subdivision is a classic divide-and-conquer strategy in computer graphics that has many applications [NeSp79]. The strategy adopted here is to divide a pixel area up recursively, depending on the behaviour of the scene illumination function over the pixel. The recursion ends on a particular sub-block of the pixel when it is found that the scene illumination function, $I(x,y)$, is intelligently-guessed to be well behaved throughout the sub-block.

Let P_{ij} be a rectangle $[a,b] \times [c,d]$. The initial partition of P_{ij} will be $\Pi = \{ B \}$, consisting of a single "subpixel" $B = S_{ij}$. As usual, the discrete intensity measure is defined as:

$$\mu_{ij}^I(V;\Pi,C) = \sum_{B \in \Pi} f(I, V, B)\mu_s(V \cap B), \tag{103}$$

where μ_s is any discrete sampling measure, and C is a coverage predicate. A *recursive intensity measure* is distinguished from the other discrete intensity measures considered above by the way f is defined. The classical recursive subdivision strategy is to sample the scene illumination at the corners of the pixel and to subdivide if their overall difference is greater than some threshold τ. We generalise this slightly. Let $M(I, B, \tau)$ be a "metric" predicate which is true if the scene illumination function I is "sufficiently well-behaved" about subpixel B. The goodness of behaviour of I about B is defined with respect to tolerance τ. There are many possibilities for M. Let $p_B \in B$ be a distinguished point in B. We define f recursively as follows:

$$f(I, V, B) = \begin{cases} I(p_B) & \text{if } M(I, B, \tau). \\ \mu_{ij}^I(V;\Pi') & \text{otherwise.} \end{cases} \tag{104}$$

The value $\tau > 0$ is a prescribed tolerance, and Π' is a partition of B that refines Π. It is defined as follows. If $B=[a,b] \times [c,d]$, then $\Pi'=\{ B_1, B_2, B_3, B_4 \}$, where

$$B_1 = \left[a, \frac{a+b}{2} \right] \times \left[c, \frac{c+d}{2} \right] \tag{105}$$

$$B_2 = \left[\frac{a+b}{2}, b \right] \times \left[c, \frac{c+d}{2} \right]$$

$$B_3 = \left[a, \frac{a+b}{2} \right] \times \left[\frac{c+d}{2}, d \right]$$

$$B_4 = \left[\frac{a+b}{2}, b \right] \times \left[\frac{c+d}{2}, d \right]$$

Assuming $M(I, B, \tau)$ is defined in a natural way, the refinement of pixel P_{ij} is finest on the region over which $I(x,y)$ varies greatly and is coarsest on regions of little intensity variation. Of course the simple 4-corner metric mentioned above is easily defeated: imagine a scene illumination function which is nearly constant around the corners of a pixel but changes dramatically towards the pixel centre. Unfortunately, this readily occurs in practice. For example, the specular highlight of a glossy surface could easily exhibit such behaviour if the highlight just happened to be in the proximity of the pixel centre. In any case, we present M formally here as an example. Let b_0, b_1, b_2, b_3 be the corner points of subpixel B. Let $\mathbf{I} =_{df} \{ I(b_i) : i = 0,1,2,3 \}$, and define the error metric as follows:

$$M(I, B, \tau) =_{df} \tau < (\max\{ \mathbf{I} \} - \min\{ \mathbf{I} \}). \tag{106}$$

An approach that does not appear to have ever been implemented is to choose sample points stochastically as described earlier. Four or more uniformly-distributed sample points could be generated over each block, replacing the use of the corner points. This technique warrants further analysis, but we defer that topic to a future report.

3.4. A Fast Rendering Approximation

In this section, we shall apply some of the formal machinery presented earlier to develop a rendering approximation that is suitable for real-time implementation. Recall from Chapter 2 that determining the visible portions of a set of N objects over each pixel requires $\Omega(N \log N)$ time. This result was shown for very simple objects: rectangles. Indeed, in cases where there is a great deal of overlap among objects, we saw that any visible object determination algorithm must take $\Omega(N^2)$ time. In practice, the number of objects in a moderately complex scene can easily exceed 100 000 polygons. It is therefore clear that an N^2 or $N \log N$ order statistic, for that matter, may impede real-time implementation.

We shall propose a simple rendering approximation that is based on the original list of objects in the scene *prior* to visible object determination. Thus we shall be dealing with objects that may overlap in various ways, a phenomenon that would be prevented if the invisible components of an object were removed. In our approximation, the process of determining the visible objects, which is essentially a sorting step, will be replaced by finding a minimum. The approximation therefore has O(N) time behaviour. A less general version of this algorithm was presented in [FiFR83], but this is the first time it is presented formally and its accuracy proven. In that paper, Fiume, Fournier and Rudolph presented a fast approximation to discrete exact-area sampling. We shall develop a family of approximations that is independent of the sampling process employed, whether discrete or continuous. In fact, it can be combined with any other approximation discussed above − coverage masks, for example.

3.4.1. Derivation

Let $\mathbf{SP} = \langle S_1, \cdots, S_N \rangle$, $S_i \subseteq S_{ij}$ be the components of each object in the scene which overlap with pixel P_{ij} *before visibility determination.* Associated with each S_i is a depth function $Z_i : S_i \rightarrow \mathbf{R}$, which gives the depth of any point in S_i. We make the following assumptions.

(0) The extent S_{ij} of each pixel P_{ij} is finite.

(1) The scene illumination is nearly constant across each S_k. Formally, we assume that for each k, $1 \le k \le N$, there exists a constant I_k such that for all $(x,y) \in S_k$, $|I(x,y) - I_k| \le \tau_1$ for a prescribed tolerance $\tau_1 > 0$.

(2) The depth of each S_k is nearly constant. That is, there exists a constant Z_k such that $|Z(x,y) - Z_k| \le \tau_2$ $\forall (x,y) \in S_k$.

(3) $\mathbf{SP}$ covers S_{ij}. That is, $\cup S_k = S_{ij}$. If this is not true, add a "background" object to fill in the parts of the pixel not covered by $\mathbf{SP}$ (see Definition 33).

These are not overly-restrictive assumptions, since several objects with differing intensities and depths could be added to $\mathbf{SP}$ to approximate a single object that contradicts assumption 1 or 2. We define w (for "winner"), $1 \le w \le N$, to be the index of the object with the smallest depth value. Like the formal definition of visibility in Chapter 2, the following formal definition for w requires some formal trickery to ensure uniqueness. In the event of a tie, we make the somewhat arbitrary convention to take w to be the smallest such index. Formally,

$$w =_{df} \min \left\{ k : Z_k = \min\{ Z_r : 1 \le r \le N \} \right\}. \qquad (107)$$

We now consider two approximate intensity measures which give the correct contribution of S_w to the intensity of pixel (i,j), and which estimate the contribution of the "losers". We shall use continuous sampling measures in this definition for notational convenience, but any discrete measure can be used as well.

Approximation 1.

$$\mu_{ij}^I(S_k; \mathbf{SP}) =_{df} \begin{cases} I_w \, \mu_s(S_w) & \text{if } k = w. \\ c_1(\mathbf{SP}) \, I_k \, \mu_s(\overline{S_w} \cap S_k) & \text{otherwise.} \end{cases} \qquad (108)$$

In this definition, μ_s is any sampling process, and c_1 is a correction factor that biases the contribution of a loser by the degree of mutual overlap of all losers with the winner. This is why c_1 is a function of all objects overlapping with the pixel.

In particular,

$$
c_1(\mathbf{SP}) =_{df}
\begin{cases}
0 & \text{if } \displaystyle\sum_{k \neq w} \mu_s(S_k \cap \overline{S_w}) = 0. \\[1.5em]
\dfrac{\mu_s\left[\displaystyle\bigcup_{k \neq w}(S_k \cap \overline{S_w}) \right]}{\displaystyle\sum_{k \neq w} \mu_s(S_k \cap \overline{S_w}))} & \text{otherwise.}
\end{cases}
\tag{109}
$$

Note that since the elements of $\mathbf{SP}$ are not disjoint, $c_1(\mathbf{SP}) \leq 1$.

Approximation 2. This approximation is slightly simpler than the above.

$$
\mu_{ij}^I(S_k; \mathbf{SP}) =_{df}
\begin{cases}
I_w\, \mu_s(S_w) & \text{if } k = w. \\
c_2(\mathbf{SP})\, I_k\, \mu_s(S_k) & \text{otherwise.}
\end{cases}
\tag{110}
$$

This time, the correction factor is defined as

$$
c_2(\mathbf{SP}) =_{df}
\begin{cases}
0 & \text{if } \displaystyle\sum_{k \neq w} \mu_s(S_k) = 0. \\[1.5em]
\dfrac{\mu_s\left[\displaystyle\bigcup_{k \neq w}(S_k \cap \overline{S_w}) \right]}{\displaystyle\sum_{k \neq w} \mu_s(S_k))} & \text{otherwise.}
\end{cases}
\tag{111}
$$

As defined above, μ_{ij}^I is not strictly a measure, for the notion of $\mu_{ij}^I(A \cup B; \mathbf{SP})$ for $A, B \in \mathbf{SP}$ is meaningless. Rather than augment the definition with extra decomposition rules for set union and intersection, we simply promise to use μ_{ij}^I independently on members of $\mathbf{SP}$. In particular, we define the approximate intensity of pixel P_{ij} as

$$
\overline{I}(i,j) =_{df} \sum_{S \in \mathbf{SP}} \mu_{ij}^I(S; \mathbf{SP}).
\tag{112}
$$

Note that $\overline{I}$ can be computed in time linear with $|\mathbf{SP}|$ if μ_s can be computed in constant time. It turns out this is possible if μ_s is a discrete exact-area sampling measure, if coverage masks are used, and if each object in $\mathbf{SP}$ is constrained to be a specific type of polygon (see Section 2.2.3 and [FiFR83; Carp84]).

3.4.2. Analysis of Approximations

We shall now show that in many cases, $\overline{I}$ is a good approximation.

Theorem 9. *Both approximations are exact when*

(a) *only one or two objects overlap with the pixel (i.e., $|\mathbf{SP}| \leq 2$), or when*

(b) *any number of mutually disjoint objects overlap with the pixel.*

Here, *exact* is taken to mean that

$$\hat{I}(i,j) = \sum_{V \in \mathbf{VP}} \mu_{ij}^l(V) = \sum_{S \in \mathbf{SP}} \mu_{ij}^l(S;\mathbf{SP}) = \overline{I}(i,j), \tag{113}$$

where $\mathbf{VP} = \{V_1, \cdots, V_N\}$ are the visible components of $\mathbf{SP}$.

Proof. We use Approximation 1. The argument is identical for Approximation 2. To prove case (a), if $\mathbf{SP}=\{S_1\}$, then S_1 is the winner and $S_1=S_{ij}=V_1$. Therefore,

$$\overline{I}(i,j) = I_1 \mu_S(S_1) = I_1 \mu_S(V_1) = \hat{I}(i,j).$$

On the other hand, if $\mathbf{SP}=\{S_1, S_2\}$, then without loss of generality let S_1 be the winner and $S_2 \neq \varnothing$ the loser such that $S_{ij}=S_1 \cup S_2$. Assume that some portion of S_2 is visible, that is, $S_2 \cap \overline{S_1} \neq \varnothing$. Then by Eq. 112,

$$\overline{I}(i,j) = I_1 \mu_S(S_1) + I_2 c_1(\mathbf{SP}) \mu(S_2 \cap \overline{S_1}). \tag{114}$$

However, $S_1=V_1$, and $S_2 \cap \overline{S_1}=V_2$. Moreover,

$$c_1(\mathbf{SP}) = \frac{\mu_s(S_2 \cap \overline{S_1})}{\mu_s(S_2 \cap \overline{S_1})} = 1. \tag{115}$$

Therefore, Eq. 114 becomes

$$\overline{I}(i,j) = I_1 \mu_S(V_1) + I_2 \mu_S(V_2) = \hat{I}(i,j). \tag{116}$$

Thus part (a) of the theorem is proved.

For case (b), let $\mathbf{SP}=\{S_1, \cdots, S_N\}$ be a set of mutually disjoint non-empty objects. Since these sets are disjoint, $\mathbf{SP}=\mathbf{VP}$. Note, moreover, that $S_l \cap \overline{S_w}=S_l$, for any loser l. Therefore, by definition of c_1 and by countable additivity of μ_s,

$$c_1(\mathbf{SP}) = \frac{\mu_s\left[\bigcup_{k \neq w}(S_k \cap \overline{S_w})\right]}{\sum_{k \neq w}\mu_s(S_k \cap \overline{S_w})} \tag{117}$$

$$= \frac{\mu_s\left[\bigcup_{k \neq w}(S_k)\right]}{\sum_{k \neq w}\mu_s(S_k)}$$

$$= \frac{\sum\limits_{k \neq w} \mu_s(S_k)}{\sum\limits_{k \neq w} \mu_s(S_k)}$$

$$= 1.$$

Hence

$$\overline{I}(i,j) = \sum_{S \in \mathbf{SP}} \mu'_{ij}(S ; \mathbf{SP}) \tag{118}$$

$$= I_w \mu_s(S_w) + \sum_{k \neq w} I_k c_1(\mathbf{SP}) \mu_s(S_k \cap \overline{S_w})$$

$$= I_w \mu_s(S_w) + \sum_{k \neq w} I_k \mu_s(S_k)$$

$$= \sum_k I_k \mu_s(S_k)$$

$$= \sum_k I_k \mu_s(V_k)$$

$$= \hat{I}(i,j).$$

Thus part (b) of the theorem is proved.

Since Approximation 1 keeps track of more overlap information, it handles a situation exactly that is not handled by Approximation 2.

Theorem 10. *Approximation 1 is exact when the winner overlaps with the losers, and the losers are disjoint.*

Proof. Observe that if S_w is the only surface that can overlap with the other elements of **SP**, then $S_k \cap \overline{S_w} = V_k$, $k \neq w$. Note also that $S_w = V_w$. By an almost identical argument to the proof of part (b) above, $c_1(\mathbf{SP}) = 1$, and $\overline{I}(i,j) = \hat{I}(i,j)$.

It remains to consider the expected accuracy of this approximation for complex scenes in which there is extensive overlap among objects. An informal discussion of a simple implementation is presented in [FiFR83], but a more formal analysis is in order. A probabilistic framework is currently being considered that will permit evaluation of these and other approximation schemes. This will be the subject of a future report.

3.5. Summary

This chapter has carefully considered the notion of rendering, its formal semantics, and some of its properties. The fundamental mathematical insight of this chapter is that rendering techniques can be defined precisely using measures. The resulting framework has allowed us to define many techniques, both old and new. We also defined approximations to these techniques, again by measure-theoretic means, and proved properties of their behaviour under realistic situations.

The future work stimulated by this chapter could follow several avenues. The crispness of the semantics of rendering provides a useful testbed for examining various existing rendering techniques and approximations. It would be of interest to augment the framework presented in this chapter by a methodology for testing rendering techniques. It would also be worthwhile to develop approximate techniques for which fast convergence properties can be proven.

In more general terms, this chapter has a moral: that abstraction and careful mathematical characterisation does not necessarily decrease relevance to real systems. We defined rendering in ideal, unimplementable terms, and then progressively transformed these idealisations into realistic rendering techniques. At any step in the process, it was entirely clear what assumptions were being made, and the effect that these assumptions would have on the efficacy of the induced rendering techniques.

4 Bit-Mapped Graphics

Let us imagine a white surface with irregular black spots on it. We then say that whatever kind of picture these make, I can always approximate as closely as I wish to the description of it by covering the surface with a sufficiently fine square mesh, and then saying of every square whether it is black or white. In this way I shall have imposed a unified form on the description of the surface. The form is optional, since I could have achieved the same result using a net with a triangular or hexagonal mesh.

−L. Wittgenstein[1]

Synopsis. Because of its convenience and growing supporting technology, a form of raster graphics called *bit-mapped graphics* is becoming increasingly widespread. A typical bit-mapped graphics environment supports the efficient manipulation of high-resolution images over a small intensity space. As such, a unique set of bit-map concepts and operations has evolved. An important problem that arises whenever a new technology is introduced is the degree to which it can be integrated or unified with existing technologies. With respect to bit-mapped graphics, this problem can be split into at least two important subproblems. First, to determine what the capabilities of bit-mapped graphics are. Second, to determine the extent to which these capabilities co-exist with, or contradict, traditional raster graphics capabilities. To attempt to solve either of these problems, a precise, mathematical formalisation of bit-mapped graphics is required. This is attempted in this chapter. In support of the formalism

---

[1] L. Wittgenstein, Prop. 6.341, *Tractatus Logico-Philosophicus* (Routledge and Kegan Paul: London, U.K.), D.F. Pears and B.F. McGuinness (trans.), 1961.

developed, a theoretical investigation of bit-mapped graphics is begun. Apart from their intrinsic interest, the results reported here constitute a first step towards arriving at a definitive understanding of the relationship between bit-mapped graphics and other raster graphics technologies. A prior version of this chapter appears in [Fium87].

4.1. Introduction

Bit-mapped graphics is a form of raster graphics technology that is increasing in popularity. Whereas raster graphics is traditionally concerned with the rendering of 3-D scenes into 2-D images which are shaded using a large intensity space, bit-mapped graphics applications typically operate on 2-D scenes over a very small set of intensity values.[2] A collection of intensity values representing an image is thought of as *bit-mapped* if there is a direct mapping from this store of intensity values to a display screen. The major applications of this technology involve the processing and synthesis of black-and-white textual and pictorial images of high spatial resolution. Consequently, a distinctive set of operations and concepts has evolved around bit-mapped graphics. The goal of this chapter is to capture mathematically some of the important members of this set. One motivation for this work is to arrive at a formal framework incorporating both bit-mapped graphics and other more traditional raster graphics technologies [AFSW82]. This is of both practical and theoretical interest. We have already mathematically considered several aspects of 3-D raster graphics, including the semantics of rendering, the visible surface problem, and scene specification. This chapter will focus on analogous topics for bit-mapped graphics: 2-D rendering, operations on bit-maps and images, and graphic transformations of bit-maps. For each topic, a semantics will be presented; as well, some interesting and occasionally non-intuitive theoretical results will be proven. The next section provides some preliminary formalism required by the remainder of the chapter. The subsequent sections are independent and may be considered in any order.

4.2. Preliminaries

Many of the definitions to follow will be familiar. The definition of an image, first encountered in Chapter 3, will be constrained slightly to reflect its meaning within the context of bit-mapped graphics. Bit-maps first arose in this book when we discussed the image store model for the visible surface problem, in Chapter 2. The notation to follow distinguishes among the notions of a scene, a bit-map, and

---

[2] In fact, this chapter shall only deal with binary (black/white) intensity spaces. The versatility and power of bit-mapped graphics over larger intensity spaces has yet to be established, although it is a simple matter to extend this chapter accordingly.

an image as in Figure 1.

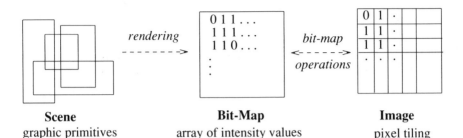

Scene	**Bit-Map**	**Image**
graphic primitives	array of intensity values	pixel tiling

Figure 1. The relationships among scene, bit-map, and image.

For the first part of this chapter, we shall consider the semantics of operations on bit-maps and images. 2-D rendering will be discussed afterwards.

We shall view a *bit-map* B as a pair (S,I), where S is a rectangle denoting the extent of B, and I is a partial function prescribing an intensity value of 0 or 1 for every (integral) point in B. This definition will be made more precise once some convenient auxiliary notation is introduced. Please note that while we shall deal exclusively with rectangular bit-maps in this chapter, it is a simple matter to extend the discussion to bit-maps of arbitrary shape provided this shape has a well-defined (and easily computable) characteristic function (see above). Later, when we consider bit-map transformations, we shall further restrict tilings to be "rigid".

Definition 1. A *pixel* P is a tuple (S_P, I_P), where $S_P \subseteq \mathbf{R}^2$ is the extent of P in the the screen plane, and $I_P \in \{0,1\}$ is its colour.

In the last chapter, an *index set* was used to enumerate the pixels in an image. Since we shall only deal with rectangular bit-maps in this chapter, we shall define a special notation for rectangular index sets.

Definition 2. A *rectangular index set*, $Rect_{x_2,y_2}^{x_1,y_1}$, denotes the set of all integral points within a rectangle with bottom-left corner (x_1,y_1) and top-right corner (x_2,y_2). That is,

$$Rect_{x_2,y_2}^{x_1,y_1} =_{df} \{ (i,j) \in \mathbf{Z}^2 : x_1 \leq i \leq x_2, y_1 \leq j \leq y_2 \}. \tag{1}$$

As we saw earlier, an image is defined by a collection of pixels having three essential characteristics: an arrangement of pixels, their shape, and their intensity.

For the purposes of this chapter, intensity space for all pixels is $\{0,1\}$. Moreover, all pixels within an image must be of the same shape defined by a prototypical pixel shape or *prototile* **P**, and the arrangement and shape of the pixels must be such that they form a tiling of the area occupied in $\mathbf{R}^2$ by the image.

Definition 3. A *pixel prototile* **P** is a finite subset of $\mathbf{R}^2$ with which it is possible to tile $\mathbf{R}^2$. That is, there exists a pixel arrangement $\mathbf{T} = \{\alpha_{ij}\mathbf{P} : (i,j) \in \mathbf{Z}^2\}$ given isometries α_{ij} such that

$$\mathbf{R}^2 = \bigcup_{P \in \mathbf{T}} P, \qquad (2)$$

and the interiors of all $P \in \mathbf{T}$ are disjoint. We shall call such a set **T** a *pixel tiling* over **P**.

Remark 1. Non-overlapping tilings are not required, but it makes the notation simpler. For example, our work can be extended to "quasi-tilings" in which pixels overlap, or in which tilings are not complete. This includes quasi-tilings such as a covering of the plane using overlapping circles, or an arrangement of non-overlapping unit circles with integral centres.

Pixel shapes on bit-mapped screens are usually thought of as rectangles occupying unit area. The most common pixel tiling is based on the unit square centred at the origin. That is,

$$\mathbf{P} =_{df} [-\tfrac{1}{2}, \tfrac{1}{2}] \times [-\tfrac{1}{2}, \tfrac{1}{2}]. \qquad (3)$$

Definition 4. The *unit-square tiling* induced by prototile **P**, denoted $\mathbf{T}_u$, has the following form:

$$\mathbf{T}_u =_{df} \{T_{ij}\mathbf{P} : (i,j) \in \mathbf{Z}^2\}, \qquad (4)$$

for translations T_{ij}.

We can now formally define the notion of an image over a pixel tiling.

Definition 5. Let **T** be a pixel tiling over prototile **P**, $\mathbf{T} = \{\alpha_{ij}\mathbf{P} : (i,j) \in \mathbf{Z}^2\}$. An *image* $R_{n_1 n_2}$ of *resolution* $(n_1+1) \times (n_2+1)$ is of the form

$$R_{n_1 n_2} = \{P_{ij} = (S_{ij}, I_{ij}) : (i,j) \in Rect_{n_1 n_2}^{0\,0}, I_{ij} \in \{0,1\}, S_{ij} = \alpha_{ij}\mathbf{P}\}. \qquad (5)$$

Definition 6. An *image space* of resolution $(n_1+1) \times (n_2+1)$, denoted by $\mathbf{R}_{n_1 n_2}$, is the set of all images $R_{n_1 n_2}$ as in Eq. (5).

Definition 7. A *bit-map* with integral bottom-left corner (x_1, y_1) and top-right corner (x_2, y_2) is of the form

$$B_{x_2 y_2}^{x_1 y_1} =_{df} (S, I),$$ (6a)

where

$$S =_{df} Rect_{x_2 y_2}^{x_1 y_1},$$ (6b)

$$I : \mathbf{Z}^2 \rightarrow \{0, 1, \omega\},$$ (6c)

such that $I(i,j) \in \{0, 1\}$ if $(i,j) \in S$ and $I(i,j) = \omega$ outside S (i.e., $\mathbf{Z}^2 - S$).

S denotes the domain of pixels represented in the bit-map. $I(i,j)$ defines the intensity of each pixel (i,j) in B. Pixels outside B (or S) are given an "undefined" intensity ω. Notice that a bit-map is tied neither to the resolution of a display image, nor to a particular pixel shape. To summarise, a bit-map is a function with domain $\mathbf{Z}^2$ that is $\{0, 1\}$-valued over a specific rectangular subset of $\mathbf{Z}^2$, and constantly ω-valued outside that rectangle.

Definition 8. Let the set of all bit-maps of form (6) for a specific (x_1, y_1) and (x_2, y_2) be denoted by $\mathbf{B}_{x_2 y_2}^{x_1 y_1}$. The set $\mathbf{B}$ of all such $\mathbf{B}_{x_2 y_2}^{x_1 y_1}$ will be called the *bit-map space*, and is defined as

$$\mathbf{B} =_{df} \bigcup_{x_1, x_2, y_1, y_2 \in \mathbf{Z}} \mathbf{B}_{x_2 y_2}^{x_1 y_1}.$$ (7)

If a bit-map $B = (S, I)$ is such that $x_1 > x_2$ or $y_1 > y_2$, then its extent S is empty and B is called an *empty bit-map*.

Definition 9. The *bit-map product space*, denoted by $\mathbf{B}^*$, is the reflexive-transitive closure of products over $\mathbf{B}$. That is,

$$\mathbf{B}^* = \bigcup_{i=0}^{\infty} \mathbf{B}^i.$$ (8)

4.3. The Semantics of Bit-Map Operations

Bit-map operations have been given some formal consideration in, for example, [NeSp79] and [GuSt82].[3] In this section, we present a thorough algebraic treatment of the semantics of bit-map operations that is somewhat more precise than

---

[3] The use of the term *bit-map operation* is synonymous with the more traditional (but less descriptive) *raster operation, rasterop,* or *bitblt* (see [NeSp79]).

previous efforts. The notational tools developed above will be very helpful. Once bit-map operations are given a solid algebraic framework, the relationship between a bit-map and an image will be precisely described.

Definition 10. A *bit-map operation* is a partial function mapping sequences of bit-maps to bit-maps. Formally, a bit-map operation $\otimes$ is a function $\otimes : \mathbf{B}^* \to \mathbf{B}$. We shall permit such functions to have other parameters over $\mathbf{Z}$ or $\mathbf{R}$.

Remark 2. Since a bit-map is a function, a bit-map operation is simply a functional (a map from functions to functions). Thus an alternative characterisation of bit-maps and operations on them would be as function spaces and functionals over them.

4.3.1. Examples of Bit-Map Operations

Recall that a bit-map B has extent S and intensity function I. $B.S$ will refer to the extent of B, and $B.I(i,j)$ will refer to the B's intensity at location (i,j).

4.3.1.1. Zero / One Bit-Map

Syntax: $Zero_{x_2 y_2}^{x_1 y_1} : \to \mathbf{B}$, $One_{x_2 y_2}^{x_1 y_1} : \to \mathbf{B}$,   where $x_1, x_2, y_1, y_2 \in \mathbf{Z}$,   and $1 \leq x_1 \leq x_2 \leq n_1$, $1 \leq y_1 \leq y_2 \leq n_2$.

Semantics: $Zero_{x_2 y_2}^{x_1 y_1} =_{df} (S, I_0)$, and $One_{x_2 y_2}^{x_1 y_1} =_{df} (S, I_1)$ where $S = Rect_{x_2 y_2}^{x_1 y_1}$. The intensity functions are defined as follows.

$$I_0(i,j) =_{df} \begin{cases} 0 & \text{if } (i,j) \in S. \\ \omega & \text{if } (i,j) \in \mathbf{Z}^2 - S. \end{cases} \tag{9a}$$

$$I_1(i,j) =_{df} \begin{cases} 1 & \text{if } (i,j) \in S. \\ \omega & \text{if } (i,j) \in \mathbf{Z}^2 - S. \end{cases} \tag{9b}$$

Remark: $Zero_{x_2 y_2}^{x_1 y_1}$ defines a bit-map of intensity all zeros with extent $Rect_{x_2 y_2}^{x_1 y_1}$. Similarly, $One_{x_2 y_2}^{x_1 y_1}$ defines a bit-map of intensity all ones.

4.3.1.2. Complement Bit-Map

Syntax: $Comp : \mathbf{B} \to \mathbf{B}$.

Semantics: Let $B \in \mathbf{B}$. Then $Comp\ B =_{df} B'$, where $B'.S = B.S$, and

$$B'.I(i,j) =_{df} \begin{cases} 1 - I(i,j) & \text{if } (i,j) \in S. \\ \omega & \text{if } (i,j) \in \mathbf{Z}^2 - S. \end{cases} \tag{10}$$

Remarks: Where suitable, let B^c abbreviate $Comp\ B$. Observe that $(B^c)^c = B$.

4.3.1.3. Composition of Bit-Map Functions

Composition of bit-map functions is permissible if functions are of matching arity, as illustrated in the following example.

Example 1. $Zero_{x_2 y_2}^{x_1 y_1} = Comp\,(One_{x_2 y_2}^{x_1 y_1})$

4.3.1.4. Restriction

We introduce a form of restriction similar to that defined for 3-D objects in Chapter 1. Let

$$\mathbf{Rect} =_{df} \{\, Rect_{x_2 y_2}^{x_1 y_1} : x_1 \le x_2,\, y_1 \le y_2 \,\}. \tag{11}$$

Regions of restriction are themselves restricted to being rectangles.

Syntax: $| : \mathbf{B} \times \mathbf{Rect} \to \mathbf{B}.$

Semantics: Let $B \in \mathbf{B},\, R \in \mathbf{Rect}$. Then $B \mid R =_{df} B'$, where $B'.S = B.\,S \cap R$, and

$$B'.I(i,j) =_{df} \begin{cases} B.\,I(i,j) & \text{if } (i,j) \in B'.S\,. \\ \omega & \text{if } (i,j) \in \mathbf{Z}^2 - B'.S\,. \end{cases} \tag{12}$$

Remark: This operation defines a bit-map B' which looks like B within a specific rectangular region, but is "undefined" outside that region.

4.3.1.5. Other Logical Bit-Map Operations

Let $\otimes$ be any binary boolean operation with 0 interpreted as **false** and 1 as **true**. We extend its semantics so that for $a \in \{0,1\}$,

$$a \otimes \omega = \omega \otimes a = \omega \otimes \omega = \omega. \tag{13}$$

Syntax: $\otimes : \mathbf{B} \times \mathbf{B} \to \mathbf{B}.$

Semantics: Let $A = (S_A, I_A),\, B = (S_B, I_B) \in \mathbf{B}$. Then $A \otimes B =_{df} (S_A \cap S_B,\, I_A \otimes I_B)$, where $I_A \otimes I_B =_{df} I_A(i,j) \otimes I_B(i,j),\, i,j \in \mathbf{Z}.$

Remarks: (0) The intersection of two rectangles, if non-empty, is always a rectangle. Therefore, $A \otimes B \in \mathbf{B}$ (since $\varnothing \in \mathbf{B}$).

(1) If $\otimes$ is associative as a binary boolean function, then it is also associative as a logical bit-map operation. Moreover, an n-ary version of $\otimes$ can be written in terms of $n-1$ compositions of corresponding binary bit-map operation. That is,

$$\otimes (B_1, B_2, \cdots, B_n) = B_1 \otimes B_2 \otimes \cdots \otimes B_n. \tag{14}$$

This is of course true of $\otimes$ as a binary boolean function. Observe that (14) does not hold for non-associative functions such as NAND.

Proposition 1. De Morgan's laws for bit-maps. *If* $A,B \in \mathbf{B}$, *then* $(A \vee B)^c = A^c \wedge B^c$, *and* $(A \wedge B)^c = A^c \vee B^c$.

Proof. The proof requires a simple application of de Morgan's laws for boolean algebras.

Remark 3. Each class of sets $\mathbf{B}_{x_2,y_2}^{x_1,y_1}$ together with the logical bit-map operations $\wedge$, $\vee$, Comp, the zero element $Zero_{x_2 y_2}^{x_1 y_1}$, and the one element $One_{x_2 y_2}^{x_1 y_1}$ is a *boolean algebra* [Halm74].

4.3.2. Bit-Maps and Images

In Section 1, bit-maps were defined to be of arbitrary size and could be in an arbitrary location. On the other hand, images are of fixed size and position. As illustrated in Figure 0, we require a mechanism to map bit-maps to images. After all, this is implicit in the term *bit-map*. So far, we have considered bit-maps and the semantics of operations over bit-maps in a straightforward functional manner. This section describes a simple extension to the notation of the previous section to capture this aspect of bit-maps without having to resort to complications such as side-effects. In effect, images will provide additional contextual information appropriate for more subtle bit-map operations. The semantics of operations such as moving a bit-map, or making a copy of a bit-map can then be expressed naturally.

Augmented Bit-Map Operation. A bit-map operation $\otimes$ is a function $a \otimes : \mathbf{B}^* \times \mathbf{R}_{n_1 n_2}^* \to \mathbf{B} \times \mathbf{R}_{n_1 n_2}$.

In defining the semantics of a bit-map operation, one image or more may be involved. One particularly simple and useful example of such an operation follows.

Extracting a Bit-Map from an Image. Bit-maps are often defined in terms of "what is already on the screen". That is, the intensity values in an image can be used to define the intensity function for a particular bit-map. We define this function as follows.

Syntax: $Extract : \mathbf{B} \times \mathbf{R}_{n_1 n_2} \to \mathbf{B}$.

Semantics: Suppose $B \in \mathbf{B}$ and $R \in \mathbf{R}_{n_1 n_2}$. Then $Extract\, B\, R =_{df} B'$, such that $B'.S =_{df} B.S \cap Rect_{n_1 n_2}^{0\ 0}$, and

$$B'.I(i,j) =_{df} \begin{cases} R.I_{ij} & \text{if } (i,j) \in B'.S. \\ \omega & \text{if } (i,j) \in \mathbf{Z}^2 - B'.S. \end{cases} \tag{15}$$

Remarks: (0) Write $B \leftarrow R$ for $Extract\, B\, R$.

(1) Bit-maps extracted from an image are allowed to overlap spatially.

Loading a Bit-Map into an Image. The converse of extracting a bit-map from an image is also very useful. Imagine taking a bit-map from "offscreen" to initialise a portion of a display image. Such an operation could be defined as follows.

Syntax: $Load : \mathbf{B} \times \mathbf{R}_{n_1 n_2} \to \mathbf{R}_{n_1 n_2}$.

Semantics: Let $B \in \mathbf{B}$ and $R \in \mathbf{R}_{n_1 n_2}$. Then $Load\, B\, R =_{df} R'$, where $\forall (i,j) \in Rect_{n_1 n_2}^{0\,0}$,

$$R'.I_{ij} =_{df} \begin{cases} R.I_{ij} & \text{if } (i,j) \notin B.S. \\ B.I\,(i,j) & \text{if } (i,j) \in B.S. \end{cases} \tag{16}$$

Remarks: (0) Write $R \leftarrow B$, for $Load\, B\, R$.
(1) If $B.S$ does not overlap with $Rect_{n_1 n_2}^{0\,0}$, then $R \leftarrow B = R$.
(2) The expression $R \leftarrow Zero_{n_1 n_2}^{0\,0}$ defines an image of intensity all zeros.

The load function has some particularly attractive formal applications. For example, the same bit-map can be mapped to images having different pixel shapes. This allows one to capture the semantics of graphics systems which allow users to modify the basic pixel shape abstraction. Many image stores support a function that sets the pixel shape to either a square or a (non-square) rectangle, while retaining the same resolution. Thus the *same* bit-map can be viewed in different ways, and our semantics can distinguish among the ways. Another useful application is that one can characterise formally the notion of buffering or queuing images for successive display.

Moving/Copying a Bit-Map. Moving and copying bit-maps are surprisingly subtle operations. Our notation facilitates a reasonably concise description of their semantics.

Syntax: $Move : \mathbf{B} \times \mathbf{R}_{n_1 n_2} \times \mathbf{Z}^2 \to \mathbf{B} \times \mathbf{R}_{n_1 n_2}$.

Semantics: Let $B \in \mathbf{B}$ and $R \in \mathbf{R}_{n_1 n_2}$. The semantics is defined only if the part of B overlapping with S has an intensity function consistent with the image intensity over that region. That is, the following precondition must hold:

$$B \leftarrow R = B \mid Rect_{n_1 n_2}^{0\,0} . \tag{17}$$

If Equation (17) holds, then $Move\, B\, R\, (x_3, y_3) =_{df} (B', R')$, where $B'.S = Rect_{x_5 y_5}^{x_3 y_3}$ such that

$$x_5 = x_3 + (x_2 - x_1)$$
$$y_5 = y_3 + (y_2 - y_1)$$

and

$$B'.I_{ij} =_{df} \begin{cases} B.I(i-x_3+x_1, j-y_3+y_1) & \text{if } (i,j) \in B'.S. \\ \omega & \text{if } (i,j) \in \mathbf{Z}^2 - B'.S. \end{cases} \tag{18}$$

The image R' is defined as follows. For all $(i,j) \in Rect_{n_1 n_2}^{0\,0}$:

$$R'.I_{ij} =_{df} \begin{cases} R.I_{ij} & \text{if } (i,j) \notin B.S \cup B'.S. \\ 0 & \text{if } (i,j) \in B.S \wedge (i,j) \notin B'.S. \\ B'.I(i,j) & \text{if } (i,j) \in B'.S. \end{cases} \tag{19}$$

Move transfers a bit-map with origin (x_1, y_1) to a bit-map with new origin (x_3, y_3). The semantics of moving B to B' above is clear. The effect on an image deserves some explanation. The first line of (19) states that the unaffected portion of the image is left unchanged in the new image. The region of the image left vacant by moving the bit-map is defined to have zero intensity. This is captured by the second line of (19). The third line gives the intensity of the bit-map in its new location. Observe that if a bit-map is moved off the image, the effect is to zero out the region it formerly occupied. Notice as well that when the old and new positions of the bit-map overlap, only that portion of the image formerly occupied by B but not occupied by B' is zeroed.

Copying a bit-map to another location is almost identical to moving it, except that the portion of the image occupied by the original bit-map is left untouched.

Syntax: $\quad Copy : \mathbf{B} \times \mathbf{R}_{n_1 n_2} \times \mathbf{Z}^2 \to \mathbf{B} \times \mathbf{R}_{n_1 n_2}.$

Semantics: $Copy\, B\, R\, (x_3, y_3) =_{df} (B', R')$, with B' as in *Move*. The only difference occurs in the definition of R'. For all $(i,j) \in Rect_{n_1 n_2}^{0\,0}$:

$$R'.I_{ij} =_{df} \begin{cases} R.I_{ij} & \text{if } (i,j) \notin B.\, S \cup B'.S. \\ R.I_{ij} & \text{if } (i,j) \in B.\, S \wedge (i,j) \notin B'.S. \\ B'.I(i,j) & \text{if } (i,j) \in B'.S. \end{cases} \tag{20}$$

4.3.3. Display Images

The semantic framework outlined above provides a uniform way of defining any desired image of a given resolution over a binary intensity space: every image $R \in \mathbf{R}_{n_1 n_2}$ is prescribed by a series of bit-map operations over a bit-map space $\mathbf{B}$ and an image space $\mathbf{R}_{n_1 n_2}$. To characterise the display of a particular graphics system, one may wish to designate a special set of names which denote the various display screens in the system and to which a particular set of images may be bound. The image space $\mathbf{R}_{n_1 n_2}$ should also be defined to model the basic pixel prototile of a particular display screen.

4.4. Rendering 2-D Scenes into Images

The most important and fundamental problem in computer graphics is that of mapping a *scene* defined over a space of arbitrarily-high resolution into an *image* of fixed resolution. A careful semantics of rendering 3-D scenes was given in Chapter 3. In this section, we consider the semantics of rendering 2-D scenes into 2-D images, since this topic involves concepts distinct from the general rendering problem. We shall employ a special term for 2-D rendering: *rasterisation*. By formalising various rasterisation schemes, it will be seen that many ostensibly intuitive approaches have some rather surprising properties.

4.4.1. Formal Development

Recall from Chapter 1 above that a *scene* S is a sequence of *objects* $(O_1, \cdots, O_N)$, where each object $O \in S$ is a tuple, (Z_O, I_O). Since we are restricting ourselves to 2-D scenes of only two intensity levels, we shall equivalently denote each object O simply by its point-set screen extent $S_O \subseteq \mathbf{R}^2$ (see Chapter 1). Any point $(x,y) \in S_O$ is assumed to have intensity one (synonyms: on, white); all other points are given intensity zero (synonyms: off, black). Since we do not wish to consider the visibility problem over 2-D scenes, we shall assume that the depth of every object is zero.

Definition 11. A *rasterisation* R of a point-set S denotes a set of pixels in an image that must be assigned intensity value 1. Such a rasterisation will be denoted by $R[S]$. An image $A \in \mathbf{R}_{n_1 n_2}$ can be defined, by extension, from a rasterisation, namely $\forall (i,j) \in Rect_{n_1 n_2}^{0\,0}$:

$$A.I_{ij} =_{df} \begin{cases} 1 & \text{if } P_{ij} \in R[S]. \\ 0 & \text{if } P_{ij} \notin R[S]. \end{cases} \tag{21}$$

Recall from Section 1 that each pixel is an instance of a pixel prototile **P**. The prototile must be such that it forms a tiling **T** of the cartesian plane.

Our definition of rasterisation admits a great many possibilities. Consider two degenerate examples.

Example 2. $\forall S \subseteq \mathbf{R}^2. R_0[S] =_{df} \varnothing.$
Example 3. $\forall S \subseteq \mathbf{R}^2. R_1[S] =_{df} \mathbf{T}.$

Rasterisation R_0 essentially says to paint the screen entirely black, while R_1 says to paint it entirely white. There are more interesting rasterisations than these, and it is desirable to classify them.

Definition 12. Let R be a rasterisation. Then

(0) R is *proper* if $\forall S \subseteq \mathbf{R}^2$, $S \subseteq \bigcup_{P \in R[S]} P$. From mathematical analysis, $R[S]$ is proper if it contains a set of pixels which form a *cover* of S. Rasterisation R_0 above is improper, while R_1 is proper.

(1) R is *uniform* if $\forall S \subseteq \mathbf{R}^2$, $P \in R[S] \Rightarrow P \cap S \neq \varnothing$. Informally, this means that a uniform rasterisation contains no "excess" pixels. Note, however, that a uniform rasterisation may omit pixels that overlap with S. A uniform, proper rasterisation is a *minimal cover* of S.

(2) R is *monotonic* if $\forall S \subseteq \mathbf{R}^2$, $S' \subseteq S \Rightarrow R[S'] \subseteq R[S]$.

The above properties all have some basis in intuition. However, it turns out that most practical rasterisations employed today fail to satisfy simultaneously all of the above constraints. Other reasonable rasterisation properties exist and are easy to specify. For example, a proximity condition could be imposed on pixels chosen. Such a condition is specified by L. Marshall in her work on the formal specification of line-drawing algorithms [Mars84]. We prefer to deal with more general rasterisations, some of which can substantially deviate from the original object. In the next section, we shall explore these properties further and present some concrete examples of rasterisations. We shall subsequently demonstrate how many rasterisation schemes fail by considering the specific case of lines. Since lines are essential to defining higher-order geometric figures such as polygons, properties of their rasterisation are usually inherited by rasterisations for these higher-order figures. We shall also study other properties of rasterisations and develop specific rasterising schemes for lines that satisfy these properties.

4.4.2. Examples of Rasterisations

Two trivial examples of rasterisations were considered earlier. Before proceeding with further development of the theory, let us first consider some reasonable examples of rasterisations over arbitrary point sets.

Example 4. Pixel P is in the rasterisation of S iff its centre is in S. Let $c_P \in \mathbf{Z}^2$ denote the centre of pixel $P \in \mathbf{T}$. Then

$$R_2[S] =_{df} \{ P \in \mathbf{T} : c_P \in S \}. \tag{22}$$

Example 5. Pixel P is in the rasterisation of S iff any part of it overlaps with S:

$$R_3[S] =_{df} \{ P \in \mathbf{T} : P \cap S \neq \varnothing \}. \tag{23}$$

Example 6. Pixel P is in the rasterisation of S iff it is more than one-half covered by S:

$$R_4[S] =_{df} \left\{ P \in \mathbf{T} : \frac{\mu(P \cap S)}{\mu(P)} > \frac{1}{2} \right\}, \tag{24}$$

where μ denotes Lebesgue measure (see Chapter 3). If the area of each pixel is normalised to 1, then the right-hand side of Eq. (24) simplifies accordingly.

Example 7. Pixel P is in the rasterisation of S iff it nontrivially overlaps with S. We assume "nontrivial overlap" means a set of positive measure.[4] Thus

$$R_5[S] =_{df} \{ P \in \mathbf{T} : \mu(P \cap S) > 0 \}. \tag{25}$$

Example 8. Pixel P is in the rasterisation of S iff P is contained in S:

$$R_6[S] =_{df} \{ P \in \mathbf{T} : P \subseteq S \}. \tag{26a}$$

An alternative, slightly more general definition is

$$R'_6[S] =_{df} \{ P \in \mathbf{T} : \mu(P \cap S) = 1 \}, \tag{26b}$$

which is to say that the overlap must be a set of full measure.

Proposition 2. *Rasterisation R_3 is proper, uniform, and monotonic.*

Proof. R_3 is trivially proper and uniform. To see that it is monotonic, let $S' \subseteq S$. If pixel $P \in R_3[S']$, then $P \cap S' \neq \varnothing$. Thus $P \cap S \neq \varnothing$, and because R_3 is proper, $P \in R_3[S]$. Hence $R_3[S'] \subseteq R_3[S]$ as desired.

Proposition 3. *Rasterisation R_4 is improper, uniform, and monotonic.*

Proof.

R_4 *is improper:* Take any S such that it no more than one-half covers some pixel P. Then $R_4[S] = \varnothing$ and clearly does not cover S.

R_4 *is uniform.* If pixel $P \in R_4[S]$, then $\mu(P \cap S) > 1/2$ which implies that $P \cap S \neq \varnothing$.

R_4 *is monotonic.* Let $S' \subseteq S$. If pixel $P \in R_4[S']$, then $\mu(P \cap S') > 1/2$. Thus $\mu(P \cap S) > 1/2$, and $P \in R_4[S]$. Hence $R_4[S'] \subseteq R_4[S]$ as desired.

---

[4] Observe that since line segments are typically defined as point sets of infinitesimal thickness (see Section 4.1 below), and since such sets have measure zero within $\mathbf{R}^2$, $R_4[L] = R_5[L] = \varnothing$ for any line segment L (or countable collection of them). Similarly, $R_2[L]$ is often empty. The use of such rasterisations makes it imperative that all graphic objects be given a thickness if they are to be visible.

4.4.3. More Properties of Rasterisations

We now continue our exploration of some basic properties of rasterisations. It was mentioned earlier that any proper and uniform rasterisation forms some sort of a minimal cover of the rasterised object. More precisely, we shall show that all rasterisations that are uniform and proper are equivalent over non-overlapping pixel tilings, all denoting the same set: the minimal pixel cover of an object.

Proposition 4. *If R is any uniform, proper rasterisation, and $S \subseteq \mathbf{R}^2$ is any object, then*

$$R[S] = \{ P \in \mathbf{T} : S \cap P \neq \varnothing \}.$$

Proof. Let $A = \{ P \in \mathbf{T} : S \cap P \neq \varnothing \}$. Since R is uniform,

$$P \in R[S] \Rightarrow P \cap S \neq \varnothing$$
$$\Rightarrow P \in A,$$
$$\therefore R[S] \subseteq A.$$

Let $Q \in \mathbf{T}$ be a pixel in A. Then $Q \cap S \neq \varnothing$. It follows that since R is proper, Q must be in $R[S]$.

$$\therefore A \subseteq R[S].$$

The proposition follows.

Proposition 5. *If rasterisation R is uniform and proper, then it is monotonic.*

Proof. Let $S' \subseteq S$. We are required to show that $R[S'] \subseteq R[S]$. Suppose $P \in R[S']$. Since R is uniform, $P \cap S' \neq \varnothing$. But this implies that $P \cap S \neq \varnothing$. Therefore, the fact that R is proper implies that P must be in the rasterisation of S; in other words, $P \in R[S]$. This establishes the result.

The above proposition establishes that any uniform and proper rasterisation is necessarily monotonic. The next two propositions show that possession of any two of these rasterisation properties does not in general mean that the third follows.

Proposition 6. *A uniform, monotonic rasterisation is not necessarily proper.*

Proof. Rasterisations R_0 and R_6 are both uniform and monotonic, but are not proper.

Proposition 7. *A proper, monotonic rasterisation is not necessarily uniform.*

Proof. Rasterisation R_1 is proper and monotonic, but is not uniform.

So far, we have discussed the rasterisation of general object point-sets, without regard to how they are created. Typically, an object is constructed from a set of simpler objects. One interesting problem that naturally arises, therefore, is that of capturing the conditions under which the rasterisation of an object is equivalent to the rasterisation of its constituent objects.

Definition 13. Let $S = \cup_i^n S_i$ be an object made up of n not necessarily distinct point-sets $S_1, \cdots, S_n$. Then a rasterisation R has the *decomposition property* if (for every such decomposition of S)

$$R[S] = \bigcup_i^n R[S_i]. \tag{27}$$

Proposition 8. *Rasterisation R_4 does not have the decomposition property.*

Proof. We let $S = S_1 \cup S_2$ be such that S_1 and S_2 are both disjoint, lie within the same pixel P, and such that $\mu(S_1) = \mu(S_2) = 3/8$. Then $\mu(S) = 3/4$ and thus $R_4[S] = \{P\}$. However $R_4[S_1] = R_4[S_2] = \varnothing$.

Proposition 9. *Any proper, uniform rasterisation has the decomposition property.*

Proof. Let $S \subseteq \mathbf{R}^2$ have arbitrary decomposition $S_1 \cup \cdots \cup S_n$, and let R be a proper, uniform rasterisation. Suppose $P \in R[S]$. Since R is uniform, $P \cap S \neq \varnothing$. So $P \cap S_i \neq \varnothing$ for at least one S_i. Hence $P \in R[S_i]$, since R is proper, and so

$$R[S] \subseteq \bigcup_i R[S_i].$$

Since R is proper and uniform, it is also monotonic. Moreover, since each $S_i \subseteq S$, $R[S_i] \subseteq R[S]$. Therefore,

$$\bigcup_i R[S_i] \subseteq R[S].$$

The proposition follows.

What is the importance of the decomposition property? Essentially, the problem with rasterisations that do not have this property is that they may thwart divide-and-conquer implementations: it may be impossible to rasterise correctly an object from its constituent components. These issues become particularly interesting in the case of rasterising line segments, for we shall soon see that it is difficult to develop line rasterisations that satisfy some form of the decomposition property.

4.5. Line Segments and Their Rasterisation

As mentioned earlier, the line segment is an essential graphic primitive in that it can be used to construct many other objects. There are many ways to rasterise (or render) line segments, and this section considers several possibilities. First, we shall define a 2-D line segment primitive formally, and consider its most common rasterisation, the so-called "optimal" line.

4.5.1. Formal Definition of a Line Segment Primitive

An extensive formal presentation of various graphic primitives was given in Chapter 1. In this section we shall restrict ourselves to the basic 2-D line segment. Let $P_0 = (x_0, y_0)$, $P_1 = (x_1, y_1) \in \mathbf{R}^2$. The object $S = \mathbf{LineSeg}(P_0, P_1) \subseteq \mathbf{R}^2$ has the following semantics:

$$\mathbf{LineSeg}(P_0, P_1) =_{df} \{ (1-t)P_0 + t P_1 : t \in [0,1] \} \tag{28}$$

For the majority of this chapter, we shall be concerned only with lines in the first octant with one endpoint being the origin. That is, we shall deal with the following set:

$$\mathbf{L} =_{df} \{ \mathbf{LineSeg}((0,0), (x,y)) : 0 \le y \le x \}. \tag{29}$$

4.5.2. The Optimal Line Segment

In this section, we commence our study of rasterisations which presume specific geometric properties of the object. In particular, the rasterisations we shall consider deal specifically with line segments which are members of **L**. The most common of these is called the *optimal line (segment)* [Spro82]. We define it formally as follows. For $x, y \in \mathbf{N}$, $y \le x$,

$$R_o[\mathbf{LineSeg}((0,0),(x,y))] =_{df} \{ P_{ir_i} \in \mathbf{T} : 0 \le i \le x, \ r_i = \langle \frac{\Delta y}{\Delta x} i \rangle \}. \tag{30}$$

The notation $\langle x \rangle$ denotes rounding real number x to the nearest integer. We introduce two abbreviations. First, the pixels involved in a line rasterisation will be denoted by a set of ordered pairs. Second, we shall write $[P_0, P_1]_o$ for $R_o[\mathbf{LineSeg}(P_0, P_1)]$. Thus Eq. (30) can be rewritten as

$$[(0,0), (x,y)]_o =_{df} \{ (i, r_i) \in \mathbf{Z}^2 : 0 \le i \le x, \ r_i = \langle \frac{\Delta y}{\Delta x} i \rangle \}. \tag{31}$$

Rasterised line segments over the other octants of the cartesian plane are generated by an appropriate set of reflections (and translations) of rasterised line segments in the first octant. The optimal line has two important properties for lines in the first octant. First, exactly one pixel is chosen in $R_o[\mathbf{L}]$ for each column of image pixels intersecting with line segment L. Second, the y values of pixels in adjacent columns in R_o never differ by more than one. These properties are easy to verify from (31). Visually, the optimal line tends to produce a jagged but fairly evenly-spaced set of pixels. Many other schemes display undesirable pixel-clustering behaviour, which results in "beaded" lines or lines that are too thick.

Example 9. *A sample optimal line segment.*

$[(0,0), (8,5)]_o = \{ (0,0), (1,1), (2,1), (3,2), (4,3), (5,3), (6,4), (7,4), (8,5) \}$.

This rasterisation is depicted in Figure 2.

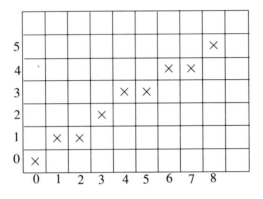

Figure 2. Optimal rasterised line segment from (0,0) to (8,5).

4.5.3. *Some New Recursive Line Rasterisations*

In this section, we shall develop two new recursive line rasterisation schemes and relate their behaviour to the optimal line rasterisation. First, we define the rasterisation of an arbitrary point $(x,y) \in \mathbf{R}^2$.

$$R_P[\{(x,y)\}] \in \{ P \in \mathbf{T} : (x,y) \in P \}. \tag{32a}$$

Remark 4. We wish the rasterisation of a point to be a single pixel. If tiles overlap, even if only at their boundaries, then $\{ P \in \mathbf{T} : (x,y) \in P \}$ may have cardinality greater than 1.

In the unit-square tiling with tiles centred at integral values, we shall write the rasterisation as:

$$R_P[\{ (x,y) \}] = \{ (\langle x \rangle, \langle y \rangle) \}. \tag{32b}$$

In the discussion to follow, we shall restrict ourselves to the unit-square tiling, which was named $\mathbf{T}_u$ in Section 1.

Definition 14. Two points are *eight-connected* if they lie within adjacent pixels. More specifically, the corresponding x and y pixel values can each differ by no more than 1. Formally,

$$8conn\,((x_0,y_0),\,(x_1,y_1))=_{df} \begin{cases} \textbf{true} & \text{if } |\langle x_0\rangle-\langle x_1\rangle|\le 1 \wedge |\langle y_0\rangle-\langle y_1\rangle|\le 1 \\ \textbf{false} & \text{otherwise} \end{cases} \tag{33}$$

Remark 5. This definition allows a point to be eight-connected to itself.

We now define an interesting recursive rasterisation scheme R_m based on dividing a line segment at its midpoint. Unlike the optimal line rasterisation of Eq. (30), it is easy to define the midpoint scheme over all of $\mathbf{R}^2$, not just those with integral co-ordinates in the first octant. Let $[P_0,P_1]_m$ abbreviate $R_m[\textbf{LineSeg}(P_0,P_1)]$. The midpoint rasterisation is defined as follows.

$$[P_0,P_1]_m =_{df} \begin{cases} R_P[P_0]\cup R_P[P_1] & \text{if } 8conn\,(P_0,P_1) \\ \left[P_0,\dfrac{P_0+P_1}{2}\right]_m \cup \left[\dfrac{P_0+P_1}{2},P_1\right]_m & \text{otherwise} \end{cases} \tag{34}$$

A particularly nice property of R_m is that it can be implemented directly as an algorithm requiring only shifts (division by two) and adds.[5] This rasterisation also has a fast parallel implementation, requiring only $P=\max(\Delta x,\Delta y)$ processors and $O(\log P)$ time. We shall consider this topic briefly later, but defer a more thorough analysis to another report. In this chapter we shall instead concentrate on the basic properties of the specification.

Example 10.

$$[(0,0),(8,5)]_m = [(0,0),(4,\tfrac{5}{2})]_m \cup [(4,\tfrac{5}{2}),(8,5)]_m$$

$$= [(0,0),(2,\tfrac{5}{4})]_m \cup [(2,\tfrac{5}{4}),(4,\tfrac{5}{2})]_m \cup [(4,\tfrac{5}{2}),(6,\tfrac{15}{4})]_m \cup [(6,\tfrac{15}{4}),(8,5)]_m$$

$$= [(0,0),(1,\tfrac{5}{8})]_m \cup [(1,\tfrac{5}{8}),(2,\tfrac{5}{4})]_m \cup [(2,\tfrac{5}{4}),(3,\tfrac{15}{8})]_m \cup [(3,\tfrac{15}{8}),(4,\tfrac{5}{2})]_m \cup$$

$$[(4,\tfrac{5}{2}),(5,\tfrac{25}{8})]_m \cup [(5,\tfrac{25}{8}),(6,\tfrac{15}{4})]_m \cup [(6,\tfrac{15}{4}),(7,\tfrac{35}{8})]_m \cup [(7,\tfrac{35}{8}),(8,5)]_m$$

---

[5] This normally presumes integer-valued endpoints, though it is not difficult to define shifting operations on fixed-point numbers. The optimal line rasterisation can also be implemented using only shifts and adds, but this is by no means obvious. The most common optimal line implementation is called *Bresenham's algorithm*, and operates over integer-valued endpoints [Spro82].

$$= R_P[(0,0)] \cup R_P[(1, \frac{5}{8})] \cup R_P[(2, \frac{5}{4})] \cup R_P[(3, \frac{15}{8})] \cup$$

$$R_P[(4, \frac{5}{2})] \cup R_P[(5, \frac{25}{8})] \cup R_P[(6, \frac{15}{4})] \cup R_P[(7, \frac{35}{8})] \cup R_P[(8,5)]$$

$$= \{ (0,0), (1,1), (2,1), (3,2), (4,3), (5,3), (6,4), (7,4), (8,5) \}.$$

In this example, the optimal and midpoint subdivision line rasterisations agree. We shall see momentarily that a sufficient condition for their agreement in the first octant is that Δx be a power of two. However, since these schemes have rather different pixel selection mechanisms, it is not reasonable to expect complete agreement. This is because the optimal line rasterisation picks a pixel for each column x whose centre deviates the least from the ideal line, whereas the midpoint subdivision selects the pixel closest to the midpoint of each subdivided ideal line segment.

Example 11. By exhaustive analysis, the shortest line segment on which the schemes differ is $L=$**LineSeg**$((0,0),(5,2))$:

$$[L]_o = \{ (0,0), (1,0), (2,1), (3,1), (4,2), (5,2) \}.$$

$$[L]_m = \{ (0,0), (1,1), (2,1), (3,1), (4,2), (5,2) \}.$$

Since R_m always draws eight-connected lines, it is never more than one pixel below or above R_o in each column. Indeed, as mentioned earlier, the two schemes agree in at least one general case (and many particular cases). This is not entirely obvious, so it will be proved.

Proposition 10. *For any line segment $L \in \mathbf{L}$ with integral endpoints such that $\Delta x = 2^k$ for some $k \geq 0$, $R_o[L] = R_m[L]$.*

Proof. We prove the proposition by induction on k. For the base step, suppose $\Delta x = 2^0 = 1$. Then if the line segment is to be in the first octant, the rightmost endpoint must be either $(1,0)$ or $(1,1)$. The argument is the same for either case, so we choose the latter without loss of generality. In this case, $\Delta y/\Delta x = 1$. Therefore, from Eq. (30),

$$R_o[\mathbf{LineSeg}((0,0),(1,1))] = \{ (i,r_i) : r_i = \langle i \rangle, \, i=0,1 \} = \{ (0,0),(1,1) \}. \quad (35)$$

On the other hand, $(0,0)$ and $(1,1)$ are eight-connected. Hence

$$R_m[\mathbf{LineSeg}((0,0),(1,1))] = R_P[(0,0)] \cup R_P[(1,1)] = \{ (0,0),(1,1) \}. \quad (36)$$

Now suppose the proposition is true for all line segments in the first octant with $0 \le \Delta x = 2^j$, where $0 < j \le k$. Consider the rasterisation of $L = \mathbf{LineSeg}((0,0),(x,y))$, where $x = 2^{k+1}$ and $y \le x$ as in Figure 3.

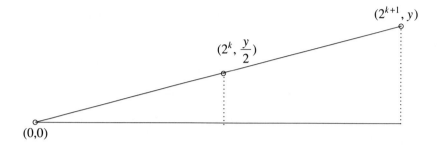

Figure 3. Rasterisation of a line segment with $\Delta x = 2^{k+1}$.

Our goal is to decompose $R_o[L]$ and reassemble it into $R_m[L]$. Observe that pixel $(2^k, \langle y/2 \rangle) \in R_o[L]$. By basic set theory, we can break the rasterisation up about this point:

$$R_o[L] = \left\{ (i, \langle \frac{y}{2^{k+1}} i \rangle): 0 \le i \le 2^k \right\} \cup \left\{ (i, \langle \frac{y}{2^{k+1}} i \rangle): 2^k \le i \le 2^{k+1} \right\}$$

$$= L' \cup L''. \tag{37}$$

Clearly $L' = [(0,0), (2^k, \langle y/2 \rangle)]_o$. Therefore, by the inductive hypothesis, $L' = [(0,0), (2^k, \langle y/2 \rangle)]_m$. Moreover, we can rewrite L'' as follows.

$$L'' = \left\{ (2^k + j, \langle \frac{y}{2^{k+1}} (2^k + j) \rangle): 0 \le j \le 2^k \right\} \tag{38}$$

$$= \left\{ (2^k, \langle \frac{y}{2} \rangle) + (j, \langle \frac{y}{2^{k+1}} j \rangle): 0 \le j \le 2^k \right\}$$

$$= T \cdot \left\{ (j, \langle \frac{y}{2^{k+1}} j \rangle): 0 \le j \le 2^k \right\}$$

$$= T \cdot L',$$

where T is a translation which maps point $(s,t) \in \mathbf{R}^2$ to $(s + 2^k, t + \langle y/2 \rangle)$. Now that $R_o[L]$ is broken up into shorter pieces, we reassemble it to form $R_m[L]$.

$$R_o[L] = L' \cup T \cdot L'' \tag{39}$$

$$= [(0,0), (2^k, \langle y/2 \rangle)]_m \cup T \cdot [(0,0), (2^k, \langle y/2 \rangle)]_m$$

by the inductive hypothesis. Using exactly the reverse argument as that employed in Eq. (37), we can rewrite this as:

$$R_o[L] = \left[(0,0), (2^k, \langle \frac{y}{2} \rangle) \right]_m \cup \left[(2^k, \langle \frac{y}{2} \rangle), (2^{k+1}, y) \right]_m$$

$$= R_m[L].$$

The above proposition has shown that the midpoint subdivision and optimal line rasterisations agree on a well-defined class of line segments. The author has implemented both algorithms in a test program that sweeps out all lines in a finite prefix of the first octant, and the results are mildly surprising. The rasterisations differ on only 1 of 15 line segments with $\Delta x \leq 5$. This error rate increases to 25% for all lines with $\Delta x \leq 10$, as line segment deviations tend to accumulate as the number of subdivisions increases. As stated earlier, the difference between the pixel chosen by each rasterisation for a given column of x is never more than 1.

We can exploit the above proposition to define another recursive subdivision line rasterisation scheme. The basic strategy is to ensure that lines are always subdivided into pieces such that each piece has Δx a power of two. This provides us with a formal definition of a line rasterisation scheme that is provably equivalent to the optimal line, but which suggests an inherently different implementation. Let $P_0(x_0, y_0), P_1(x_1, y_1)] \in \mathbf{R}^2$. Then

$$[P_0, P_1]_d =_{df} \begin{cases} R_P[P_0] \cup R_P[P_1] & \text{if } 8conn(P_0, P_1) \\ [P_0, (x,y)]_m \cup [(x,y), P_1]_d & \text{otherwise} \end{cases} \tag{40}$$

where

$$x =_{df} x_0 + 2^k \ni 2^k \leq \Delta x < 2^{k+1} \tag{41}$$

$$y =_{df} y_0 + \frac{\Delta y}{\Delta x} 2^k.$$

The values (x, y) are defined by similar triangles as illustrated in Figure 4. The value k can be calculated by finding the most significant 1-bit in Δx. An alternative is to use a look-up table indexed by integral values of Δx. The slope of the line can be precomputed with an implicit decimal point to the left of the digits (in the first octant). Therefore, calculating a new y value requires one shift and one add.

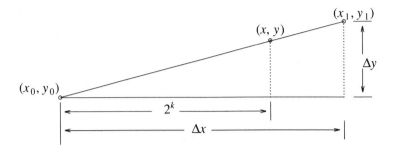

Figure 4. Geometry of the power-of-two subdivision rasterisation.

Proposition 11.   *For   any   line   segment $L \in \mathbf{L}$ with   integral   endpoints,*
$R_o[L] = R_d[L]$.

Proof. The theorem follows easily by induction from the above proposition.

A direct implementation of R_d does not appear to have any significant advantages over the optimal line. However, in a multiple processor environment, the specification of R_d provides a useful basis from which to form an O(log n) algorithm using n processors. With each subdivision, the current processor informs one other to begin work on a subdivided line segment. Research has just begun on parallel implementations of traditional optimal-line algorithms such as Bresenham's. The obvious approach is to split a long line into pieces of constant size, which may then be "stroked out" individually. This forms the basis of a *multipoint algorithm* [Spro82]. Such algorithms can run in O(1) time with O(n) processors. However, a stroked multipoint implementation may exhibit deviations from the optimal line at the boundaries between strokes. The reason for this, as will be seen later, is that the optimal line rasterisation itself does not have a certain weak monotonicity property which is necessary to being able to subdivide the rasterisation arbitrarily. The subdivision rasterisation, R_d, takes advantage of the fact that a more careful choice of subdivision points will yield the correct result.

4.5.4. *More Properties of Line Rasterisations*

Line rasterisations can occasionally display somewhat curious behaviour in practice. For example, a rasterisation may exhibit excessive jagginess, or uneven, nonmonotonic spacing. For these reasons, and many others, a thorough theoretical understanding of line rasterisations will help us to better assess their practical behaviour and perhaps, as in the case of the subdivision rasterisation of the previous section, will lead us to new algorithms. As in the section for general rasterisations, this section gives a brief taxonomy of the line rasterisations introduced earlier with respect to the properties formally defined in Section 4.1 above.

Proposition 12. *Both R_o and R_m are improper on the unit square tiling* $\mathbf{T}_u$.

Proof. Recall that a rasterisation is proper if an aribitrary point-set $S \subseteq \mathbf{R}^2$ is covered by its rasterisation R[S]. Consider $L = LineSeg((0,0),(8,5))$. By the examples above, P_{43} is in both $R_o[L]$ and $R_m[L]$. This pixel covers the region $[3.5,4.5] \times [2.5,3.5]$. However, the point $Q(29/8, 145/64) \in L$, but $Q \notin P_{43}$, lying, in effect, just under this pixel. Since there is no other pixel chosen by either rasterisation for this column, $x = 4$, point Q is not covered by either rasterisation.

Remark 6. Since R_d was shown to be equivalent to R_o, any property true of the optimal line is obviously true of the power-of-two subdivision rasterisation.

Remark 7. A proper line rasterisation tends to produce beaded lines, or lines with clumps of pixels about regions where the line overlaps with several pixels over a small area (e.g., near pixel corners). The fact that both R_o and R_m are improper is implied by the fact that they tend to thin out, as it were, the choice of pixels. In the case of the optimal line, this thinning-out rule is that precisely one pixel per column in the first octant is chosen.

Proposition 13. R_o *is uniform on* $\mathbf{T}_u$.

Proof. Let $L = \mathbf{LineSeg}((0,0),(x,y))$, $y \le x$, be in $\mathbf{L}$. We are required to show that if pixel $P \in [L]_o$, then $P \cap L \neq \emptyset$. Suppose $P_{ij} \in [L]_o$. Then by the definition of the optimal line, $j = \langle (y/x) i \rangle$. Now P_{ij} is a unit square centred at $(i,j) \in \mathbf{Z}^2$:

$$P_{ij} = [i - \tfrac{1}{2}, i + \tfrac{1}{2}] \times [j - \tfrac{1}{2}, j + \tfrac{1}{2}]. \qquad (42)$$

It therefore suffices to show that $(y/x) i \in [j - \tfrac{1}{2}, j + \tfrac{1}{2}]$. This follows directly from the definition of the rounding operation, namely,

$$\left| \frac{y}{x} i - \langle \frac{y}{x} i \rangle \right| \le \tfrac{1}{2}. \qquad (43)$$

Expanding,

$$-\tfrac{1}{2} \le \frac{y}{x} i - \langle \frac{y}{x} i \rangle \le \tfrac{1}{2}, \qquad (44)$$

$$\langle \frac{y}{x} i \rangle - \tfrac{1}{2} \le \frac{y}{x} i \le \langle \frac{y}{x} i \rangle + \tfrac{1}{2}. \qquad (45)$$

Therefore, $(y/x) i \in [j - \tfrac{1}{2}, j + \tfrac{1}{2}]$ as required. Hence $P_{ij} \cap L \neq \emptyset$.

Proposition 14. R_m *is uniform on* $\mathbf{T}_u$.

Proof. Let $L = \mathbf{LineSeg}((0,0),(x,y))$, $y \le x$, be in $\mathbf{L}$. Suppose $P_{ij} \in [L]_m$. By Equations (32b) and (34), $\exists (x,y) \in L : (i,j) = (\langle x \rangle, \langle y \rangle)$. By the same argument as above, therefore, $x \in [i - \frac{1}{2}, i + \frac{1}{2}]$, and $y \in [j - \frac{1}{2}, j + \frac{1}{2}]$. Hence $(x,y) \in P_{ij}$, and so $P_{ij} \cap L \ne \varnothing$.

Remark 8. Sharing rasterisation properties such as uniformity and properness is not a sufficient condition for the equivalence of line rasterisations (e.g., R_o and R_m).

Proposition 15. *Neither* R_o *nor* R_m *have the decomposition property.*

Proof. Recall that a rasterisation R has the decomposition property if the rasterisation of any union of objects is the union of the individual rasterisations. From the proof of Prop. 12, the point $Q(29/8, 145/64) \in L$, where $L = \mathbf{LineSeg}((0,0),(8,5))$, but Q is not contained in any pixel in $R_o[L]$. It is a simple matter to split L into two line segments, L_0 from $(0,0)$ to Q, and L_1 from Q to $(8,5)$. Clearly $L = L_0 \cup L_1$. Thus $P_{42} \in R_o[L_0], R_o[L_1]$, where $(4,2) = (\langle 29/8 \rangle, \langle 145/64 \rangle)$. However, $P_{42} \notin R_o[L]$.

Remark 9. This proposition essentially says that R_o and R_m are unsatisfactory rasterisations for those applications that require that all scene specifications denoting the same scene must also, under a rasterisation, denote the same image. This anomaly suggests that subtle nonmonotonicities are at play in rasterisations R_o and R_m. We further explore this issue in the next section.

4.5.5. Line Monotonicity

One of the most important criteria of a line rasterisation scheme is the extent to which it satisfies certain properties of monotonicity. We began our consideration of monotonic rasterisations in Section 3.1. Since we have been dealing in this section with a more explicit graphic primitive, the line segment, we can define more specific monotonicity conditions and examine whether or not they are satisfied by line rasterisations. Again, it turns out that this study has some practical significance, in that the by now well-known line rasterisations fail on reasonably intuitive monotonicity conditions. This possibility was just suggested by Proposition 15. It is therefore of interest to consider families of line rasterisations that do satisfy the conditions and examine their expected deviation from the ideal or optimal line.

4.5.5.1. Simple Line Monotonicity

The monotonicity property defined in Section 3.1 is much too strong when dealing only with line segments, but it is an easy matter to make it more reasonable.

Definition 15. A line rasterisation R is *simple-line monotonic* (SLM) if

$$\forall L, L' \in \mathbf{L} : L' \subseteq L \Rightarrow R[L'] \subseteq R[L]. \tag{46}$$

Remark 10. From the proof of Prop. 15, it is clear that neither R_m nor R_o are simple-line monotonic.

4.5.5.2. Raster Line Monotonicity

A slight variation on simple-line monotonicity yields a very interesting and practical property, which has attracted the attention of others (e.g. [Pavl82; Luby87]).

Definition 16. A rasterisation R is *raster-line monotonic* or *R-monotonic* if for any line segment $L = \mathbf{LineSeg}((0,0),(x,y)) \in \mathbf{L}$,

$$P_{i_0 j_0}, P_{i_1 j_1} \in R[L] \Rightarrow R[\mathbf{LineSeg}((i_0, j_0), (i_1, j_1))] \subseteq R[L]. \tag{47}$$

We shall also call any R-monotonic rasterisation *stable*. If the condition on rasterisation R is relaxed to

$$P_{i_1 j_1} \in R[L] \Rightarrow R[\mathbf{LineSeg}((0, 0), (i_1, j_1))] \subseteq R[L], \tag{48}$$

then we shall call this rasterisation *R-semimonotonic*, or *origin-stable*.

R-monotonicity (or stability) means that a rasterised line drawn between any two pixels in $R[L]$ must itself be embedded in $R[L]$, whereas R-semimonotonicity (or origin-stability) means that the rasterisation is R-monotonic on any prefix of $R[L]$. R-monotonicity is clearly stronger than R-semimonotonicity.

Although stability constraints are somewhat stringent, there are naturally-occurring situations in which it would be convenient to have a stable line-drawing algorithm. For example, if a line segment is drawn onto a screen, one might wish to erase a portion of that line segment. To accomplish this in many systems, one requires the ability to rewrite that portion with the background colour, without hitting any other pixels and without missing any pixels in that portion. A similar problem can arise in window management systems. Suppose a window is placed over a set of line segments, partially obscuring portions of them. If the window is subsequently removed, these portions should be regenerated. Can this be accomplished using the optimal-line rasterisation? The most appropriate solution in practice appears to be that of storing the overlaid image elsewhere, rather than recalculating the obscured line segment portions. However, it would be of interest to determine whether the well-known line rasterisation schemes are stable, and if not, to develop schemes which are.

Proposition 16. *Neither R_o nor R_m are stable.*

Proof. Recall from the examples above that $R = [(0,0),(8,5)]_m = [(0,0),(8,5)]_o$. The pixels (0,0) and (7,4) are in both rasterisations. However it is easy to verify that while $[(0,0),(7,4)]_m \neq [(0,0),(7,4)]_o$, neither rasterisation is embedded in R.

The above proposition forces us to conclude that our favourite line rasterisation schemes do not satisfy this particularly useful property. The natural questions to ask, of course, are:

(a) Are there any R-monotonic rasterisation schemes?

(b) If so, are there any practical and accurate ones?

The answer to question (a) is yes. The answer to question (b) is probably.

4.5.5.3. Some Very Simple Stable Rasterisations

As usual, we shall restrict our discussion to line segments over the first octant (i.e., the set **L**). Let us consider some R-monotonic line rasterisations, ordered by increasing interest.

Example 12. The degenerate rasterisations R_0 and R_1 from Examples 2 and 3: for any line segment L, paint the entire screen entirely black or entirely white. It is difficult to imagine less useful rasterisations. Notice, however, that one of these is also a proper rasterisation, while the other is uniform.

Example 13. Let $L = \mathbf{LineSeg}((0,0),(x,y)) \in \mathbf{L}$. Then define $R_|$ as follows.

$$R_| [L] =_{df} [(0,0),(x,0)]_o \cup [(x,0),(x,y)]_o. \tag{49}$$

Given any line segment from (0,0) to (x,y) to rasterise, $R_|$ draws a horizontal row of pixels followed by a vertical column of pixels, as in Figure 5. From this figure, it is easy to see that $R_| [L]$ is stable.

Example 14. Let $L = \mathbf{LineSeg}((0,0),(x,y)) \in \mathbf{L}$. Define $R_/$ as follows.

$$R_/[L] =_{df} [(0,0),(x-y,0)]_o \cup [(x-y,0),(x,y)]_o. \tag{50}$$

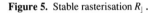

Figure 5. Stable rasterisation $R_\rfloor$.

Given any line segment from (0,0) to (x,y) to rasterise, $R_/$ draws a row of pixels until x matches y, followed by a 45° line of pixels, as in Figure 6.

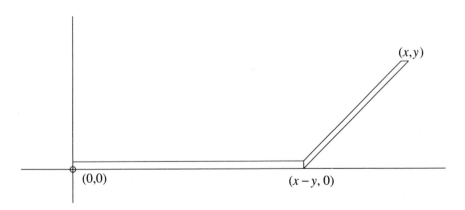

Figure 6. Stable rasterisation $R_/$.

It is again easy to see that $R_/[L]$ is stable.

So far, we have seen somewhat unreasonable stable rasterisations. One useful criterion for reasonableness is a measure of deviation from the ideal line or the optimal line. We introduce such a measure below and reflect on whether there exist any reasonable stable rasterisations. Before that discussion, however, we shall first consider a few more interesting rasterisations.

4.5.5.4. An Interesting Family of Origin-Stable Rasterisations

We shall consider some less trivial line rasterisations in this section. First, however, we prove an interesting proposition. Whereas we saw above that any uniform and proper rasterisation is monotonic, it will be shown that any stable rasterisation cannot be *both* uniform and proper. The proof is actually quite easy because of the equivalence result stated in Proposition 4 above.

Proposition 17. *A stable line rasterisation cannot be both proper and uniform.*

Proof. Let $L \in \mathbf{L}$ and let R be a uniform and proper rasterisation. By Prop. 4,

$$R[L] = \{ P \in \mathbf{T} : L \cap P \neq \varnothing \},$$

which is to say that $R[L]$ is a minimum pixel cover (which is unique if the pixel tiling is non-overlapping). Let $L = \mathbf{LineSeg}((0,0),(6,4))$, and consider $R[L]$. It is easy to show that pixels $(1,1)$ and $(5,3)$ are in $R[L]$. However, $R[\mathbf{LineSeg}((1,1),(5,3))]$ contains pixel $(2,0)$, which is not in $R[L]$. Thus R is not stable.

Let us now consider a family of origin-stable line rasterisation schemes. It is worthwhile to consider such schemes for two reasons. First, like the optimal line, an origin-stable rasterisation can be translated or reflected, thus allowing one to draw lines over all of $\mathbf{Z}^2$. Second, the family to be presented provides us with some clue to the nature of good stable rasterisations.

The basic strategy of each rasterisation scheme in the family is the same: given a line segment $L \in \mathbf{L}$ to rasterise, start from the top-right endpoint, and trace out an eight-connected set of pixels to the origin. The schemes are memory-less, in that no information regarding where it has been is used in choosing the next pixel. Only the current pixel and the ultimate destination play roles in the choice of the next pixel.

More formally, let $L = \mathbf{LineSeg}((0,0),(x,y)) \in \mathbf{L}$. Then

$$R_w^N[L] =_{df} \{ (x_0,y_0), \cdots, (x_n,y_n) \}, \tag{51}$$

where each (x_i,y_i) is given by the following rules:

$$(x_0,y_0) = (0,0) \tag{52a}$$

$$(x_n,y_n) = (x,y) \tag{52b}$$

$$(x_{i-1},y_{i-1}) = \begin{cases} (x_i,y_i) - (0,1) & \text{if } wd_i = M_i \\ (x_i,y_i) - (1,0) & \text{if } wl_i = M_i \ \wedge \ wd_i \neq M_i \\ (x_i,y_i) - (1,1) & \text{if } wb_i = M_i \ \wedge \ wd_i, wl_i \neq M_i \end{cases} \tag{52c}$$

The values of *wd*, *wl*, and *wb* are weights which indicate if the next pixel to be chosen should, respectively, be one pixel down, one pixel left, or both left and down. M_i denotes the maximum of these values for a given pixel. More precisely,

$$wd_i = \frac{y_i^N}{(x_i+y_i)^N} \qquad (52d)$$

$$wl_i = \frac{x_i^N}{(x_i+y_i)^N} \qquad (52e)$$

$$wb_i = 1 - wd_i - wl_i \qquad (52f)$$

$$M_i = \max\{\, wd_i, wl_i, wb_i \,\}. \qquad (52g)$$

A different value or power of $N > 0$ gives a different line rasterisation. Observe, moreover that the three alternatives in Eq. (52c) are mutually exclusive.

Some basic relationships among N, x and y in Eqs. (52d-g) will facilitate a clearer understanding of R_w^N. When N is large, then *wl* and *wd* are small, and *wb* dominates. Thus lines with large N tend to $R_{/}$ (see Figure 7).

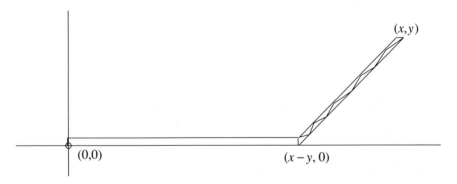

Figure 7. R_w^N, N large.

When N is small, *wb* tends to be smaller than *wl* and *wd*. In the limiting case of $N = 1$,

$$wd = \frac{y}{x+y}, \quad wl = \frac{x}{x+y}, \quad wb = 0. \qquad (53)$$

Line rasterisations for this case are as in Figure 8. Putting these effects together, Figure 9 illustrates the effect of N on R_w^N.

Despite the obvious visual defects of R_w^N for extremal values of N, the lines defined by more moderate values of N are often very good, especially for

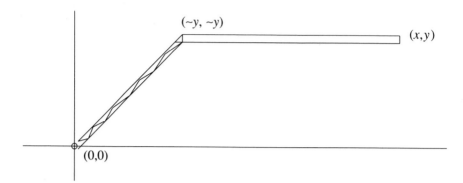

Figure 8. R_w^N, $N = 1$.

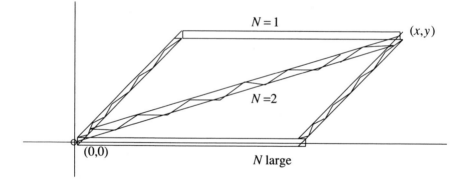

Figure 9. Overall behaviour of R_w^N, N varying.

reasonably short lines of, for example, $\Delta x \leq 32$. In fact, the author for some time was fooled by the extremely good performance of R_w^2 into believing that it has only $O(n)$ worst-case error (see below). It will be seen that this is not the case.

Proposition 18. $\forall N > 0$, R_w^N is origin stable.

Proof. This is easily proved by induction on Δx. However, a completely formal proof is slightly tedious, so instead a proof sketch will be offered. The intuition behind the proof is clear. For a given N, R_w^N prescribes a unique path of pixels from (x,y) to $(0,0)$. When at position $(x+1,y)$, the rules above prescribe exactly one neighbouring pixel to be part of the line; the pixel chosen is one of (x,y),

$(x, y-1)$, or $(x+1, y-1)$. If one of the first two cases is chosen, the remainder of the line is unique, by the inductive hypothesis. In the latter case, the pixels subsequently chosen either

(a) chain down to $(x+1, 0)$. In this case the next pixel chosen after $(x+1, 0)$ can only be $(x, 0)$.

(b) contains one of $(x, y-1)$ or $(x, y-2)$.

In either case, the situtation is reduced to one with $\Delta x = n$, and we can thus appeal to the inductive hypothesis.

4.5.5.5. A Line Rasterisation Error Metric

At this point, many line rasterisations have been introduced, some of which appear to define very poor lines, and others which perform somewhat less poorly. Clearly a formal metric assessing the error inherent in a particular line rasterisation scheme should exist. While one cannot expect any such metric to correspond exactly with human visual satisfaction with a rasterisation, such metrics are useful first-order indicators. The metric defined in this section measures the maximal deviation of a line rasterisation from the ideal line.

Definition 17. The *cumulative error* of a rasterisation R over an arbitrary line segment in the first octant rooted at the orgin is defined to be

$$\epsilon(R[L], L) =_{df} \sum_{(i,j) \in R[L]} \left| \frac{\Delta y}{\Delta x} i - j \right|. \tag{54}$$

The worst-case error metric we shall be using can now be defined in terms of this function.

Definition 18. For a given rasterisation R and natural number n, the *worst-case cumulative error* of R is

$$\epsilon_{\max}(R, n) =_{df} \max\{ \epsilon(R[L], L) : L \in \mathbf{L}, \Delta x \leq n \}. \tag{55}$$

Let us consider the error of several line rasterisations. To be true to its name, the optimal line should indeed yield optimal results.

Proposition 19. R_o *has* $O(n)$ *cumulative worst-case error.*

Proof. By definition of the optimal line,

$$\varepsilon(R_o[L],L) \;=\; \sum_{(i,j)\in R[L]} \left| \frac{\Delta y}{\Delta x} i - \langle \frac{\Delta y}{\Delta x} i \rangle \right|. \qquad (56)$$

For any line segment L and integer i,

$$\left| \frac{\Delta y}{\Delta x} i - \langle \frac{\Delta y}{\Delta x} i \rangle \right| \le \frac{1}{2}. \qquad (57)$$

Since there are exactly $n = \Delta x$ pixels in $R_o[L]$,

$$\forall L \in \mathbf{L} : \varepsilon(R_o[L],L) \le \frac{n}{2}. \qquad (58)$$

Therefore $\varepsilon_{\max}(R_o,n)$ is $O(n)$, and the proposition follows.

Remark 11. There are line segments for which the error in R_o is $\Omega(n)$. We leave a proof of this fact to the reader.[6] Thus R_o has $\Theta(n)$ error.

Our error metric confirms that $R_{\rfloor}$ is indeed a poor rasterisation scheme (as if that were required).

Proposition 20. $R_{\rfloor}$ has $\Theta(n^2)$ worst-case error.

Proof. Recalling Figure 5, the maximum error in $R_{\rfloor}$ occurs on the rasterisation of the line $y = x$. Let $L = \mathbf{LineSeg}((0,0),(n,n))$. Then it is easy to see that

$$\varepsilon(R_{\rfloor}[L],L) \;=\; \sum_{j=0}^{n} j \;+\; \sum_{j=0}^{n-1} j \qquad (59)$$

$$= \frac{n(n+1)}{2} + \frac{(n-1)n}{2}$$

$$= \frac{n(n+1+n-1)}{2} \;=\; \frac{2n^2}{2}$$

$$= n^2.$$

Proposition 21. $R_{/}$ has $\Theta(n^2)$ worst-case error.

Proof. Consider Figure 6. Clearly the maximum cumulative error is never more than that of $R_{\rfloor}$. A suitable worst-case line segment is any with slope $\tfrac{1}{2}$, that is, on the rasterisation of the line $y = x/2$. Let $L = \mathbf{LineSeg}((0,0),(n,n/2))$, with n

---

[6] Hint: consider a line segment from $(0,0)$ to $(2n,1)$, $n>0$.

divisible by 4. After a short inspection, it can be readily seen that

$$\varepsilon(R_{/}[L],L) = \sum_{j=1}^{n} \frac{j}{2} + \sum_{j=1}^{n} \frac{j-1}{2} \tag{60}$$

$$= \frac{1}{2} \cdot \frac{n(n+1)}{2} + \frac{1}{2} \cdot \frac{(n-1)n}{2}$$

$$= \frac{n^2}{2}.$$

The proposition follows.

Despite the comment above that R_w^2 often produces very good lines, its worst-case behaviour is not good.

Proposition 22. *For any $N > 0$, the rasterisation R_w^N has $\Theta(n^2)$ worst-case error.*

Proof. We prove this result for $N = 2$, since it appears to give the best-looking lines. Again, observe that the maximum error is bounded above by $O(n^2)$. A worst-case for R_w^2 is obtained for any line segment having slope $\frac{1}{4}$. Consequently, let $L = \textbf{LineSeg}((0,0), (n,n/4))$, letting n be divisible by 4. If $x > 2y$, then $wl > wb > wb$. Thus R_w^2 will choose pixels

$$\left\{ (n, \frac{n}{4}), (n-1, \frac{n}{4}), \cdots, (\frac{n}{2}, \frac{n}{4}) \right\}$$

as the right half of the rasterisation. The error in the right half of $R[L]$ therefore approximates the area of the triangle in Figure 10.

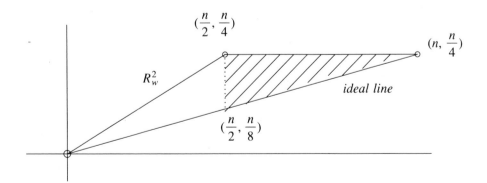

Figure 10. Triangle of error.

The exact area of this triangle is

$$A = \frac{1}{2} \cdot base \cdot height$$

$$= \frac{1}{2} \cdot \frac{n}{8} \cdot \frac{n}{2} \tag{61}$$

$$= \frac{n^2}{32}.$$

More precisely, the error on the right-half of the rasterisation is

$$E_n = \sum_{i=n/2}^{n} \frac{n}{4} - \frac{i}{4}$$

$$= \frac{1}{4} \sum_{i=n/2}^{n} (n-i) \tag{62}$$

$$= \frac{n(n+2)}{32}.$$

Since $E_n \le \varepsilon_{max}(R_w^2, n)$, the proposition follows.

4.5.5.6. Conclusions and Conjectures

This section has introduced the basic semantics and theory of line rasterisations. We first considered a formal definition of the line segment and the line rasterisation. Several such rasterisations were presented and some of their properties were proved. We then considered monotonicity properties, and examined the error behaviour of many line rasterisations. Time and space does not permit us to explore this area more deeply, but it is clear that there is a great deal of interesting and important work to be done.

The negative results shown above concerning the worst-case error performance of many line rasterisations leads one to wonder if there are any good (i.e., $O(n)$ error) stable or origin-stable line rasterisations. We end this section with several nontrivial questions and conjectures.

- Does there exist a stable rasterisation R with $\varepsilon_{max}(R,n) = O(n)$? *Conjecture:* No.

- Does there exist an origin-stable rasterisation R with $\varepsilon_{max}(R,n) = O(n)$? *Answer:* Yes. M. Luby has developed a clever scheme which exhibits $O(1)$ deviation of any pixel in the rasterisation from the ideal line [Luby87]. Thus the cumulative worst-case error of such rasterisations would be $O(n)$.

- Does there exist a stable or origin stable rasterisation with worst-case error strictly between $O(n)$ and $O(n^2)$? *Answer:* There exists a stable rasterisation with worst-case error of $O(n \log n)$. Luby has demonstrated a stable rasterisation scheme that exhibits a maximal pixel deviation of $O(\log n)$, which would give rise to a cumulative error statistic of $O(n \log n)$.

While we are forced to leave this topic with many interesting questions as yet unsettled, it is of some consolation that we now have the notational tools to express these problems succinctly, and have developed a body of results that is interesting in its own right.

4.6. Image Transformations and Their Rasterisation

Throughout this book, we have maintained that a *scene* represents a real-world picture, and that an *image* is a particular rendering of a scene. So far, we have thought of images as static entites that, once computed, just take up space on a display screen. It is often the case, however, that images are taken as graphic primitives themselves and that operations are performed on them. In this section, we shall consider only one class of image operations: geometric transformations. Certainly other useful operations exist, but it is reasonable to start with those that are the most basic and common. In two recent papers, for example, T. Duff and T. Porter present a semantics of *compositing*, a well-known technique in animation and film in which images are blended together in various ways to create a composite image [PoDu84;Duff85]. Such blending processes are very easy to express mathematically.[7] In this section, we shall discuss the formal semantics of image transformations and their rasterisation.

As we saw in Chapter 1, the notion of transforming a scene prior to rendering is well understood. After defining image transformations, or transformations of scenes *after* rendering, we shall attempt to settle a basic, practical, and interesting question: to what extent can image transformations replace scene transformations? For example, what is the set of rotations which achieve identical results on both scenes and images? We shall classify the set of transformations that can operate over images and yet still remain "faithful" to the corresponding scene transformation. It is important to determine this set, for there are many graphics systems which rapidly perform image transformations in hardware or microcode. Optimal use of the system may be made, and the image display enviroment can be made more dynamic, if it is known what transformations can be deferred to a stage after rendering. Unfortunately, it will be seen that this set is rather small, and only the most basic transformations can be correctly applied after rendering. This

---

[7] In the interest of giving credit where it is properly due, we note that there exists a body of research in the semantics of picture composition which precedes the work of Duff and Porter, a fact which goes unmentioned in their papers. Although their work is not well known in computer graphics, W. Mallgren together with A. Shaw presented a more general formalism in [MaSh78] and [Mall82a,b].

conclusion presumes, as we have throughout this chapter, a two-valued intensity space. Many more transformations can be made to look correct by digitally filtering the transformed image [CaSm80]. This requires a large intensity space.

The research in this section was originally motivated by a paper by Guibas and Stolfi [GuSt82] whose main theme was that operations on bit-mapped images should assume equal prominence with scene operations. This prompted the author to begin a study of the capabilities of bit-map operations in order to assess their claim. The conclusion of this section is that, while many very useful and surprising operations can be performed on bit-maps, the higher-level notion of performing operations on scenes cannot be replaced in general.

It has recently come to the attention of the author that some of the results of section 5.2 on "faithful" transformations are similar to the work of J. Serra in his book *Image Analysis and Mathematical Morphology* [Serr82]. The results were discovered independently, and are derived with respect to different formalisms. For example, we shall relate faithfulness to symmetry groups, while [Serr82] does not.

4.6.1. Basic Definitions

Definition 19. A two-dimensional *geometric transformation*, hereafter called a transformation, is a continuous bijection $\alpha : \mathbf{R}^2 \to \mathbf{R}^2$. If $S \subseteq \mathbf{R}^2$, then

$$\alpha S = \{ \alpha p : p \in S \}. \tag{63}$$

Many-one mappings will not be considered here, although in Chapter 1 we saw that projections, such as perspective projections, are relevant to computer graphics.

Definition 20. A transformation α is a *rigid motion*, or an *isometry*, if it preserves distance. That is, if $d(p,q)$ is the familiar euclidean distance metric, then

$$p,q \in \mathbf{R}^2 \implies d(p,q) = d(\alpha p, \alpha q). \tag{64}$$

Remark 12. If a transformation preserves distance, then it preserves area.

Definition 21. An isometry α is a *symmetry* of a set $P \subseteq \mathbf{R}^2$ if $\alpha P = P$. The set of all symmetries of a set $P \subseteq \mathbf{R}^2$, denoted $\mathbf{S}(P)$, is a group under the operation of composition [Mart82]. $\mathbf{S}(P)$ is called the *symmetry group* of P.

Remark 13. $S(P)$ is always non-empty, regardless of the choice of P, since the identity function is a symmetric transformation of any set.

Example 15. *A 2-D Translation.* Three-dimensional translations were defined in Chapter 1. A 2-D translation $T_{uv} : \mathbf{R}^2 \to \mathbf{R}^2$, $u,v \in \mathbf{R}^2$ has the following semantics.

$$T_{uv}(x,y) =_{df} (x+u, y+v).$$
(65)

Obviously, every translation is an isometry.

Proposition 23. *If A, $B \subseteq \mathbf{R}^2$ and α is an isometry, then*

$$\alpha(A \cup B) = \alpha(A) \cup \alpha(B),$$

and

$$\alpha(A \cap B) = \alpha(A) \cap \alpha(B).$$

Proof. The theorem follows directly from naive set theory and Eq. (63).

Recall from Section 1 that an image is defined over a pixel tiling $\mathbf{T}$ of a rectangular portion of $\mathbf{R}^2$ using a single pixel prototile $\mathbf{P}$.[8] Tiles (i.e., pixels) in $\mathbf{T}$ are assumed to be addressable using a two-dimensional indexing (i,j), $i,j \in \mathbf{Z}$. Each pixel is defined to have an intensity of either zero or one. In this section, we shall impose one additional restriction on the nature of the tiling $\mathbf{T}$: all pixels in the tiling must have the same orientation. We call such a tiling a *rigid pixel tiling*, and define it formally as follows.

Definition 22. A *basis* for a pixel tiling $\mathbf{T}$ is a pair of linearly independent vectors $(\overline{e}_0, \overline{e}_1)$ such that the centre c_{ij} of each $P_{ij} \in \mathbf{T}$ is given by $c_{ij} = i\,\overline{e}_0 + j\,\overline{e}_1$.

Definition 23. A pixel tiling $\mathbf{T}_P$ is *rigid* over prototile $\mathbf{P}$ if it can be expressed in the following form:

$$\mathbf{T_P} = \{\, \alpha_{ij}\,\mathbf{P} : (i,j) \in \mathbf{Z}^2 \,\},$$
(66)

where α_{ij} is a translation mapping the centre, $(0,0)$, of $\mathbf{P}$ to the centre of pixel P_{ij}. More specifically,

---

[8] Owing to their generality, the following definitions are somewhat technical. On first reading, the reader may wish to consider the results to follow only within context of the unit square pixel tiling, since it is the most common pixel arrangement abstraction and since the results apply to all similarly "rigid" pixel arrangements.

$$\alpha_{ij} =_{df} T_{(i\overline{e}_0+j\overline{e}_1)}, \tag{67}$$

Example 16. The unit square tiling, $\mathbf{T}_u$, is rigid since it has basis $\overline{e}_0 = (1,0)$ and $\overline{e}_1 = (0,1)$, with $\alpha_{ij} = T_{ij}$. Similarly, a rectangular tiling based on prototile $\mathbf{P} = [-\frac{1}{2}, \frac{1}{2}] \times [-\frac{3}{4}, \frac{3}{4}]$ has basis $\overline{e}_0 = (1,0)$ and $\overline{e}_1 = (0, 1\frac{1}{2})$.

It is easy to construct rigid rectangular or hexagonal tilings. On the other hand, tilings based on triangles are not rigid, since every other triangle in a row of a tiling must be rotated as well as translated. Note, however, that triangular tiles can be grouped into parallelograms, which do form a rigid pixel tiling (see Figure 11).

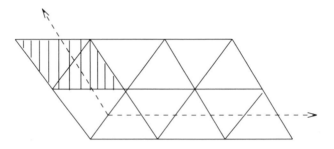

Figure 11. Grouping triangular tiles into parallelograms. A basis is indicated by the dashed lines.

Therefore, the results proved of rigid pixel tilings will also apply to paired-triangular tilings.

Definition 24. Let $\mathbf{T}_\mathbf{P}$ be a pixel tiling over prototile $\mathbf{P}$. Let α be a geometric transformation, and suppose $P_{ij} \in \mathbf{T}_\mathbf{P}$ is the pixel containing the image of the centre of $\mathbf{P}$ under α. That is, suppose $\alpha(0,0) \in P_{ij}$. We define the *normalising transformation* α_n of α as

$$\alpha_n =_{df} T_{norm}\, \alpha, \tag{68}$$

where T_{norm} is a translation mapping the image of the origin under α back to the origin, except that the steps in the translation are relative to the pixel spacing. Formally,

$$T_{norm} =_{df} T_{-(i\overline{e}_0+j\overline{e}_1)}. \tag{69}$$

The overall effect of α_n is to allow one to relate the behaviour of α about a pixel or set of pixels back to that original pixel or set.

Example 17. In the unit square tiling, if $\alpha(0,0) = (x,y) \in P_{ij}$, then

$$T_{norm} = T_{-(i,j)}.$$

4.6.2. Some Basic Results

Our goal is to discover the general conditions under which a rasterisation R and transformation α commute over an arbitrary point-set $O \subseteq \mathbf{R}^2$. That is, when is it true that

$$\alpha R[O] = R[\alpha O]? \tag{70}$$

Definition 25. If a transformation α satisfies property 70, then α is a *faithful transformation* with respect to a rasterisation R.

We shall assume that R is the proper, uniform rasterisation (R_3 from Section 3.2 above). Recall from Proposition 4 that regardless of the myriad ways of writing down a proper, uniform rasterisation, they all denote the same set of pixels. Also recall that a proper, uniform rasterisation has the decomposition property. These facts, taken with Proposition 23 makes the proofs simpler, since we can decompose the case of transforming or rasterising an object overlapping with many pixels into many similar instances over individual pixels. It is therefore sufficient to consider the behaviour of transformations only over pixel-sized objects. Throughout this discussion, let α be an isometry, and let **T** be a rigid pixel tiling of $\mathbf{R}^2$.

Remark 14. We are concerned only with *isometric* transformations because it is clear that this property is necessary for faithfulness. Consider a non-isometric transformation such as scaling by constant factors in x and y, for example. Given specific scale factors s_x and s_y, it is easy to construct an object O such that Eq. (70) does not hold. This is by no means a proof of the necessity of isometry to faithfulness, but it does provide some intuition.

Example 18. Any integral translation is faithful over T_u.

The following proposition relates the faithfulness of α_n with that of α.

Proposition 24. *Let $O \subseteq P \in \mathbf{T}$. Then*

$$\alpha R[O] = R[\alpha O] \iff \alpha_n R[O] = R[\alpha_n O].$$

Proof. Observe that since $\alpha_n = T\alpha$ for translation T_{norm}, $\alpha = T_{norm}^{-1}\alpha_n$, where T_{norm}^{-1} is also a translation. We know such an inverse exists because all translations are invertible. It therefore suffices to prove the proposition only one direction.

Suppose $\alpha R[O] = R[\alpha O]$. Multiplying both sides by T_{norm},

$$T_{norm}\,\alpha R[O] = T_{norm}\,R[\alpha O].$$

$$\therefore \alpha_n R[O] = T_{norm}\,R[\alpha O].$$

The proposition will follow if we show that $T_{norm}\,R[\alpha O] = R[\alpha_n O]$. Let

$$R[\alpha O] = \{\,P_1,\,\cdots,P_N \in \mathbf{T}\,\} \tag{71}$$

be the rasterisation of αO. Then

$$T_{norm}\,R[\alpha O] = \{\,T_{norm}\,P_1,\,\cdots,T_{norm}P_N\,\}.$$

$$= \{\,Q_1,\,\cdots,Q_N\,\},$$

where each $Q_i = T_{norm}\,P_i$ is also a pixel in the tiling (since T_{norm} is an integral translation with respect to the pixel spacing). Since R is proper, αO is covered by $R[\alpha O]$. We can therefore decompose αO into pieces $S_1, S_2, \cdots, S_N$ such that

$$S_i = \alpha O \cap P_i.$$

That is, each $S_i \subseteq P_i$ is simply the part of αO overlapping with pixel P_i. Clearly $S_1 \cup \cdots \cup S_N = \alpha O$. Therefore,

$$R[\alpha_n O] = R[T_{norm}\,\alpha O] \tag{72}$$

$$= R[T_{norm}\,\underset{i}{\cup}\,S_i]$$

$$= R[\underset{i}{\cup}\,T_{norm}\,S_i] \qquad \text{(by Prop. 23)}$$

$$= \{\,R[T_{norm}\,S_1],\,\cdots,R[T_{norm}\,S_N]\,\} \quad \text{(decomposition rule)}$$

$$= \{\,Q_1,\,\cdots,Q_N\,\}.$$

Thus $T_{norm}\,R[\alpha O] = R[\alpha_n O]$. The proposition follows.

We now follow with an important result, namely that a transformation is faithful if and only if its corresponding normalising transformation is in the symmetry group of the pixel prototile.

Proposition 25. *Let $O \subseteq P \in \mathbf{T}$, and let α be an isometry. Then*

$$\alpha R[O] = R[\alpha O] \;\Leftrightarrow\; \alpha_n \in \mathbf{S}(P).$$

Proof. (only if) Suppose $\alpha R\,[O\,]=R\,[\alpha O]$, and assume for the purposes of contradiction that $\alpha_n \notin \mathbf{S(P)}$. Then by definition, $\alpha_n\,P \neq P$, for some pixel P. Write $\alpha_n\,P = A \cup B$, where $A \subseteq P$ is the portion of $\alpha_n\,P$ lying within P, and B is the portion lying outside P, $B \cap P = \varnothing$, as in Figure 12.

$$A \cup B = \alpha_n \mathbf{P}$$

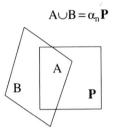

B   A   P

Figure 12. Relationship of $\alpha_n\,P$ to P.

If $B = \varnothing$, then either $\alpha_n\,P = P$, or $\alpha_n P \subset P$. Clearly the former case contradicts the fact that α_n is not a symmetry. In the latter case, however, it is clear that α_n is not surjective, a contradiction.[9] Therefore, we are forced to conclude that $B \neq \varnothing$. Recall that R has the decomposition property. Since R is proper, $B \neq \varnothing \Rightarrow R\,[B\,] \neq \varnothing$. Hence

$$R\,[\alpha_n P] \;=\; R\,[A \cup B\,] \;=\; R\,[A\,] \cup R\,[B\,] \;=\; P \cup R\,[B\,], \tag{73}$$

since $R\,[A\,] = P$. Define

$$Q \;=_{df}\; \alpha_n^{-1}\,A \tag{74}$$
$$=\; \{\,p \in \mathbf{R}^2 : \alpha p \in A\,\} \;\subseteq\; P.$$

Observe that $Q \neq \varnothing$ (since $A \neq \varnothing$, and α is 1-1), and that $R\,[\alpha_n Q\,] = P$. However,

$$\alpha_n R\,[Q\,] = \alpha_n P = P \cup R\,[B\,] \neq R\,[\alpha_n Q\,],$$

since we established earlier that $R\,[B\,] \neq \varnothing$. Moreover, by Proposition 24,

$$\alpha_n R\,[Q\,] \neq R\,[\alpha_n Q\,] \;\Rightarrow\; \alpha R\,[Q\,] \neq R\,[\alpha Q\,],$$

---

[9] Indeed, a stronger result can be shown, namely that if α is only required to be continuous and injective, but not necessarily surjective, such that $\alpha P \subset P$, then α cannot be an isometry. The argument is subtle, and we only give an informal outline. Recall that an isometry also preserves area, so that if we show that $\mu(P)$, the Lebesgue measure (intuitively, the area) of P, is greater than $\mu(\alpha P)$, we can conclude that α is not an isometry. Let point $p \in P - \alpha P$. Since α is continuous, p cannot be an isolated point. That is, there exists a neighbourhood $N\,(p)$ of points about p such that $N\,(p) \subset P - \alpha P$. However, $\mu(N\,(p)) > 0$ and $\mu(P)$ is finite. Therefore $\mu(P - \alpha P) > 0$. It follows that $\mu(P) \neq \mu(\alpha P)$.

a contradiction. Therefore $\alpha_n \in \mathbf{S}(\mathbf{P})$.

To prove the "if" part of the theorem, suppose $\alpha_n \in \mathbf{S}(\mathbf{P})$. It suffices to show that for any object O, $O \subseteq \mathbf{P} \Rightarrow \alpha R[O] = R[\alpha O]$. Let $O \subseteq \mathbf{P}$ be arbitrary. There are two cases to consider.

Case: $R[O] = \varnothing$. Then

$$\alpha R[O] = \alpha \varnothing = \varnothing.$$

Moreover, since R is uniform,

$$R[\alpha O] = R[\varnothing] = \varnothing.$$

Case: $R[O] \neq \varnothing$. Then since R is proper, $R[O] = P$, and moreover $O \neq \varnothing$. Furthermore, α_n is 1-1 and a symmetry of $\mathbf{P}$. Therefore $\alpha_n O \subseteq \mathbf{P}$ and $\alpha_n O \neq \varnothing$. It follows that $R[\alpha_n O] = \mathbf{P} = \alpha_n R[O]$, and so, by Proposition 24, $R[\alpha O] = \mathbf{P} = \alpha R[O]$.

These two cases establish the "if" part of the proposition, and thus the proposition follows.

What does this proposition imply? It implies that the set of faithful transformations is determined only by the symmetry group of the pixel prototile. For the unit square prototile, $\mathbf{P} = [-\frac{1}{2}, \frac{1}{2}] \times [-\frac{1}{2}, \frac{1}{2}]$, for example, $\mathbf{S}(\mathbf{P})$ includes

- rotations by $\dfrac{k\pi}{2}$ radians, $k \in \mathbf{Z}$,
- reflections across $y = \pm x$, and $y = r$ or $x = r$, where $r \in \{0, \frac{1}{2}, 1\}$,
- the identity mapping.

Therefore, the set of faithful transformations is any integral translation (recall the definition of α_n above) of any $\alpha \in \mathbf{S}(\mathbf{P})$. Although this result is perhaps not altogether surprising, it offers a precise methodology for determining the set of faithful transformations for a given pixel prototile. A different prototile will yield a different set. Notice that the above set for the unit square contains very few interesting rotations. The symmetry group for the unit hexagon, for example, contains a slightly richer set of rotations: any rotation of the form $\dfrac{k\pi}{3}$ radians, $k \in Z$.

The above two propositions examined the effect of a transformation on the entire pixel. Suppose instead we define a *raster transformation* as one whose behaviour on a set $Q \subseteq P \in \mathbf{T}$ is determined by its mapping of a single point $p \in P$.

Definition 26. A *raster transformation* α^R has the following form:

$$\alpha^R Q =_{df} R_P[\alpha c_P], \tag{75}$$

where c_P is the centre of pixel P, $Q \subseteq P$, and R_P is the point rasterisation defined in

Eq. (32) above.

The following proposition allows us to make a similar conclusion for faithful raster transformations as Proposition 25 above does for general geometric transformations.

Proposition 26. *Let α^R be a raster transformation defined as in Equation (75). Then*

$$\alpha^R Q = R\,[\alpha Q] \iff \alpha_n \in S(\mathbf{P}).$$

Proof.
(*if*) Let $\alpha_n \in S(\mathbf{P})$, and let $Q \subseteq \mathbf{P}$. By Proposition 25, $\alpha R\,[Q] = R\,[\alpha Q]$. The rasterisation R is proper; thus $R[Q] = \mathbf{P}$. Since α_n is a symmetry,

$$\alpha_n R\,[Q] = \alpha_n \mathbf{P} = \mathbf{P}.$$

Since α_n is an integral translation of α, $\alpha R\,[Q] = P_{ab}$, for exactly one pixel $P_{ab} \in \mathbf{T}$, $a,b \in \mathbf{Z}$. Observe that $c_P \in R\,[Q] = \mathbf{P}$. Therefore, $\alpha c_P \in P_{ab}$. It follows that

$$\alpha^R Q = R_P[\alpha c_P] = P_{ab} = R\,[\alpha Q].$$

(***only if***) Now suppose $\alpha^R Q = R\,[\alpha Q]$. Then clearly $\alpha^R \mathbf{P} = R\,[\alpha \mathbf{P}]$. Indeed,

$$\alpha^R Q = \alpha^R \mathbf{P} = R\,[\alpha c_{\mathbf{P}}] = P_{ab}, \tag{76}$$

for some $a,b \in \mathbf{Z}$. We are required to show that $\alpha \mathbf{P} = P_{ab}$. Suppose this is not the case. Define

$$B = \{\, p \in \mathbf{P} : \alpha p \in P_{ab} \,\},$$

and put $A = \mathbf{P} - B$. Obviously $A \cup B = \mathbf{P}$. We consider two cases.

Case: $\alpha \mathbf{P} \subset P_{ab}$. Then α is not an isometry (see above), a contradiction.

Case: $\alpha \mathbf{P}$ overlaps with P_{ab} and other pixels, as in Figure 13.

By construction,

$$\alpha \mathbf{P} = \alpha(A \cup B) = \alpha A \cup \alpha B. \tag{77}$$

Since $\alpha_R Q = P_{ab}$ by Eq. (76), and since by assumption, $\alpha^R \mathbf{P} = R\,[\alpha \mathbf{P}]$, clearly

$$\alpha^R \mathbf{P} = P_{ab} = R\,[\alpha \mathbf{P}].$$

However, by Eq. (77)

$$R\,[\alpha \mathbf{P}] = R\,[\alpha A] \cup R\,[\alpha B]$$
$$= C \cup P_{ab}.$$

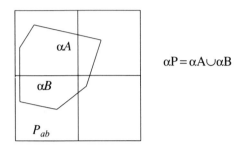

Figure 13. The case in which αP is not wholly contained in P_{ab}.

But $A \neq \emptyset$, and $A \cap P_{ab} = \emptyset$. Hence $C = R[\alpha A] \neq \emptyset$, since R is proper. Since C is nonempty, clearly $C \cup P_{ab} \neq P_{ab}$, and so

$$\alpha^R \mathbf{P} \neq R[\alpha \mathbf{P}],$$

a contradiction.

The only alternative remaining is that indeed, $A = \emptyset$, and that $B = \mathbf{P}$, from which it follows that $\alpha \mathbf{P} = P_{ab}$. Hence $\alpha_n \in \mathbf{S}(\mathbf{P})$, and the proposition follows.

Remark 15. By Propositions 25 and 26, the class of faithful raster transformations and the class of faithful geometric transformations agree. This is a useful property, for it means that to transform an image, only one representative from each pixel is required.

4.6.3. Summary and Conclusions

This section has established some basic facts regarding the relationship between faithful geometric or raster transformations and the symmetry group of the pixel prototile, under the proper, uniform rasterisation. The results are important, for they allow one to determine easily the set of faithful transformations and decide if this set is sufficiently rich for one's application to replace higher-level scene transformations. It is of course impossible to answer in general whether or not this is the case, but it is clear that the set of faithful transformations is relatively small.

Once again, much interesting work remains. We have only considered one rasterisation in this section, on which our results are highly dependent, and only general point sets. Can we get richer sets of (useful) faithful transformations under less restrictive rasterisations and over more specific graphic primitives like line segments? The author believes that the answer to this question is essentially negative, but this has yet to be established formally.

4.7. Summary

This chapter has touched on many aspects of bit-mapped graphics. We have developed a semantics that carefully distinguishes among scenes, bit-maps, and images. Operations on bit-maps have also been given a concise, algebraic formulation. Within this framework, two-dimensional renderings called rasterisations were defined, and many interesting properties of rasterisations over general scenes, and over line segments were proved. We were then able to develop line rasterisation schemes which have useful monotonicity properties, and (sometimes pessimistic) error bounds were established. Our last topic dealt with the classification of transformations which are faithful to images.

5 Illumination Models

Socrates: *You may have the power of vision in your eyes and try to use it, and colour may be there in the objects; but sight will see nothing and the colours will remain invisible in the absence of a third thing peculiarly constituted to serve this very purpose.*

Glaucon: *By which you mean—?*

Socrates: *Naturally I mean what you call light; ... No one could say that light is not a precious thing.*

—Plato[1]

Synopsis. An illumination model defines the shade of every visible point in a scene. The model may be local in nature, using only the light sources and local information in prescribing the intensity of a point. Alternatively, a model may utilise global scene information. A framework for specifying illumination models of either variety is presented in this chapter.

5.1. Introduction

In Chapter 1, we saw that every point on or in an object can be given a colour value. When rendered as such, these objects typically have solid colours and look highly unnatural. More realistic images require an *illumination model* which simulates some (small) subset of natural lighting and shading effects. The development of realistic illumination models is one of the most active and

---

[1] Plato, *The Republic* (Oxford University Press: London, U.K.), F.M. Cornford (trans.), 1941.

exciting areas of computer graphics today. Unfortunately, as indicated in the next chapter, a general version of these models is probably intractable. This chapter lays the foundation for this result, presenting a framework in which all known illumination models can be expressed.

Informally, an illumination model prescribes an intensity value, $I(x,y,z)$, for every visible point, (x,y,z) in a scene of objects, relative to an eye position and a set of light sources. Ultimately, we wish to define an illumination function $I(x,y)$, which is the result of projecting $I(x,y,z)$ onto the screen plane (see Chapter 1). This function over $\mathbf{R}^2$ may then be sampled in order to render the scene into an image (see Chapter 3).

The first step in our development will be to give a general schema for illumination models which define an intensity based only on information local to the object and the light sources. The second step is to develop a structure in which global information is used to define an intensity value. These *global illumination models* are required to model convincingly effects such as refraction, multiple reflections, and diffraction (the latter of which has yet to be realistically modelled in computer graphics). *Local illumination models* from the first step are used in a recursive manner to synthesise an overall intensity value for each point in scene. While our semantics describes a two-tiered approach to illumination, which is common practice, it is a straightforward extension of the model to generalise to several levels.

The study of realistic illumination models for computer graphics began with the work of Bui Tuong Phong [BuiT75], who incorporated a specular, or glossy, illumination component into his model. Prior to Bui Tuong's work, all objects in a scene were shaded diffusely, according to Lambert's law (see below). Bui Tuong's model was extended by J. Blinn [Blin77] to produce more realistic specular reflections; increasingly complex physical illumination models have been proposed ever since, with the reflectance model of Cook and Torrance being perhaps the most realistic [CoTo82]. Many variations on these models also exist. Coincidentally with this work, T. Whitted popularised a (quasi-)global illumination model called *ray tracing*, a technique that has produced the most spectacular computer-synthesised images to date. In the quest for increasing realism, Whitted incorporated the basic physics of classical ray optics in which rays of light emanating from a light source are traced throughout a scene [Whit80]. The intensity of reflected and refracted light rays is determined by a physical local illumination model. Those ray traces which hit the eye determine the scene illumination from a given eye point. In practice, ray-tracing implementations approximate ideal ray tracing by following paths in the opposite direction, namely from the eye to a light source.

A complementary illumination model based on radiosity is becoming increasingly popular [CoGr85]. Semantically speaking, this technique does not differ from ideal ray tracing, which assumes that rays of light are traced from the light sources into the scene. Indeed, radiosity should be viewed as an another approximation to ideal ray tracing.

The next section gives a very brief overview of the general structure of local illumination models. We subsequently discuss a framework for specifying global illumination models based on ray tracing. Our framework generalises ray tracing as it is now understood. To demonstrate its generality, an idealisation of Whitted's model is specified. Lastly, we discuss various implementation issues, describing alternative ways to model light sources, and considering the effect of the placement of an illumination model at various stages in the graphics pipeline.

The discussion in this chapter is not intended to give a thorough account of illumination models in computer graphics, and is moreover not particularly rigorous. To do so would require an excursion into colour theory and into the physics of illumination. The interested reader is invited to consult one of the basic textbooks, as well as the recent *SIGGRAPH* proceedings, for more practical information. The recent monograph by R. Hall is also a useful introduction to the application of illumination theory to computer graphics [Hall89]. Our intention is instead to give a general framework within which arbitrary illumination models can be specified, and to introduce a ray-tracing framework that is used, in the next chapter, to consider the complexity of ray tracing.

5.2. Local Illumination Models

Definition 1. Given a set **L** of light sources, a *local illumination model* prescribes a function $I_L(P)$ that maps the incoming light from **L** that strikes visible point $P \in \mathbf{R}^3$ in a scene, to an outgoing intensity (in one or more directions).

Remark 1. The adjectives *local* and *global* are to some extent qualitative. Our distinction will be that local illumination models define a mapping from "input" light and local object information to "output" light, whereas a global illumination model accounts for *both* incoming and outgoing light. In this sense, it is natural to define global models in terms of cascaded local models.

Remark 2. The term *intensity* is perhaps one of the most misused words in computer graphics, and it requires much more than a passing remark to remedy the situation. While the semantics of illumination discussed here is insensitive to precise quantities and units, we adopt the physical convention that intensity is *power* per unit *area*. Power, in turn, is *energy* per unit *time*. Typical units would be joules for energy, watts for power, and watts per square metre for intensity. A careful consideration of these terms is not mere pedantry. Observe that under this model it is possible to increase intensity while conserving power or energy (by, for example, focusing a beam of light into a smaller area).

All local illumination models in current use divide the problem of determining the intensity $I(P)$ of a visible point $P \in \mathbf{R}^3$ on the surface of an object into three or four subproblems [Blin77; NeSp79]:

$$I =_{df} I_a + I_d + I_s \, [+I_t], \tag{1}$$

where:

- I_a is the *ambient* illumination at point P. This term models the diffusely scattered light hitting every object.

- I_d is the *diffuse* illumination at point P. This term models the dull reflection of the light sources and other objects about P.

- I_s is the *specular* illumination at point P. This term models the glossy reflection that may be present at point P.

- I_t is an optional approximation to light that is *refracted* or *transmitted* through the object, striking point P. It can be used to model transparency or translucency (although a global illumination model is required to do this task accurately).

This constitutes a fairly gross approximation to reality, since there is really a continuum between diffuse and specular reflection. Furthermore, any reasonable approximation to the ambient component itself requires a global illumination model. A local illumination model can be used either as a primary illumination model, or as part of a global scheme, as we shall see below.

5.3. Global Illumination Models Based on Ideal Ray Tracing

5.3.1. Strategy

In this section, we shall present a general framework for specifying a large class of global illumination models. *Ray tracing*, a technique popularised by Whitted in [Whit80] is central to this framework. As was mentioned above, however, the semantics of ideal ray tracing also characterises radiosity approaches [CoGr85]. We shall give ideal ray tracing a formal foundation. To encompass wide variety of other ray-tracing approaches, our model is quite general, and we shall formalise Whitted's model as an example. The basic intuition behind the model is as follows. A scene is thought of as a set of objects, a set of initial light sources, and a view point. Light rays are emitted by the light sources, and these rays travel about the scene and change in intensity according to a set of prescribed rules. In such a global scheme, *all objects* are potential light sources.

In addition to a scene specification as outlined in Chapter 1, the illumination model requires some additional information about each object:

- a reflection relation, which gives the set of rays emitted in response to an incident ray.
- a local illumination model, which defines the intensity of these emitted rays. The model can use information such as the direction and intensity of the incoming ray, the object's defined colour, and other physical properties of the object such as its glossiness or opacity.

The set of rays hitting the eye is used to determine the illumination of the scene. It is assumed that the scene is in the desired viewing orientation, but that perspective transformation has not been applied. The intensity function $I(x,y,z)$ defined by this approach will give an intensity value for every visible point in the scene. A perspective transformation could then be applied to this function and to the remainder of the scene as in Chapter 1. This would result in a function $I(x,y)$ over the screen plane, which would be suitable for defining the semantics of rendering (Chapter 3). The definition of this function is given below.

5.3.2. *Formalisation*[2]

Notation. A *point* in $\mathbf{R}^2$ or $\mathbf{R}^3$ will be denoted by an upper-case roman character (e.g. $P(x,y,z) \in \mathbf{R}^3$). A *vector* in $\mathbf{R}^3$ is denoted by an upper-case roman character with a bar over it (e.g., $\bar{N} = (x,y,z) \in \mathbf{R}^3$). Where ambiguous, the components of a vector $\bar{N}$ are denoted by x_N, y_N, $z_N \in \mathbf{R}$. A *ray* in $\mathbf{R}^3$ is a rooted, directed line segment and is denoted by an italic lower-case letter (e.g., r). A ray r is defined by a point of origin $C_r \in \mathbf{R}^3$ and a (unit) direction vector $\bar{D}_r$, and prescribes the following set:

$$r =_{df} \{ C + m\bar{D} : m \in \mathbf{R}^3, m \geq 0 \}. \tag{2}$$

Where unambiguous, the subscript for a ray component will be omitted (as in the above equation). The *dot product* of two vectors will be expressed by the familiar notation

$$\bar{A} \cdot \bar{B} =_{df} x_A x_B + y_A y_B + z_A z_B \in \mathbf{R}. \tag{3}$$

The *magnitude* of a vector $\bar{A}$ is denoted by $|\bar{A}|$ and is defined as

$$|\bar{A}| =_{df} (x_A^2 + y_A^2 + z_A^2)^{1/2} \tag{4}$$
$$= (\bar{A} \cdot \bar{A})^{1/2}.$$

---

[2] The following section is rather technical and requires a number of auxiliary formal mechanisms. If the reader is interested only in the complexity of ray-tracing rather than its full 3-D semantics, then the reader is advised to go on to the next chapter, where a simpler non-geometric subset of this model is redeveloped. The full generality of the model presented in this section is not required to establish the complexity result.

From Chapter 1, assume we have a scene $S = (O_1, \cdots, O_N)$. We shall augment the scene with a set $\mathbf{L}$ of light sources and a point $E \in \mathbf{R}^3$ denoting the eye position. This augmented scene is denoted by S^*.

Definition 2. A *light source* $L \in \mathbf{L}$ is a tuple

$$L =_{df} (l, I_L),\tag{5}$$

where l is a ray defining the path of light emitted by L, and $I_L \in \mathbf{C}$, for colour space $\mathbf{C}$, is its intensity. The set $\mathbf{L}$ can be uncountable.

As indicated above, we extend the definition of each object $O \in S^*$ to contain a *ray-emittance relation*, which may be thought of as an operator that maps incoming light rays to outgoing rays.

Definition 3. A *ray-emittance relation* for each object $O \in S^*$ has the following form.

$$R_O : \mathbf{R}^3 \times \mathbf{R}^3 \times \mathbf{C} \to 2^{\mathbf{R}^3 \times \mathbf{R}^3 \times \mathbf{C}}\tag{6}$$

such that for any incident ray r_0 with intensity I_0,

$$R_O(r_0, I_0) = \{ (a, I_a), (b, I_b), \cdots \}.\tag{7}$$

Many rays can be emitted in response to a single ray. Indeed, the set of emitted rays may be uncountable. While by no means essential to the semantics, a practical model must impose a finite bound on the size of any R_O, possibly tying this bound to the expected resolution or the dynamic range of the display device. Other implementation issues are discussed below. The intensity of each emitted ray is defined by an illumination model for each object. If desired, the intensity of a ray can also be made a function of distance from its origin. For example, one might wish the model to be faithful to the law of physics which states that light intensity at any point along the ray is in an inverse-square relationship with the distance from its origin. Since each object may contain a different local illumination model, this framework provides a very flexible distributed mechanism for controlling and defining realistic (or surrealistic) optical effects.

All light sources and the viewpoint are also thought of as objects with trivial ray-emittance relations:

- if $L = (l, I_L) \in \mathbf{L}$, then for any incident ray r of intensity I,

$$R_L(r, I) =_{df} \{ (l, I_L) \}.\tag{8}$$

- the viewpoint $E \in \mathbf{R}^3$ is an object such that for any ray r of intensity I,

$$R_E(r, I) =_{df} \varnothing. \qquad (9)$$

In other words, a light source emits a ray in only its defined direction and intensity, and the viewpoint of course does not emit light rays; it consumes them. It is easy to extend the definition of a light source to include point and area light sources.

Definition 4. A *ray trace* is a finite sequence of rays with origin some light source in **L**, with the viewpoint as its terminus. We denote such a trace by

$$t = \langle (r_0, I_0, O_0), \cdots, (r_m, I_m, O_m) \rangle, \qquad (10)$$

as illustrated by Figure 1.

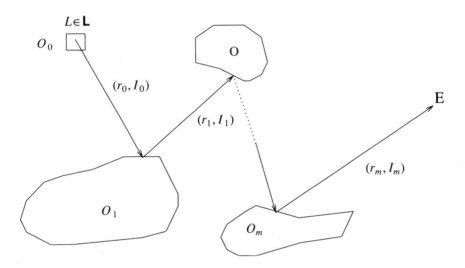

Figure 1. A sample ray trace within a scene.

We denote the *final intensity* of a trace t by F_t. In the trace t above, $F_t = I_m$. A trace t as defined in Eq. (10) must satisfy the following properties.

(0) The origin must be a light source. Namely, for some $L = (l, I_L) \in \mathbf{L}$,

$$O_0 = C_l \quad (\text{recall } l = (C_l, \overline{D}_l)),$$

$$r_0 = l,$$

$$I_0 = I_L.$$

(1) The trace terminates at the eye:

$$O_m = E.$$

(2) Each ray in the trace must be in the emittance rule of the previous ray, and must intersect with a point on the surface of the object (see Figure 1):

$$\forall\, 0 \leq i < m : (r_{i+1}, I_{i+1}) \in R_{O_{i+1}}(r_i, I_i) \;\wedge\; Intersection\,(r_i, r_{i+1}, O_{i+1}).$$

Let $r_1 = (C_1, \overline{D}_1)$, and $r_2 = (C_2, \overline{D}_2)$ be two rays. Then the intersection predicate is defined as

$$Intersection(r_1, r_2, O) =_{df} \tag{11}$$

$$C_2 \in r_1 \cap Z_O \;\wedge\; \forall P \in r_1 \cap Z_O \left(P \neq C_2 \Rightarrow d(C_1, C_2) < d(C_1, P) \right),$$

where $d(P,Q)$ is the euclidean distance between points P and Q, and Z_O is the extent of object O in $\mathbf{R}^3$ (see Chapter 1). Figure 2 illustrates the behaviour of this predicate.

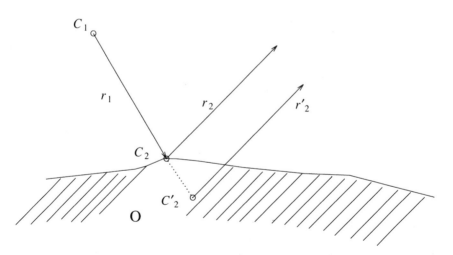

Figure 2. The geometry of intersection. Intersect(r_1, r_2, O) is true, and Intersect(r_1, r'_2, O) is false, because C_2 is closer to C_1 than C'_2.

Definition 5. *Trace* (S^*) denotes the set of all traces t of the form given in Eq. (10). This is the set of all ray traces which begin at a light source and reach the viewpoint.

The vast majority of traces do not reach the eye.

Definition 6. A projection of $Trace\,(S^*)$, $Tr_{S^*}(P)$, for any $P \in \mathbf{R}^3$, denotes the set of ray traces whose penultimate ray terminus is P. Formally,

$$Tr_{S^*}(P) =_{df} \{\, \langle (r_0,I_0,O_0), \cdots, (r_m,I_m,O_m) \rangle \in Trace\,(S^*) : C_{r_m} = P \,\}. \quad (12)$$

Pictorially, $Tr_{S^*}(P)$ contains ray traces of the form depicted in Figure 3.

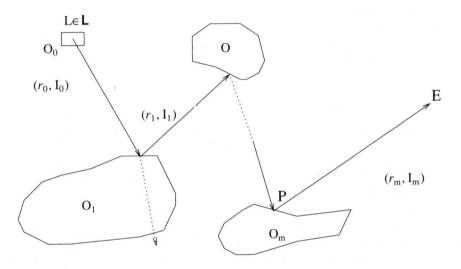

Figure 3. Traces in $Tr_{S^*}(P)$.

Observe that if P is not on the surface of an object in S^*, then $Tr_{S^*}(P) = \emptyset$. Indeed, P must be a point visible from E for the trace set to be non-empty. We are finally in position to define the semantics of a scene illumination function.

Definition 7. Let S^* be an augmented scene as defined above, and let $\mathbf{C}$ be a colour space (see Chapter 1). Then a *ray-traced scene illumination function* $I_{S^*} : \mathbf{R}^3 \to \mathbf{C}$ is of the form

$$I_{S^*}(P) =_{df} \bigotimes_{t \,\in\, Tr_{S^*}(P)} F_t, \quad (13)$$

where $P \in \mathbf{R}^3$, F_t is the final intensity of trace t (see above), and $\otimes$ is an arithmetic function on these intensities. Most frequently, $\otimes$ is simple summation.

The projection of the illumination function from $\mathbf{R}^3$ into screen space is straightforward. It can be done uniquely, because the only points of interest in I_{S*} are those that are visible from the view point, and there is at most one such point for each $(x,y) \in \mathbf{R}^2$ (see Chapter 2). This screen-space intensity function can be defined as

$$I(x,y) =_{df} \begin{cases} I_{S*}(x,y,z) & \text{if } (x,y) \in Vis_S(O) \text{ for some } O \in S. \\ 0 & \text{otherwise.} \end{cases} \tag{14}$$

This states that the intensity of screen position $(x,y) \in \mathbf{R}^2$ is given by the illumination at the point $(x,y,z) \in \mathbf{R}^3$ that is visible from the view point. The set $Vis_S(O)$ is defined in Chapter 2. The screen-space scene illumination function can be used by any rendering mechanism defined in Chapter 3 to determine an image corresponding to scene S.

5.4. An Example: Whitted's Global Illumination Model

The global ray-tracing semantics presented above is very general. To illustrate that fact, we present the semantics of Whitted's original global illumination model, which is the seminal and most popular ray-tracing scheme used today [Whit80]. The semantics presented here is an idealisation of Whitted's model, since ours does not take into account implementation heuristics such as the fact that Whitted traces rays backwards from the eye to the light sources.[3]

To specify an implementation model in our framework, we must specify the behaviour of the ray emittance relation R_O for each object O in the scene, and we must demonstrate how the final trace intensities are used to define the ultimate intensity at each point. In Whitted's model, a ray striking an object typically results in two emitted rays: a *reflected* ray, and a *refracted* ray. [Whit80] also mentions the possibility of simulating duller specular reflections by emitting many reflected rays in different directions. This is a straightforward extension, so we shall omit it from our formalisation of Whitted's model. The scenario we shall assume, then, is illustrated in Figure 4.

The ray-emittance rule for every object defines the rays r_1 and r_2 as follows. Assume we have available the intersection point $P \in \mathbf{R}^3$ on the surface of O, and direction of the normal, $\overline{N}$, to the surface at P. Then $r_1 =_{df} (C_1, \overline{D}_1)$, where

$$C_1 = P \tag{15}$$

and

---

[3] In practice this often yields a significant reduction in the number of rays traced. However, it will yield incorrect results for shadows and for all diffuse and secondary illumination effects [FiFo88].

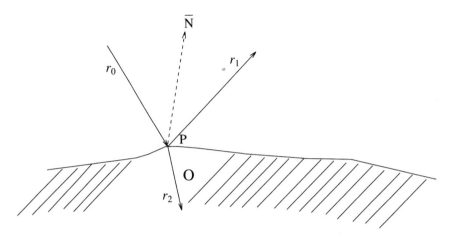

Figure 4. Classic optical reflection/refraction geometry. $\overline{N}$ is the normal to intersection point P on object surface, r_0 is the incident light ray $(C_0, \overline{D}_0)$, r_1 is the reflected light ray $(C_1, \overline{D}_1)$, and r_2 is the refracted light ray $(C_2, \overline{D}_2)$.

$$\overline{D}_1 = \overline{V} + 2\overline{N}. \tag{16}$$

The auxiliary vector $\overline{V}$ is defined as

$$\overline{V} = \frac{\overline{D}_0}{|\overline{D}_0 \cdot \overline{N}|}. \tag{17}$$

The refracted ray r_2 is defined to be $(C_2, \overline{D}_2)$, where

$$C_2 = P \tag{18}$$

and

$$\overline{D}_2 = \frac{(\overline{N} + \overline{V})}{(\eta^2 |\overline{V}|^2 - |\overline{V} + \overline{N}|^2)^{\frac{1}{2}}} - \overline{N}, \tag{19}$$

and η is the index of refraction. The reflection direction given by Eq. (16) simply states that the object is thought of as a perfect mirror: the angle of incidence is equal to the angle of reflection. The refraction direction given by Eq. (19) is Snell's law: an incident ray is transmitted into an object in a direction determined by the object's index of refraction.

Two simple local illumination models are used to define the intensities of the above rays:

$$I_{r_1} =_{df} I_a + I_d + I_s, \tag{20}$$

and

$$I_{r_2} =_{df} I_t. \tag{21}$$

The first model defines the intensity of a reflected ray, and the second defines the intensity of a transmitted ray. These parameters have the following meaning.

I_a is a term approximating the ambient light equally illuminating all objects in the scene. This is often set to an *ad hoc* value.

I_d is the diffuse (non-glossy) reflection at point P. As noted by Whitted, in an ideal model, it would include a term for reflections of nearby objects, but for computational reasons, he defines the diffuse component of the reflectance model as a simple Lambert's law equation (which is essentially a cosine law):

$$I_d =_{df} k_d \sum_{L \in \mathbf{L}} (\bar{N} \cdot \bar{D}_L), \tag{22}$$

where $\bar{D}_L$ is the direction vector of light source L, and k_d is a diffuse reflection factor. Very good approximations for I_a and I_d can be found in the radiosity literature (e.g., [CoGr85]).

I_s is the specular (glossy) reflection at point P:

$$I_s =_{df} k_s S, \tag{23}$$

where S is the intensity of light from $\bar{D}_1$, the direction of r_1, and k_s is the specular reflection constant. S may itself be an expression modelling the local specular properties of the object at P.

I_t is the light transmission through the object from point P:

$$I_t =_{df} k_t T, \tag{24}$$

where T is the intensity of light from $\bar{D}_2$, the direction of r_2, and k_t is the transmission coefficient. As with S above, T can be an expression modelling local refractive behaviour.

Both k_s and k_t are held constant in Whitted's model, but should actually vary to model the Fresnel reflection law.[4] Whitted discusses several other ways of varying the parameters of the above model to achieve interesting effects.

Whitted's model is completely specified once we indicate how rays in the same trace set $Tr_{S*}(P)$ are combined to define $I(P)$. In this case, summation is used. That is,

$$I_{S*}(P) =_{df} \sum_{t \in Tr_{S*}(P)} F_t. \tag{25}$$

---

[4] Very loosely, this law states that the above coefficients should vary with the incidence angle of r_0, and with the physical composition of the object being modelled.

5.5. Discussion

5.5.1. Illumination and Rendering

In our characterisation of the structure of raster graphics, the notions of visibility, rendering, and illumination have been treated separately. This separation does not generally exist in practice. Typically, graphics systems will interleave these components so that an image can by synthesised as quickly as possible. In Chapter 3, we were careful to distinguish between *what* is to be sampled, namely an illumination function, from *how* this function is to be sampled to derive an intensity for a given pixel. The coupling is a close one, and clearly there is little point in evaluating an illumination function about some point or area if a rendering scheme makes no use of the result. Consequently, it is advisable to employ lazy evaluation on an illumination function, that is, computing an illumination value only when a renderer insists on it. A complementary approach is to derive shading algorithms that facilitate the use of incremental techniques for quickly evaluating illumination functions. Two examples of this are so-called *Phong* and *Gouraud* shading [NeSp78; FoDa82].[5] While such approaches are still effective in traditional scan-line graphics systems, they are not particularly useful for speeding up implementations of illumination models that based on ray tracing or radiosity. This is because the basic assumptions of screen-space *coherence* on which these shading algorithms are based tend not to extend to the 3-D sampling of space required by global illumination models.

5.5.2. Alternative Models for Light Sources

In the semantics of illumination models presented above, light sources were modelled as point sources that each emit a single, infinitesimally-thin beam of light in a specific direction, and of a specific intensity. This would be somewhat akin to aiming a very thin laser beam of a given colour in a given direction. Normally, one would require a very large number of rays for the model to be realistic. There are many other possible ways to model light sources which can easily be incorporated into our semantics. Let us consider some useful alternatives.

Ray Coherence. Instead of thinking of huge numbers of single light rays bouncing around in a scene, one might consider grouping them into geometrically tractable entities. This is another example of a coherence assumption in computer graphics: the grouping is effective if large numbers of spatially close rays behave similarly. This approach has some useful benefits, such as the ability to produce soft shadows in a relatively easy way. Several researchers have developed ray-coherence schemes: J. Amanatides, who uses cones, and Heckbert and Hanrahan, who use parallelopipeds [Aman84; HeHa84]. Amanatides was the first to develop

---

[5] This is as distinct from *Phong illumination*, which was discussed above.

simulations of umbral and penumbral shadow regions as well as area-sampling rendering techniques within a ray-traced environment. Formally, these approaches are extensions of the notion of a ray, and easily fit into our scheme, at the expense of more complicated semantics. In particular, the semantics of intersection becomes more complex, since one now must consider areas of intersection. While cones and parallelopipeds are relatively tractable objects, their intersection with surfaces in all but very simple cases yields complex geometric results. On the whole, the structure of the semantics above is not affected by such ray-coherence methods, although its implementation may become more problematic [Aman88].

Light Ray Distributions. Under the semantics above, the only way of modelling a light source which illuminates a broad region of space is by defining a large set of rays approximating the region covered by the light source. The coherence schemes mentioned above are possible alternatives, as is modelling the light source by a relation which emits a set of light rays in accordance with some defined light distribution relation. The same approach can be taken to model the distribution of rays resulting from a ray intersection [Blin77; CoTo82]. This scheme fits nicely into our semantics.

More Realistic Illumination Models. It has been often mentioned that more realistic illumination models are obtained if the wavelengths of the light travelling around a scene are also considered (e.g. [Blin77; CoTa82]). What this translates into in practice is a more complicated intensity calculation for rays reflecting off or refracting into objects. Assuming this effect can be captured mathematically, our model certainly accommodates its specification.

5.6. Conclusions

This chapter has presented a basic structure for specifying the semantics of arbitrary local and global ray-oriented illumination models. As an example, an idealisation of Whitted's global illumination model was presented. Also considered was the relationship between illumination and rendering within a graphics system. It was concluded that a lazy evaluation of an illumination function at the rendering stage is likely to be of greatest practical benefit. It was also seen that our framework can be extended quite naturally to alternative representations of light sources.

6 The Complexity of Abstract Ray Tracing

For the case of surfaces aligned in such a way that a branch of a tree [of ray tracings] has infinite depth, the branch is truncated at the point where it exceeds the allotted storage.

−T. Whitted[1]

Synopsis. Ray-tracing algorithms, while capable of producing images of great realism and visual complexity, are computationally expensive in practice. Until now, the computational complexity of the ray-tracing problem has not been considered formally. In this chapter, we show that an abstract form of the problem is in fact PSPACE-complete, which puts its complexity status at or beyond NP-completeness. Thus the abstract ray-tracing problem is probably intractable. This complexity result is established by demonstrating that any polynomially space-bounded deterministic Turing machine can be transformed in polynomial time to an instance of the ray-tracing problem. Also considered are more general forms of the ray-tracing problem and their relationship to natural and graphical illumination. This chapter is independent of the previous chapter, which allows the definition of ray-tracing models of much greater power than those considered here.

---

[1] T. Whitted [Whit80:p345].

6.1. Introduction

Ray-tracing algorithms are now widespread in computer graphics systems, and have been used to generate some of the most vivid computer-synthesised images to date. The basic operation of these algorithms is very simple [Whit80]. The illumination of a scene is determined by following the paths taken by rays of light emanating from light sources, as they are reflected or refracted by objects in the scene. These paths, or *ray traces*, can be of arbitrary length. The traces which ultimately reach the eye determine the intensity of the pixel through which these traces pass. Informally, the *ray-tracing problem* is that of computing the intensity of each pixel with respect to a given scene containing a set of objects and light sources. The intensity of each pixel is a function of the intensities of all rays passing through the pixel and reaching the eye. To reduce the number of traces to be considered, ray-tracing algorithms often work in reverse, tracing rays back from the eye to a light source. However, reversed ray tracing is not always correct. Indeed, Fiume and Fournier [FiFo88] prove the following distressing facts about the limits to the correctness of traditional ray tracing (from the eye):

- The computed intensity of a pixel can be incorrect by an arbitrary amount.

- The size of a ray-trace tree, can, under realistic conditions, be extremely large.

- The uncertainty of intersection calculations can grow extremely quickly.

Under the circumstances, it appears worthwhile to develop formal models of ray tracing and to examine further their expected behaviour.

In effect, ray tracing embodies a particle model view of natural scene illumination. As described in Chapter 5, it is a sufficiently general approach to permit the accurate modelling of glossy objects, multiple reflections, refraction, and shadows (to some extent). However, a price is paid for such realism: ray-tracing algorithms are computationally expensive. It seems that there is no obvious way of making the process of tracing the rays through a general scene efficient, that is, computable in polynomial time with respect to the size of the scene description. This has led us to consider the computational complexity of ray tracing in a more theoretical way.

Our approach will be as follows. A formal model for ray tracing will be defined. Objects in the model are endowed with the power to compute ray-emission functions. When these functions are allowed to be polynomial-*time* computable in this model, it will be seen that the problem of determining whether or not a single ray originally emitted from a light source reaches the eye is polynomial-*space* complete. This result is presented in Section 2. In Section 3, we consider general classes of ray tracing problems which are parameterised by the complexity class allowed for object ray-emission functions. Our ultimate goal of this structural investigation is to classify the ray-emission behaviour of objects both natural and artificial in terms of their computational complexity, and to determine the induced complexity of the ray-tracing problem. While we only scratch the surface of this ambitious goal, a foundation for such an undertaking is laid in this chapter. In Section 4, we discuss the relevance of our model to illumination in nature and in computer graphics. The next section presents some basic notions from computational complexity and defines an abstract ray-tracing model.

6.2. Preliminaries

6.2.1. Computational Complexity Terminology

This chapter assumes some familiarity with basic notions of complexity theory such as deterministic and nondeterministic Turing machines, polynomial-time reductions, and NP-completeness [GaJo79]. A problem Π is in *PSPACE* if Π is computed by a deterministic Turing machine M_Π such that the number of tape squares used by M_Π is bounded by a polynomial $p(n)$, where n is the input size. In this chapter, we shall only consider Turing machines that have a single tape which is infinite to the right. The initial input string is assumed to be placed in the n leftmost tape squares, and computation begins on the rightmost character of the input string. The number of tape squares used by a Turing machine is given by the furthest tape position to the right the machine ever reaches during its computation. PSPACE includes all of NP, including of course the NP-complete problems, as Figure 1 suggests.

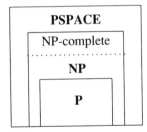

Figure 1. Complexity class hierarchy.

It is conjectured that $P \subset NP \subset PSPACE$ [GaJo79]. A problem Π is *PSPACE-hard* if every problem in PSPACE polynomially reduces to Π. This means that any polynomially space-bounded deterministic Turing machine M can be transformed in polynomial time to an instance of Π. Π is *PSPACE-complete* if it is PSPACE-hard and if Π is itself in PSPACE. The computation time of a Turing machine solving a problem in PSPACE may be exponential, and it is believed that this is indeed the case for PSPACE-complete problems.

6.2.2. An Abstract Ray-Tracing Model

The framework defined in the last chapter allows one to define obviously intractable ray-tracing models. We shall instead work with a more abstract model and problem in order to highlight some critical aspects of ray tracing. The benefits and shortcomings of the model are discussed later. An instance of the *abstract ray-tracing problem* (ARTP) is given by a tuple $R = \langle S, E, \{O_1, O_2, \cdots, O_n\}\rangle$, where S is a light source description, E is the eye, and each O_i is an object in the scene. For conceptual simplicity, we shall denote rays by their source or destination. The notation $\rightarrow O$ means that a ray is directed to object O, $O \rightarrow$ means that object O has emitted a ray, and $O_j \rightarrow O_k$ means that O_j has directed a ray to O_k. We shall indicate the intensity i of the ray in this notation by

$$O_j \underset{i}{\rightarrow} O_k .$$

This notation allows us to avoid a formal definition of ray-object intersection (see Chapter 5), which, while very time-consuming in practice, we have chosen to abstract away. S and E are in effect special objects in that S can only transmit rays (but not receive), and E can only receive (but not transmit). A ray tracing is initiated by the following action of the light source S:

$$S \underset{i_0}{\rightarrow} O .$$

$S \rightarrow O$ is a single ray of intensity $i_0 \in \mathbf{N}$ emitted to a specific object $O \in \{O_1, \cdots, O_n\}$. Each object $O \in \{O_1, \cdots, O_n\}$, is endowed with a *ray-emittance function* R_O which is made up of a set of rules of the form:

$$R_O(O_j \rightarrow, i_1) = (\rightarrow O_k, i_2), \tag{1a}$$

or

$$R_O(\rightarrow O, i_1) = (\rightarrow O_k, i_2). \tag{1b}$$

for objects O_j, O_k and integers i_1, i_2. A rule of form 1(a) states that if a ray of intensity i_1 from object O_j is directed to (i.e., incident with) O, then O will emit a ray of intensity i_2 to object O_k. A rule of form 1(b) is a shorthand for

$$\forall 1 \leq j \leq n \ \big(R_O(O_j \rightarrow, i_1) = (\rightarrow O_k, i_2)\big) . \tag{1c}$$

Rather than providing an explicit enumeration of all intensity values over which a ray-emission rule is defined, it is permissible instead to write a function mapping free variables O_j and i_1 to values O_k and i_2. Examples of such rules can be found below. If a ray-emission function is not defined for an incoming ray of a given intensity, then no ray is emitted in response. Note that we permit the direction of an outgoing ray to be dependent on the incoming ray's orientation and intensity. However, we insist that R_O for every object O be computable in time polynomially bounded in the number of objects and intensity size in bits. More specifically, we assume that the model of computation for each of the n R_O's is a circuit which realises a function mapping an incident direction and m-bit intensity to an emitted direction and m-bit intensity. The size of each R_O in gates is restricted to being $O(p(m+n))$ for some polynomial p. Thus the circuit also runs in time $O(p(m+n))$. This expression involves n, the number of objects, because directions are given in terms of objects. We define the size of the scene instance R as the sum of the sizes of all such R_O's, S, and E. It will be seen that our main PSPACE-completeness result only requires ray-emission functions that can perform a single compare operation on a constant number of bits (after their location is found from among a polynomial number of bits) and a constant number of bit rearrangements.

We define $Trace_R(S,O)$ to be the set of distinct *ray traces*, or sequences of ray transmissions, in scene R from the light source S to object O. All traces $t \in Trace_R(S,O)$ are of the form

$$S \underset{i_0}{\to} O_1 \underset{i_1}{\to} \cdots \underset{i_m}{\to} O, \qquad (2)$$

such that for $1 \leq j < m$,

$$R_{O_j}(O_{j-1} \to, i_j) = (\to O_{j+1}, i_{j+1}),$$

with $S = O_0$ and $O = O_{m+1}$. In the present model, the cardinality of any trace set is zero or one. An alternative model defined later will permit much larger trace sets. If $t \in Trace_R(S,O)$, we define F_t to be the *final intensity* of the ray t striking O (e.g., F_t in equation (2) is i_m).

Remark 1. It is not important in which direction the ray tracing is performed. That is, if R^* is R with reversed ray-emission rules, then $Trace_R(S,O) = Trace_{R^*}(O,S)$.

We are now in a position to define our first problem precisely.

Abstract Ray-Tracing Problem (ARTP)
INSTANCE: Scene $R = \langle S,E,\{ O_1, \cdots, O_N \} \rangle$ as defined above.
QUESTION: Is $Trace_R(S,E)$ non-empty? That is, does there exist in R a trace

$$S \underset{i_0}{\to} O_1 \underset{i_1}{\to} O_2 \underset{i_2}{\to} \cdots \underset{i_{m-1}}{\to} O_m \underset{i_m}{\to} E? \qquad (3)$$

Later, we shall discuss the relationship between this ray-tracing problem and illumination effects encountered in computer graphics and nature.

6.3. The Results

6.3.1. The Complexity of ARTP

We now state and prove the basic result of this chapter.

Theorem 1. *ARTP is PSPACE-complete.*

Remark 2. This result is an instance of a more general class of ray-tracing problems. We discuss this class in Section 4.

Proof. First, we note that ARTP is in PSPACE. Observe that there is precisely one ray that can be emitted by an object after receiving a ray whose intensity and orientation is in the domain of its ray-emission function. Thus a naive ray-tracing procedure need only follow the path of the trace by referring to successive ray-emission functions. The entire trace, which could easily be exponential in length, need not itself be stored. Rather, only the previous ray in the trace is needed in order to compute the next ray. Thus our storage requirements are clearly dominated by the circuit size of the ray-emission functions, which are certainly in PSPACE. Hence ARTP is in PSPACE.

In passing, note from the above discussion that it is not at all obvious that ARTP is in NP, for a possible trace that is "guessed" may require exponential verification time and may be exponentially long.

We now show that ARTP is PSPACE-hard. We are given an arbitrary deterministic Turing machine $M = (Q, \Sigma, \delta, s, h)$, and input string $w = \sigma_1 \sigma_2 \cdots \sigma_n \in \Sigma^*$, where $Q = \{ q_1, \cdots, q_r \}$ is the state set, Σ is the tape alphabet, δ is the state-transition function, $s \in Q$ is the start state, and $h \in Q$ is the (accepting) halt state. We further suppose that M has a single one-way infinite tape and that the amount of space used by M is bounded by a polynomial $p(n)$ with respect to input size n.[2] The language accepted by M is denoted by L_M. Our goal is to transform M in polynomial time to an instance R_M of the ARTP such that

$$w \in L_M \iff Trace_{R_M}(S, E) \neq \varnothing.$$

In our reduction, S will correspond to the start state, s, of M, and also depends on w; E corresponds to the halt state, h, of M. Our strategy is to encode the contents of M's tape as an intensity and define a set of objects in instance R_M such

---

[2] In fact, the problem of determining whether or not a deterministic Turing machine which never uses more than n tape squares accepts its input is PSPACE-complete. Thus we could restrict our argument to such Turing machines (i.e., those with $p(n)=n$) [Karp72; GaJo79].

that a state transition in M corresponds to a ray emission in R_M. We must be careful to ensure that the description of R_M is of polynomial size, for otherwise our transformation of M to R_M would be non-polynomial.

Construction. Given M as above, we define R_M to have $O(p(n))$ objects. In fact, one object is computationally sufficient to perform the entire Turing machine simulation; this would involve encoding M's tape contents, current state, and current tape head position into a single intensity value. However, the simulation we shall use has an appealing geometric configuration (should that be desirable) in which a state change in M results in a ray-emission to a nearby object; moreover, the complexity of each object is very easy to see. For each possible tape head position, character under tape head, and state (other than h) in M, we shall define an object. Each object encodes a possible *state configuration* of M. We denote such an object by $q : \sigma : x$, $q \in Q$, $\sigma \in \Sigma$, and $1 \leq x \leq p(n)$. It is easy to orient these objects in $\mathbf{N}^3$ such that any two objects corresponding to configurations of M whose tape positions differ by 0 or 1 can be linked by a line segment (i.e., ray) without hitting another object.[3] One possibility is to place each object on one of $p(n)$ digital circles which decrease in radius as the tape position increases. All objects denoting the same tape position are placed on the same circle. Arcs to the left of a given circle x correspond to tape positions $y < x$, and similarly with arcs to the right of x. The light source is placed on circle n (the tape position of the initial configuration). The eye is placed sufficiently far away from the circles so that it may be linked to any object by an uninterrupted line segment. Figure 2 illustrates the arrangement.

Each digital circle must contain a constant number of distinct objects (points or small areas). Straightforward linear-time algorithms exist to draw circles [NeSp79], and exactly $p(n)$ such circles are required. Thus the orientation of all objects in R_M can be accomplished in polynomial time.

Formally, given M, we define an instance of ARTP, R_M, as follows.

$$R_M =_{df} \langle S, E, \{ q : \sigma : i \mid q \in Q - \{ s, h \}, \sigma \in \Sigma, 1 \leq i \leq p(n) \} \rangle. \qquad (4)$$

We shall refine this definition presently. Since the number of tape squares used by M is bounded by $p(n)$, only the first $p(n)$ tape squares of M need be considered in any computation of M with an input string of size n. Therefore, the relevant portion of M's tape can be coded into an integer of size $O(p(n))$, and in particular of size $\log(|\Sigma|)p(n)$ bits.[4] The ray-tracing instance of M, R_M, will

---

[3] This is not strictly necessary, since we have abstracted intersection details from the ray-tracing model; however, it is a useful exercise to show that this model is in fact geometrically valid.

[4] We assume that at any point in the computation, the unused portion of the tape at the right-hand end is padded with blanks. See also footnote 2. Later, we shall address the issue of the *precision* re-

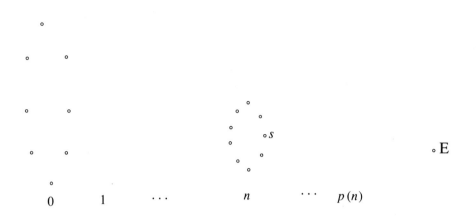

Figure 2. Geometric representation of Turing machine states. Each small circle represents a possible state of the machine at a specific tape head position from 0 to $p(n)$.

encode the tape contents into the intensities of the rays being traced. If $w \in \Sigma^*$ denotes the current tape contents, then $[w] \in \mathbf{N}$ refers to its encoding. The notation $[w]@i$ denotes the encoding of the ith character on the tape (numbering from the left-hand end). Since these encodings are just natural numbers, the elements of a coding can quickly be extracted, moved, or changed either by using basic logic gate operations or by using the usual integer arithmetic operations on $\mathbf{N}$. To be entirely precise, objects of the form $q : \alpha{:}\, i$ should actually be labelled $q :[\alpha]{:}\, i$, but we will use the former labelling for clarity.

The light source S initiates the ray tracing by emitting the following ray:

$$S \underset{i_0}{\rightarrow} O ,$$

where $i_0 = [wB_n]$, w is the string input to the Turing machine M, and B_n is $p(n) - n$ blanks. The destination object O is chosen as per the rules to follow.

The state-transition function of M will be simulated by the ray-emission functions belonging to each object in R_M, which we shall now define. Let $ua\underline{\alpha}bv$ denote the tape contents of M at some arbitrary stage in its computation, where $u, v \in \Sigma^*$, $a, b, \alpha \in \Sigma$, and the underscore refers to the tape position. The notation

$$u_0\, \underline{\alpha}v_0 \vdash_M u_1\, \beta v_1$$

indicates the change to the tape contents after exactly one step (or transition) in the execution of M. There are three types of non-halting transition rules in M: the tape head can be moved to the right, it can be moved to the left, or a character can be written in the tape square currently pointed to by the tape head. We now define the ray-emission rules based on these possible transitions.

(1) $\delta(p,\alpha)=(q,R)$, $q \neq h$. This corresponds to the transition $ua\underline{\alpha}bv \vdash_M ua\alpha\underline{b}v$. In this case, for all objects of the form $p : \alpha{:}\, j$, $1 \leq j \leq p\,(n)$,

$$R_{p\,:\,\alpha{:}\,j}(\rightarrow p : \alpha{:}\, j, i_1) =_{df} (\rightarrow Q, i_2), \text{ where}$$

> if $i_1@\mathrm{j} = [\alpha]$ then
> $\quad i_2 = i_1,$
> $\quad Q = q : i_1@k{:}k \quad (k = j+1)$
> else
> $\quad$ no ray emitted.

The above rule states that if the incoming intensity has an α encoded at position j of the tape, then emit a new ray of the same intensity as the incident ray (since the tape is unchanged), and direct the ray to the object which encodes a configuration with the tape head position moved one square to the right. Otherwise, no ray is emitted. Since M is deterministic, *all* objects of the form $p{:}\alpha{:}1, \cdots, p{:}\alpha{:}p\,(n)$ have only this easily computable rule in their ray-emission tables.

(2) $\delta(p,\alpha)=(q,L)$, $q \neq h$. This corresponds to the transition $ua\underline{\alpha}bv \vdash_M u\underline{a}\alpha bv$. In this case, for all objects of the form $p : \alpha{:}\, j$, $1 \leq j \leq p\,(n)$,

$$R_{p\,:\,\alpha{:}\,j}(\rightarrow p : \alpha{:}\, j, i_1) =_{df} (\rightarrow Q, i_2), \text{ where}$$

> if $i_1@\mathrm{j} = [\alpha]$ then
> $\quad i_2 = i_1,$
> $\quad Q = q : i_1@k{:}k \quad (k = j-1)$
> else
> $\quad$ no ray emitted.

(3) $\delta(p,\alpha)=(q,\beta)$, $q \neq h$, $\beta \in \Sigma$. This corresponds to the transition $ua\underline{\alpha}bv \vdash_M ua\underline{\beta}bv$. In this case, for all objects of the form $p : \alpha{:}\, j$, $1 \leq j \leq p\,(n)$,

$$R_{p\,:\,\alpha{:}\,j}(\rightarrow p : \alpha{:}\, j, i_1) =_{df} (\rightarrow Q, i_2), \text{ where}$$

> if $i_1@\mathrm{j} = [\alpha]$ then
> $\quad i_2@k = i_1@k, \text{ for } k \neq j$
> $\quad i_2@j = \beta,$
> $\quad Q = q {:}\beta{:}j$
> else
> $\quad$ no ray emitted.

(4) We now handle halting configurations: $\delta(p, \alpha) = (h, \beta)$, $\beta \in \Sigma \cup \{ L, R \}$. This corresponds to the transition $ua\underline{\alpha}bv \vdash_M w$ where w is the appropriate terminating configuration depending on the value of β. In this case, we define a rule to emit a ray to the eye. All objects of the form $p : \alpha: j$, $1 \leq j \leq p(n)$, will send a ray directly to object E, since our construction has ensured that an uninterrupted line segment can join any object and E. Thus we have:

$$R_{p : \alpha: j}(\to p : \alpha: j, i_1) =_{df} (\to E, i_2), \text{ where}$$

> if $i_1 @ j = [\alpha]$ then
> $\quad i_2 = w \quad$ (see (1)-(3) above),
> else
> $\quad$ no ray emitted.

To complete the construction, we must state how the tracing commences. If $w = \sigma_1 \cdots \sigma_n \in \Sigma^*$ is the input to M, we define the light source S in R_M to have initial intensity $i_0 = [\sigma_1 \cdots \sigma_n B_n]$, where B_n is $p(n) - n$ blanks. S will direct a single light ray to object $p : \alpha: m$, where $p \in Q$ is the state for which the transition $\delta(s, \sigma_n) = (p, \beta)$ is in M, and (α, m) is one of $([\sigma_{n-1}], n-1)$, $([\sigma], n)$, or $([` `], n+1)$, depending on whether β is 'L', $\sigma \in \Sigma$, or 'R' (see points (1)-(3) above).

Although rather detailed, the transformation of M to R_M can be accomplished in polynomial time, for R_M contains $O(p(n))$ objects, each with a small, fast rayemission function. Indeed, a circuit realising a ray-emission function only requires the ability to set a constant number of bits to a constant value (passing the other bits unchanged), and a single compare operation on a constant number of bits, after finding the appropriate location in the intensity value for the comparison. These functions can be generated directly from M's state-transition table (which itself can be encoded with constant space complexity with respect to $|\Sigma|$ and $|Q|$). Moreover, note that all integers in R_M are of length at most $\log|\Sigma| p(n)$ (i.e., integers are $O(p(n))$ in size). Thus the transformation of M to R_M takes $O(p(n))$ time.

Lemma 1. $w \in L_M \Leftrightarrow Trace_{R_M}(S, E) \neq \emptyset$.

Proof. Suppose $w = \sigma_1 \cdots \sigma_n \in L_M$. Then M accepts w, and so there is a sequence of configurations which trace the computation of M on w. Let this sequence be $\omega_0 \vdash_M \omega_1 \vdash_M \cdots \vdash_M \omega_m$, where each ω_i is a pair of the form (q_i, w_i), $w_i = u_i \underline{\alpha_i} v_i \in \Sigma^+$, $q_i \in Q$, $\alpha_i \in \Sigma$, $u_i, v_i \in \Sigma^*$. In particular, $\omega_0 = (s, \sigma_1 \cdots \underline{\sigma_n} B_n)$, and $\omega_m = (h, w_m B_{|w_m|})$. Let $T_i = |u_i| + 1$, which is the tape position of α_i). Then by the construction of R_M, there must exist a trace

$$S \underset{W_0}{\to} q_1 : \alpha_1 : T_1 \underset{W_1}{\to} \cdots \underset{W_{m-1}}{\to} q_m : \alpha_m : T_m \underset{W_m}{\to} E,$$

where W_i stands for $[w_i B_{|w_i|}]$.

Thus $Trace_{R_M}(S,E)$ is non-empty. An identical argument establishes the converse. Thus the lemma and theorem follow.

6.3.2. An Alternative Ray-Tracing Model

The ray-emission rules within the simple ray tracing model defined above allow the direction of an emitted ray to be a function of both the incident ray's direction and intensity. The proof of Theorem 1 relies on this, since a ray is directed to an object on the basis of the tape contents, which is encoded as an intensity. While we argue below that this is not a shortcoming of either the model or proof, it might be argued that this is not a common property of current ray-tracing algorithms.

In this section, we show that even if this assumption is replaced by a more "realistic" one, ray-tracing is still PSPACE-complete. We shall make one change to the ray-tracing model, and one to the nature of the question asked in the problem. The model is changed by prohibiting object ray-emission rules to direct emitted rays on the basis of incident intensity. However, we *do* allow a bounded number of rays to be emitted in response to a single incident ray. This is entirely consistent with ray-tracing algorithms of today, since this is the technique commonly used to simulate dull reflections, for example (see below and [Whit80; CoPC84]). Formally, we redefine the ray-emission function, R_O, for a given object O, to be a relation:

$$R_O(\overline{O}\rightarrow, i) = \{ (\rightarrow O_1, i_1), \cdots, (\rightarrow O_K, i_K) \};\qquad(5)$$

for all objects O, $\overline{O}$, $|R_O(\overline{O}\rightarrow, i)| \leq N$. The set $Trace_R(S,E)$ can now contain a large number of valid traces rather than just one or zero. The circuit model described above for ray-emission functions can be extended in the obvious way to relations.

Ray-tracing is concerned not only with whether or not a ray reaches the eye, but also with whether its contribution to the intensity of the pixel is non-negligible. That is, does a trace have an intensity greater than a given threshold? We shall incorporate this notion into the statement of a "realistic" ray-tracing problem.

"Realistic" Ray-Tracing Problem (RRTP)

INSTANCE: Scene $R = \langle S, E, \{ O_1, \cdots, O_N \} \rangle$ with modified ray-emission rules as defined in (5) above and $\varepsilon > 0$.
QUESTION: Does there exist a trace $t \in Trace_R(S,E)$ such that $F_t > \varepsilon$? That is, does there exist in R a trace

$$S \to O_1 \to O_2 \to \cdots \to O_m \to E$$
$$i_0 \quad i_1 \quad i_2 \quad\quad i_{m-1} \quad i_m$$

such that $i_m > \varepsilon$?

Theorem 2. *RRTP is PSPACE-hard.*

Proof. Given deterministic Turing machine M as defined earlier, we construct an instance R_M of RRTP in an almost identical fashion to that in the above proof. We shall note some of the changes. The intensity of a ray will still be used to encode the tape contents. However, we shall be encoding the tape in base $|\Sigma|+2$ rather than in base $|\Sigma|$, reserving the digits 0 and 1 for other purposes. Instead of directing a single ray on the basis of the incident intensity (i.e., the encoded value of the current tape contents), each state will emit $|\Sigma|$ rays, but only special rays will be assigned intensities corresponding to correct tape configurations of M. The other rays will be given intensity ε which we shall set to the integer 1 followed by $p(n)-1$ zeros. Note that every valid tape configuration must have an integral encoding greater than ε. Thus R_M will contain a trace with final intensity greater than ε given initial intensity $[w]$ if and only if M accepts w.

To illustrate how the new ray-emission rules are constructed, we consider the rules corresponding to the following transition in M:

$$\delta(p,\alpha) = (q,\beta), \quad \alpha,\beta \in \Sigma, \; p,q \in Q.$$

Each object in R_M of the form $p : \alpha{:}\, j, \; 1 \le j \le p(n)$ is defined to have the following ray-emission rule:

$$R_{p:\alpha:j}(\to p : \alpha{:}\, j, i) = \{ (\to q : \sigma_1{:}\, j, i_1), \; \cdots, (\to q : \sigma_{|\Sigma|}{:}\, j, i_{|\Sigma|}) \},$$

where $\forall\, 1 \le k \le |\Sigma|$,

    if $i@j = [\alpha]$ and $[\sigma_k] = [\beta]$ then
        $i_k = i$,
        $i_k@j = \beta$,
    else
        $i_k = \varepsilon$.

The idea is that given an incident ray from a specific object, rays are always transmitted to the same set of objects. However, only one ray transmits the correct encoded tape configuration. The other rays are each given intensity ε which remains unchanged on the subsequent ray emissions in the trace.

For a right-tape transition, $\delta(p,\alpha) = (q,R)$, at most one i_k in $R_{p:\alpha:j}(\to p : \alpha{:}\, j, i)$ is set to i, corresponding to the state $q : \sigma_k{:}\, i_k$ such that $i@j = [\alpha]$ and $i@(j+1) = [\sigma_k]$. All other intensities are set to ε. Similarly for left tape transitions.

Clearly, this is a polynomial-time reduction and furthermore,

$$w \in L_m \Leftrightarrow \exists\, t \in Trace_{R_M}(S,E) : I_t > \varepsilon.$$

The theorem follows.

Remark 3. It appears difficult to establish an upper bound that RRTP is indeed in PSPACE. See the following discussion on counting ray traces.

6.3.3. Counting Ray Traces

Until now we have considered the problem of whether at least one ray trace exists between a light source and the eye in a given scene. Since every ray-tracing procedure must compute such a predicate, the negative complexity results proved above are persuasive evidence that a polynomial-time algorithm for ray-tracing will not be discovered. However, the situation appears to be even worse, for as will be seen in this section, the problem of counting the number of ray traces between the light source and the eye is PSPACE-hard, and perhaps not even in PSPACE. Since the problem of computing the intensity of a pixel involves knowing how many rays pass through that pixel on their way to the eye, the overall complexity of the ray-tracing problem is at least as bad. Let $RT(R, \varepsilon)$ denote the set of ray traces in R with final intensity greater than ε. Formally,

$$RT(R, \varepsilon) =_{df} \{ t \in Trace_R(S,E) : F_t > \varepsilon \}. \tag{6}$$

Ray-Trace Counting Problem (RTCP)
INSTANCE: Scene R and $\varepsilon > 0$ as in RRTP.
QUESTION: What is $|RT(R, \varepsilon)|$?

Theorem 3. *RTCP is PSPACE-hard.*

Proof. This is obvious, since given R and ε, an instance of RRTP is solved by asking whether $|RT(R, \varepsilon)| > 0$. Thus RRTP polynomially reduces to RTCP, and since RRTP is PSPACE-complete by Theorem 2, RTCP must be PSPACE-hard.

Showing that RTCP is in PSPACE does not appear to be easy to establish. This is because one must be able to count the number of ray-traces (which could each require exponential space to store) without duplication. We must therefore find some canonical enumeration of such ray traces. An alternate approach would be to use ARTP repeatedly on slightly modified instances of the given scene. However, it is not clear how to derive an overall count from the counts of specific sub-problems.

As the last topic of this section, we finally define a more general ray-tracing problem formally and state a rather obvious result. For the purposes of this chapter, we shall assume that all valid traces pertain to a single pixel whose intensity we wish to compute. Obviously the complexity of computing the intensity of all pixels in a display differs by only a constant factor.

Ray-Tracing Problem (RTP)
INSTANCE: Scene R, $\varepsilon > 0$ as in RRTP.
QUESTION: What is the intensity of the pixel, defined as

$$I =_{df} \sum_{t \in RT(R,\varepsilon)} F_t? \tag{7}$$

Theorem 4. *RTP is PSPACE-hard.*

Proof. Once again, an instance of RRTP is easily transformable to RTP, and asking if $I > \varepsilon$.

6.3.4. Further Changes to the Ray-Tracing Model

There is still some insight to be gained by further examining modifications to the ray-emission functions of the ray-tracing model. Suppose we relax our constraints so that the circuit realisations of ray-emission rules can use any number of gates. Not surprisingly, the ray-tracing problem based on this model becomes impossibly difficult.

General Ray-Tracing Problem (GRTP)
INSTANCE: Scene R as in RRTP, except with general ray-emission functions, and $\varepsilon > 0$.
QUESTION: Does there exist a trace $t \in Trace_R(S,E)$ such that $F_t > \varepsilon$?

Theorem 5. *GRTP is undecidable.*

Proof. We show that the halting problem for an arbitrary deterministic Turing machine M and input w can be transformed to an instance R_M of GRTP. The reduction is by now familiar, except that only $|\Sigma| \times |Q| + 2$ objects are required, which will denote the current state of the Turing machine and character currently under the tape head. Since the polynomial-time constraint has been dropped, ray intensities will now encode both the tape head position and the tape contents. We define a non-ε ray emission only if the character under the tape head matches the current state. In this case, the tape head position is advanced accordingly. If one wishes to avoid the problem of an object emitting a ray to itself, just double the number of objects to toggle rays back and forth in the case of loops. It is therefore clear that

$$w \in L_M \Leftrightarrow \exists\, t \in Trace_{R_M}(S,E): F_t > \varepsilon.$$

All versions of the ray-tracing model presented thus far allow rays to be emitted which have an intensity greater than that of the incident ray. While we argue below that such amplification is not unnatural, it is of some interest to consider the effect of forcing an emitted intensity to be of magnitude less than the corresponding incident intensity. Formally,

$$\forall O_1, O_2, \overline{O}. \ \ \text{if}\ R_{\overline{O}}(O_1 \rightarrow, i_1) = (\rightarrow O_2, i_2), \ \text{then}\ i_2 < i_1. \tag{7}$$

Monotonic Ray-Tracing Problem (MRTP)
INSTANCE: Scene R as in RRTP, with ray-emission functions obeying Eq. 7 above, and $\varepsilon > 0$.
QUESTION: Does there exist a trace $t \in Trace_R(S,E)$ such that $F_t > \varepsilon$?

Theorem 6. *MRTP is NP-hard.*

Remark 4. Is MRTP in NP? Given an instance $R = \langle S, E, \{\, O_i \,\} \rangle$ and $\varepsilon > 0$ of MRTP, note that there is an upper bound on the length of any trace t with $F_t > \varepsilon$. This bound is clearly $b = i_0 - \varepsilon$. To decide an instance of MRTP, a nondeterministic Turing machine need only guess a sequence t of rays of length $\leq b$ and verify that $t \in Trace(S,E)$ with $F_t > \varepsilon$. Since ray-emission functions are computable in polynomial time, the time required to verify t is bounded by $b\,r(n)$, where $r(n)$ is the circuit complexity of the "most complex" ray-emission function. Verification of t is thus computable in polynomial time, and therefore MRTP $\in$ NP, if b is polynomially bounded. Unfortunately, it is not. If the number of bits required to store the initial intensity i_0 dominates the size of instance R's description, then the value of b is exponential in the size of R. The algorithm just outlined actually runs in what is known as *pseudo-polynomial* time [GaJo79]. It appears to be difficult to show that MRTP is strictly in NP. It is not so difficult to demonstrate that it is NP-hard.

Proof. Let $L_M \in NP$ be an language computed by an arbitrary nondeterministic Turing machine M. Then there exists a polynomial $p(n)$ such that for any $w \in L_M$, the length of the shortest computation of M accepting w is bounded by $p(|w|)$. Using p and M, we define an instance R_M of MRTP as in the proof of Theorem 2. The only difference in the reduction is that for each object $p : \alpha : j$, we allow non-ε emissions for *any* transition in M of the form $\delta(p, \alpha) = (q, \beta)$. R_M thus simulates every possible execution of M simultaneously. The outgoing intensity will record a decreasing "step counter" as well as the encoded tape contents.

6.4. Classes of Abstract Ray-Tracing Problems

Because of its potential relevance to the complexity of natural and graphical illumination, and to the classification of both graphic and natural objects in terms of their "computational complexity", it is worthwhile to examine the structural properties of ray-tracing problems over many different classes of objects. The investigation of the last section is only an instance of a very rich set of problems.

Problem 0. Find complexity classes C_0 and C_1 such that if all object ray-emission functions in the ARTP have complexity C_0, then the ARTP is C_1-hard. When is the ARTP is C_1-complete?

Theorem 1 has established that polynomial time (C_0) and polynomial space (C_1) are related in this way. A similar class of ray-tracing problems is the following.

Problem 1. Given a class of functions C, if all objects in ARTP are computable in C-time, then is the ARTP C-space hard? When is the ARTP C-space complete?

Again, Theorem 1 supplies a solution for Problem 1: when C is the class of polynomial functions.

These more general views of the ARTP are not just of considerable theoretical interest: they enable us to pose structural questions about the essence of the problem and its relationship to ray tracing objects from nature or computer graphics. For example, it would be worthwhile to determine the *smallest* complexity class C_0 for ray-emission functions such that the ARTP is complete for another class C_1. As a specific example, does there exist a class $C_0 \subset P$ that still gives rise to the PSPACE-completeness of ARTP? If it is believed that endowing ray-emission functions with the full power of polynomial-time computability is excessive, then clearly the smaller we can make C_0 holding C_1 constant (and the stronger the argument that this captures more closely the desired or observed power of ray-emission functions), the more profound its implications are on the complexity of "more natural" ray tracing. We have only begun this investigation by assuming that objects are polynomial-time computable. A great deal of work remains to discover results for other complexity classes. As an example, consider the following theorem.

Theorem 7. *When C_0 is the class of linear-time computable functions, the ARTP is still PSPACE-complete.*
Proof. Following Karp [Karp72] and Garey and Johnson [GaJo79], the problem of determining whether or not a deterministic Turing machine, which never uses

more than *n* tape squares, accepts its input is PSPACE-complete. By restricting the proof of Theorem 1 above to such Turing machines, it is easy to verify that the reduction of any such machine to an instance of the ARTP requires $O(n)$ time, and that ray-emission functions run in $O(n)$ time.

Remark 5. If the class P is considered too powerful for ray-emission functions, then so must be linear-time computability.

Another possible line of attack to discover the essential aspects of the ray tracing problem is to devise similar but ostensibly simpler problems over very restricted environments. For example, imagine a simple polygon in $\mathbf{R}^2$ in which the $n > 2$ interior polygon edges are to be thought of as perfect mirrors. Let one of the edges have a slit in it and let a single ray of light enter the 2-D "chamber" defined by the polygon, and consider whether or not the ray ever re-emerges from the slit after a number of intersections. What is the complexity or computability of this problem? Is the problem easier if the polygon is forced to be convex? There is a straightforward generalisation of this problem to polyhedra in $\mathbf{R}^3$.

6.5. Does Nature "Solve" Intractable Problems in "Real" Time?

The ray-tracing models presented above are not intended primarily to model "reality". Instead, their intent is to model the potential behaviours of objects in computer graphics – behaviours that can diverge rather arbitrarily from reality. After developing abstract models, we showed that ray-tracing in these models is very complex. This section has two goals: first, to argue that this result has some bearing on computer graphics, and second, to discuss aspects of the model which are or are not natural. We wish to persuade the reader that as objects in computer graphics increase in complexity, and as we attempt to model more illumination effects in nature more precisely, we should be prepared for intractable problems.

Since ray-tracing generally models natural processes, one might be tempted to conclude that nature "solves" very difficult, possibly intractable problems in "real time". The author does not believe this chapter provides justification for this conclusion. However, before dealing with this issue, let us justify that not all of our models are as unnatural as one might first think.

One possible objection to several of our models is that they allow objects to amplify incident intensities. Since these objects do not increase the total luminous energy of the system (i.e., they only emit rays of light in response to incident rays), one might argue that this is unnatural. This is not a valid criticism. First, in the MRTP, ray intensities always decrease and yet the complexity result remains pessimistic. Second, a ray is actually only an abstraction of a *beam* or *cone* of light, which is in effect a ray of finite thickness and spread (e.g., [Aman84,88;

HeHa84]). It is entirely possible for an emitted cone, for example, to be narrower or wider in thickness than its incident width, depending on the objects involved. For example, a lens or convex mirror may narrow a cone. A narrowing of the cone results in an increased intensity, and a spreading constitutes a decreased intensity. Thus an amplification of intensity can be achieved without adding energy to the system. In our proof we only require the ability to amplify an incident intensity by a constant factor of at most $|\Sigma|$.

Another possible objection to the ARTP is that the direction of emitted rays can be made dependent on both the incoming ray intensity and object direction. It might be thought that such objects do not exist in reality. In fact, they do. There exist crystals whose emitted intensity *and* direction vary with the incident intensity. In effect, their index of refraction varies with incoming intensity. Such substances are important to the now well-established field of *optical computing*, in which various computer architectures based on purely optical mechanisms have been proposed and are being constructed [AbSS83;Huan80,83].[5] Admittedly, objects made of these substances do not form the bulk of objects ray-traced in computer graphics today. However, it provides some evidence that this behaviour is not inconsistent with natural (or artificial) illumination, and it provides some justification that a model should allow such behaviour.

There are other reasons for allowing the above ray-emission behaviour. The ARTP only allows for a single light ray to be emitted in response to an incident ray. However, there are a number of natural diffractive optical phenomena that are best modelled by splitting a beam of light into a set of constituent wavelengths, amplitudes, and phases. Each component could then be treated as a "ray" (or more correctly, a wave-front). The reflective behaviour of objects can often depend on the *amplitude* of light at different wavelengths, particularly in accounting for light rays that just graze an object surface (e.g., at a very small incidence angle) or light passing through thin passages in objects. For this reason, the RRTP model was introduced, and not surprisingly, the complexity results are at least as poor as those for the ARTP. In the sense that our model allows objects to vary emitted ray direction on the basis of incident intensity, the model is not overly deficient. An interesting aspect of the proofs above is that the obvious geometric interpretation of the objects' configuration is such that state changes result in rays being emitted only to nearby objects. This could be used to provide a bound for the amount of variation required in the emitted ray direction.

---

[5] See also the survey in the July, 1984 *Proceedings of the IEEE* on optical computing. For further information, the journal *Applied Optics* and the regular International Optical Computer Conference both contain a variety of reports on optical computing architectures, algorithms, and number representations. Very few optical computers have as yet made it past the paper design stage.

There is further justification for experimenting with ray-emission relations rather than functions. With functions, it is difficult to model the optical behaviour of materials other than pure reflectors, and it is certainly impossible to account for translucent and semi-opaque objects, those with both reflective *and* refractive behaviour. Another difficult illumination characteristic to model with a single light ray is diffused reflective properties. Normally, one would model diffuse reflection by emitting many distributed rays in response to a single ray [Whit80; CoPC84]. However, J. Amanatides has shown how to simulate some of these effects using cones, which can be represented in our model [Aman84].

An interesting outgrowth of optical computing is that, while the number of practical applications is still quite small, several fairly sophisticated optical pattern-matching mechanisms appear to be feasible [Huan83]. The comparison operations required in the objects of the proof above are essentially equivalent to pattern-matching small binary images representing the particular (constant-length) characters to be compared. The optical mechanisms currently being proposed are constructed from objects like lenses and beam splitters, which are well-known in computer graphics. Thus it might be possible to perform more powerful object operations by the appropriate combination of other objects with simple optical properties.

There exist artificial objects in computer graphics that cannot be easily ray-traced. The ray-emission behaviour for objects like fractals, for example, which can be everywhere non-smooth, can only be defined precisely in the limit (or probabilistically). The best solution in practice is to approximate the behaviour by limiting the depth of the iterative process generating the fractal. In many other graphical objects, a significant degree of departure from physical validity is often required to compensate for deficiencies in other models or to achieve the desired "look" in the image. Regardless of the physical rules being violated, the validity of the technique is largely determined by how good the finished product looks.

An aspect of the model which is debatable is the choice of the complexity class P (or linear-time computability) for characterising the computational complexity of ray-emission functions. From our discussion in this section, it is clear that these functions should be allowed *some* non-trivial computational power. The questions are: how much is reasonable, and can it be easily classified? It is quite possible that the behaviour of natural objects cuts across our traditional complexity classes. Moreover, optical computing appears to be demonstrating the potential for coercing light into computing nontrivial functions, though it is still not clear if these proposals are entirely feasible. The author feels that, researchers in optical computing notwithstanding, the class P (and linear-time computability) is probably excessively powerful (particularly for the reason given below). As indicated in the previous section, there are many possible research directions in which to go that may help to settle this issue.

The most serious problem when trying to apply the results from the abstract model to reality lies in the *precision* required. Although our reduction of Turing machines to instances of the ray-tracing problem is formally sufficient, the precision required of these instances is likely to make them unverifiable experimentally. In these instances, the size of the numbers required depends on the tape storage requirements. Since our optical simulation of Turing machines would require n-bit precision, it is clear that the practical construction and measurement of all but very trivial instances is impossible. In the limit, moreover, the degree of precision to which we can measure practical constructions of such instances is constrained by the Uncertainty Principle.[6] We therefore conclude that while our results show that abstract ray-tracing models of natural illumination give rise to PSPACE-hard problems for computers, the results have little to say about the natural processes being modelled. A more plausible conclusion is that the ray-tracing models of this chapter and of computer graphics are probably too demanding. Moreover, this chapter has spawned an interesting set of abstract ray-tracing problems whose solution could yield insights into our computational models of natural and artificial phenomena.

---

[6] Again this applies to measuring the real world. Predicting it with computation still can require a polynomially-large number of bits [FiFo88].

7   The Last Word

Mathematics, of course, is a human activity, like philosophy or the design of computers; like these other activities, it is carried on by humans using natural languages. At the same time mathematics has, as a special feature, the ability to be well described by a formal language, which in some sense mirrors its contents precisely. It might be said that the possibility of putting a mathematical discovery into a formal language is the test of whether it is fully understood.

–P.J. Davis and R. Hersh[1]

After having gone through the graphics pipeline once, this appears to be an appropriate place to stop and reflect on what has been achieved. The basic tenet we have set about to justify is that raster graphics can be made rigorous, and that there are many problems within it that are mathematically interesting. It is unlikely that the list of such problems will soon be exhausted.

A criticism often levelled at formal specification efforts is that the objects in the specification have little similarity to the actual objects being characterised. In our case, however, we have been careful to define abstract objects so that they are highly related to their actual counterparts; consequently, the properties we have proven say something directly about real graphics systems. This is especially true of Chapters 3 and 4.

The mathematical framework developed in this book was designed to capture the semantics of the important aspects of practical raster graphics systems. For

---

[1] P.J. Davis and R. Hersh, *The Mathematical Experience*, Birkhäuser, Boston MA, 1981.

each distinct set of concepts, a notation was adopted that suited that set as best as possible. No attempt was made to develop a single formal specification language that captured all concepts, unless one is willing to consider the language of mathematics as fitting into that category. Some of the intuitive notions for which a precise meaning was given are:

- scene, image, object, pixel, texture mapping, clipping, colour mapping, visibility, interpenetration, illumination, rendering, rasterisation, bit-map, bit-map operation, image transformation, area sampling, point sampling, super-sampling, filtering, stochastic sampling, coverage, intensity contribution, ray tracing.

Once a mathematical characterisation of these notions was established, a number of interesting problems could be posed. Some of these were answered fairly completely. These include:

- what is conformal texture mapping, and why is it interesting?
- how is sorting related to the visible surface problem?
- what are some approximations to ideal rendering techniques, and under what conditions are they equal?
- what is the complexity of some simple ray-tracing models?
- find some interesting properties that common rasterisations have (or lack).
- characterise the transformations that are faithful to images.
- what are stable line rasterisation schemes, and why are they interesting? Give some examples; what is their error behaviour?
- what is the expected convergence rate of stochastic point sampling?
- why is it important to separate scenes from images, and bit-maps from images and scenes?

Some problems that were posed during the research for this book have been more or less answered (not necessarily by the author). For example:

- are there any practical conformal maps?
- what is the optimal lower bound for the RVSP under the output list model?
- what is the best possible error behaviour for stable line rasterisations?

Some problems have as yet not been answered:

- what is the expected behaviour of rendering approximations on realistic scenes?

- what is the complexity/computability status of ray-tracing reachability problems over restricted classes of objects such as mirrors?

- will the notations employed in this book be of use to the formal specification of graphics standards, reference models, or programming languages?

Lastly, there remain many unanswerable or (until now) unasked questions:

- when is a rendering or rasterisation good?

- what is the complexity of the visible surface problem over surfaces other than polygons?

- can a rigorous framework for input and interaction, the "other" side of computer graphics, be developed?

- what about the integration of video and other technologies with raster graphics?

- why do soccer players prefer ice-cold beer to freezing beer?

In time, the author may attack several of these problems in earnest. Of the others, the author recalls the closing sentence of that famous and strange work by Wittgenstein, *Tractatus Logico-Philosophicus*, which, in the most poetic of its many possible translations, reads "Whereof we cannot speak, thereof we must be silent."

References

AFSW82   Acquah, J., J. Foley, J. Sibert, and P. Wenner, "A Conceptual Model of Raster Graphics Systems", *Proceedings of SIGGRAPH '82,* also published as *Computer Graphics 16,* 3 (July 1982), 321-328.

AbSS83   Abraham, E., S.T. Seaton, and S.D. Smith, "The Optical Computer", *Scientific American 248,* 2 (Feb. 1983),85-93.

AbWW85   Abram, G., L. Westover, and T. Whitted, "Efficient alias-free rendering using bit-masks and look-up tables", *SIGGRAPH 1985 Conference Proceedings,* also published as *ACM Computer Graphics 19,* 3 (July, 1985), 53-59.

AhHU74   Aho, A.V., J.E. Hopcroft, and J.D. Ullman, *The Design and Analysis of Computer Algorithms,* Addison-Wesley, Reading, Mass., 1974.

Aman84   Amanatides, J., "Ray tracing with cones", *SIGGRAPH 1984 Proceedings,* also published as *ACM Computer Graphics 18,* 3 (July 1984), 129-136.

Aman88   Amanatides, J., *A Solid Angle Approach to Ray Tracing in Computer Graphics,* Ph.D. Thesis, Department of Computer Science, University of Toronto, Toronto, Canada, M5S 1A4, 1988.

BaPe83   Barwise, J., and J. Perry, *Situations and Attitudes,* MIT Press, Cambridge, Massachusetts, 1983.

Barr84   Barr, A.H., "Global and Local Deformation of Solid Primitives", *SIGGRAPH 1984 Proceedings,* also published as *ACM Computer Graphics 18,* 3 (July 1984), 21-30.

Blin77   Blinn, J.F., "Models of Light Reflection for Computer Synthesized Pictures", *SIGGRAPH 1977 Proceedings,* also published as *ACM Computer Graphics 11,* 2 (July 1977), 192-198.

Blin78   Blinn, J.F., "Simulation of Wrinkled Surfaces", *SIGGRAPH 1978 Proceedings,* also published as *ACM Computer Graphics 12,* 3 (Aug.

1978), 286-292.

BuiT75   Bui Tuong, P. "Illumination for Computer Generated Pictures", *Commun. ACM 18*, 6 (June 1975), 311-317.

CaSm80   Catmull, E., and A.R. Smith, "3-D Transformations of Images in Scanline Order", *SIGGRAPH 1980 Proceedings*, also published as *ACM Computer Graphics 14*, 3 (July 1980), 279-285.

Carn58   Carnap, R., *Meaning and Necessity*, The University of Chicago Press, Chicago, IL, 1958.

Carp84   Carpenter, L., "The A-buffer, an Antialiased Hidden Surface Method", *SIGGRAPH 1984 Proceedings*, also published as *ACM Computer Graphics 18*, 3 (July 1984), 103-108.

Cars83   Carson, G.S., "The Specification of Computer Graphics Systems", *IEEE Computer Graphics and Applications 3*, 6 (Sept 1983), 27-41.

Cars84   Carson, G.S., "An Approach to the Formal Specification of Computer Graphics Systems", *Computers and Graphics 8*, 1 (1984), 51-57.

Catm75   Catmull, E.A., "Computer Display of Curved Surfaces", *Proceedings Conference on Computer Graphics, Pattern Recognition, and Data Structure* (May 1975), 11-17.

CoGr85   Cohen, M., and D. Greenberg, "The hemi-cube: a radiosity solution for complex environments", *SIGGRAPH 1985 Conference Proceedings*, also published as *ACM Computer Graphics 19*, 3 (July, 1985), 31-40.

CoPC84   Cook, R., T. Porter, and L. Carpenter, "Distributed ray tracing", *SIGGRAPH 1984 Proceedings*, also published as *ACM Computer Graphics 18*, 3 (July 1984), 137-145.

CoTo82   Cook, R.L, and K.E. Torrance, "A Reflectance Model for Computer Graphics", *ACM Transactions on Graphics 1*, 1 (Jan. 1982), 7-24.

Cook86   Cook, R.L., "Stochastic Sampling in Computer Graphics", *ACM Transactions on Graphics 5*, 1 (Jan. 1986), 51-72.

Crav82   Craven, B.D., *Lebesgue Measure and Integration*, Pitman Publishing Co., Marshfield, Mass., 1982.

Crow77   Crow, F.C., "The Aliasing Problem in Computer-Generated Shaded Images", *Commun. ACM 20*, 11 (Nov. 1977), 799-805.

vanD88   van Dam, A., "PHIGS+ Functional Description, Revision 3.0", *ACM Computer Graphics 22*, 3 (July 1988), 125-218.

DeHN85   Demko, S., L. Hodges, and B. Naylor, "Construction of Fractal Objects with Iterated Function Systems", *SIGGRAPH 1985 Proceedings*, also published as *ACM Computer Graphics 19*, 3 (July 1985),

271-278.

DiWo85   Dippe, M.A., and E.H. Wold, "Antialiasing through Stochastic Sampling", *SIGGRAPH 1985 Proceedings*, also published as *ACM Computer Graphics 19*, 3 (July 1985), 69-78.

DoLR76   Dobkin, D.P., R.J. Lipton, and S.P. Reiss, "Excursions into geometry", Tech. Report #71, Department of Computer Science, Yale University, 1976.

DuFM88   Duce, D.A., E.V.C. Fielding, and L.S. Marshall, "Formal Specification of a small example based on GKS", *ACM Transactions on Graphics 7*, 3 (July 1988), 180-197.

DuFi84   Duce, D.A., and E.V.C. Fielding, "Better Understanding through Formal Specification", Technical Report RAL-84-128 (1984), Rutherford Appleton Laboratory, Oxford, England.

Duff85   Duff, T., "Compositing 3-D Rendered Images", *SIGGRAPH 1985 Proceedings*, also published as *ACM Computer Graphics 19*, 3 (July 1985), 41-44.

Fell66   Feller, W., *An Introduction to Probability Theory and Its Applications, Vol. I*, Third Edition, John Wiley and Sons, New York, 1966.

Fell68   Feller, W., *An Introduction to Probability Theory and Its Applications, Vol. II*, Second Corrected Printing, John Wiley and Sons, New York, 1968.

FiFC87   Fiume, E., A. Fournier, and V. Canale, "Conformal Texture Mapping", *Proceedings of Eurographics '87* (August 1987), Elsevier Science Publishers (North-Holland), 53-64.

FiFR83   Fiume, E., A. Fournier, and L. Rudolph, "A Parallel Scan Conversion Algorithm with Anti-Aliasing for a General-Purpose Ultracomputer", *ACM Computer Graphics 17*, 3 (July, 1983), 141-150.

FiFo84   Fiume, E., and A. Fournier, "A Programme for the Development of a Mathematical Theory of Computer Graphics", *Proceedings of Graphics Interface '84*, 251-256.

FiFo88   Fiume, E., and A. Fournier, "The complexity of abstract ray tracing", submitted for publication, 1988.

Fium86   Fiume, E., *A Mathematical Semantics and Theory of Raster Graphics*, Ph.D. Thesis, Department of Computer Science, University of Toronto (May 1986); published as Technical Report CSRI-185, Computer Systems Research Institute, University of Toronto, Toronto, Canada, M5S 1A4.

Fium87   Fiume, E., "Bit-mapped graphics: a semantics and theory", *Computers and Graphics 11*, 2 (April 1987), 121-140.

FoAm84   Fournier, A., and J. Amanatides, "Three-Dimensional Texture Mapping", presented at the *International Conference on Engineering and Computer Graphics*, Beijing (Aug. 1984).

FoDa82   Foley, J.D., and A. van Dam, *Fundamentals of Interactive Computer Graphics*, Addison-Wesley, Reading, Massachusetts, 1982.

FoFC82   Fournier, A., D. Fussell, and L. Carpenter, "Computer Rendering of Stochastic Models", *Commun. ACM 25*, 6 (June 1982), 371-384.

FoFi88   Fournier, A., and E. Fiume, "Constant-Time Filtering with Space-Variant Kernels", *SIGGRAPH 1988 Proceedings*, also published as *ACM Computer Graphics 22*, 4 (Aug. 1988), 229-238.

FoFu88   Fournier, A., and D. Fussell, "On the Power of the Frame Buffer", *ACM Transactions on Graphics 7*, 2 (April 1988), 103-129.

FoMo84   Fournier, A., and D.Y. Montuno, "Triangulating Simple Polygons and Equivalent Problems", *ACM Transactions on Graphics 3*, 2 (April 1984), 153-174.

Four84   Fournier, A., "Primitives in Computer Graphics", *Proceedings of Graphics Interface '84* (May 1984), 51-52.

GKS84   Technical Committee X3H3-Computer Graphics, "Draft Proposed American National Standard Graphical Kernel System", *ACM Computer Graphics*, Special GKS Issue (Feb. 1984).

GSPC79   SIGGRAPH-ACM (GSPC), "Status Report of the Graphics Standards Planning Committee", *ACM Computer Graphics 13*, 3 (Aug. 1979).

GaJo79   Garey, M.R., and D.S. Johnson, *Computers and Intractability - A Guide to the Theory of NP-Completeness*, W.H. Freeman, New York, N.Y., 1979.

Gard85   Gardner, G.Y., "Visual Simulation of Clouds", *SIGGRAPH 1985 Proceedings*, also published as *ACM Computer Graphics 19*, 3 (July 1985), 297-303.

Gazd79   Gazdar, G., *Pragmatics*, Academic Press, New York, 1979.

Gilo78   Gilloi, K., *Interactive Computer Graphics*, Prentice-Hall, Englewood Cliffs, NJ, 1978.

Gnat84   Gnatz, R., "Approaching a Formal Framework for Graphics Software Standards", *Computers and Graphics 8*, 1 (1984), 39-50.

Gold73   Goldstein, L.J., *Abstract Algebra*, Prentice-Hall Inc., Englewood Cliffs, N.J., 1973.

Grin84   Grindal, D.A., *The Stochastic Creation of Tree Images*, M.Sc. Thesis, Department of Computer Science, University of Toronto, 1984.

GuHo78 Guttag, J.V., and J.J. Horning, "The Algebraic Specification of Abstract Data Types", *Acta Informatica 10*, 1 (Jan. 1978), 27-52.

GuSt82 Guibas, L.J., and J. Stolfi, "A Language for Bitmap Manipulation", *ACM Transactions on Graphics 1*, 3 (July 1982), 191-214.

HaHa64 Hammersley, J.M., and D.C. Handscomb, *Monte Carlo Methods*, Methuen and Co. (London), or John Wiley and Sons (New York), 1964.

Hall89 Hall, R., *Illumination and Color in Computer Generated Imagery*, Springer-Verlag, New York, 1989.

Halm70 Halmos, P.R., *Measure Theory*, Second Edition, Springer-Verlag, New York 1970.

Halm74 Halmos, P.R., *Lectures on Boolean Algebras*, Springer-Verlag, New York, 1974.

HeHa84 Heckbert, P.S., and P. Hanrahan, "Beam tracing polygonal objects", *SIGGRAPH 1984 Proceedings*, also published as *ACM Computer Graphics 18*, 3 (July 1984), 119-128.

Heck86 Heckbert, P.S., "Survey of Texture Mapping", *IEEE Computer Graphics and Applications 6*, 11 (Nov. 1986), 56-67.

Hosk79 Hoskins, R.F., *Generalised Functions*, Ellis Horwood Ltd., distributed by Halstead Press (John Wiley and Sons), New York, 1979.

Huan80 Huang, A., "Design for an Optical General Purpose Digital Computer", *Proceedings of International Optical Computing Conference*, Vol. 232, Book II, 1980.

Huan83 Huang, A., "Parallel Algorithms for Optical Digital Computers", *Proceedings of International Optical Computing Conference*, Vol. 422, 1983.

Jone80 Jones, C.B., *Software Development: A Rigorous Approach*, Prentice-Hall, Englewood Cliffs, NJ, 1980.

Jone82 Jones, D.S., *The Theory of Generalised Functions*, Second Edition, Cambridge University Press, Cambridge, 1982.

Karp72 Karp, R.M., "Reducibility among combinatorial problems", in *Complexity of Computer Computations*, Plenum Press, New York, R.E. Miller and J.W. Thatcher (eds.), 1972, 85-103.

Knut76 Knuth, D.E., "Big Omicron and Big Omega and Big Theta", *ACM SIGACT News 8*, 2 (Apr. 1976), 18-24.

KoBa83 Korein, J., and N.I. Badler, "Temporal anti-aliasing in computer-generated animation", *SIGGRAPH '83 Proceedings*, also published as *ACM Computer Graphics 17*, 3 (July 1983), 377-386.

LeRU85   Lee, M.E., R.A. Redner, and S.P. Uselton, "Statistically optimized sampling for distributed ray tracing", *SIGGRAPH 1985 Proceedings*, also published as *ACM Computer Graphics 19*, 3 (July 1985), 61-68.

Luby87   Luby, M., "Grid geometries which preserve properties of euclidean geometry: A study of graphics line drawing algorithms", in *Theoretical Foundations of Computer Graphics and CAD*, R.A. Earnshaw (ed.), Springer-Verlag, Berlin, 1987, 397-432.

MaSh78   Mallgren, W.R., and A.C. Shaw, "Graphical Transformations and Hierarchic Picture Structures", *Computer Graphics and Image Processing 8*, 2 (Oct. 1978), 237-258.

MaTh81   Magnenat-Thalmann, N., Thalmann, D., "A Graphical Pascal Extension Based on Graphical Types", *Software-Practice and Experience 11*, 1 (Jan. 1981), 53-62.

Mall82a   Mallgren, W.R., *Formal Specification of Interactive Graphics Programming Languages*, MIT Press, Cambridge, Massachusetts, 1982.

Mall82b   Mallgren, W.R., "Formal Specification of Graphic Data Types", *ACM Transactions on Programming Languages and Systems 4*, 4 (Oct. 1982), 687-710.

Mand83   Mandelbrot, B.B., *The Fractal Geometry of Nature*, W.H. Freeman and Co., San Francisco, CA, 1983.

Mars73   Marsden, J.E., *Basic Complex Analysis*, W.H. Freeman and Co., San Francisco, CA, 1973.

Mars74   Marsden, J.E., *Elementary Classical Analysis*, W.H. Freeman and Co., San Francisco, CA, 1974.

Mars84   Marshall, L.S., "A Formal Specification of Line Representations on Graphics Devices", Department of Computer Science, University of Manchester, 1984.

Mart82   Martin, G.E., *Transformation Geometry*, Springer-Verlag, New York, NY, 1982.

McKe87   McKenna, M., "Worst-case optimal hidden-surface removal", *ACM Transactions on Graphics 6*, 1 (Jan. 1987), 19-28.

Mitc87   Mitchell, D.P., "Generating Antialiased Images at Low Sampling Densities", *SIGGRAPH 1987 Proceedings*, also published as *ACM Computer Graphics 21*, 4 (July 1987), 65-72.

Nayl81   Naylor, B.F., *A Priori Based Techniques for Determining Visibility Priority for 3-D Scenes*, Ph.D. Dissertation, Program in Mathematical Sciences, University of Texas at Dallas, 1981.

NeSp79   Newman, W.M., and R.F. Sproull, *Principles of Interactive Computer Graphics*, 2nd ed., McGraw-Hill, New York, 1979.

Nort82   Norton, A., "Generation and Display of Geometric Fractals in 3-D", *SIGGRAPH 1982 Proceedings*, also published as *ACM Computer Graphics 16*, 3 (July 1982), 61-67.

OtWW82   Ottmann, T., P. Widmayer, and D. Wood, "A Worst-Case Efficient Algorithm for Hidden Line Elimination", Technical Report CS-82-33, Department of Computer Science, University of Waterloo, 1982.

Pavl82   Pavlidis, T., *Algorithms for Graphics and Image Processing*, Computer Science Press, Rockville, MD, 1982.

Peac85   Peachey, D.R., "Solid Texturing of Complex Surfaces", *SIGGRAPH 1985 Proceedings*, also published as *ACM Computer Graphics 19*, 3 (July 1985), 279-286.

Perl85   Perlin, K., "An Image Synthesizer", *SIGGRAPH 1985 Proceedings*, also published as *ACM Computer Graphics 19*, 3 (July 1985), 287-296.

PoDu84   Porter, T., and T. Duff, "Compositing Digital Images", *SIGGRAPH 1984 Proceedings*, also published as *ACM Computer Graphics 18*, 3 (July 1984), 253-259.

Poly74   Polya, G., *Complex Variables*, John Wiley and Sons, New York, NY, 1974.

PrSh85   Preparata, F.P., and M.I. Shamos, *Computational Geometry*, Springer-Verlag, New York, 1985.

Prat78   Pratt, W.K., *Digital Image Processing*, John Wiley and Sons, New York, 1978.

Quin80   Quine, W.V.O., *From a Logical Point of View*, Second Edition, Harvard University Press, Cambridge, Massachusetts, 1953 (revised 1961, 1980).

Rose74   Rosenblatt, M., *Random Processes*, Second Edition, Springer-Verlag, New York, NY, 1974.

Schm81   Schmitt, A., "On the Time and Space Complexity of Certain Exact Hidden Line Algorithms", Technical Report 24/81, Fakultat fur Informatik, Universitat Karlsruhe, 1981.

Serr82   Serra, J., *Image Analysis and Mathematical Morphology*, Academic Press, 1982.

Sham78   Shamos, M.I., *Computational Geometry*, Ph.D. Dissertation, Department of Computer Science, Yale University, New Haven CT, 1978.

Shou79   Shoup, R.G., "Color Table Animation", *SIGGRAPH 1979 Proceedings*, also published as *ACM Computer Graphics 13*, 3 (July 1979), 8-13.

Smit84   Smith, A.R., "Plants, Fractals, and Formal Languages", *SIGGRAPH 1984 Proceedings*, also published as *ACM Computer Graphics 18*, 3 (July 1984), 1-10.

Spro82   Sproull, R.F., "Using Program Transformations to Derive Line-Drawing Algorithms", *ACM Transactions on Graphics 1*, 4 (Oct. 1982), 257-273.

SuSS74   Sutherland, I.E., R.F. Sproull, and R.A. Schumacker, "A characterization of ten hidden-surface algorithms", *ACM Computing Surveys 6*, 1 (March 1974), 1-55.

Watk70   Watkins, G.S., *A Real-Time Visible Surface Algorithm*, Technical Report UTEC-CSc-70-101, Computer Science Deptartment, University of Utah, 1970.

Whit80   Whitted, T., "An Improved Illumination Model for Shaded Display", *Commun. ACM 23*, 6 (June 1980), 343-349.

Index

Bold page numbers indicate the term's definition.